UNDERGRADUATE RESEARCH FOR STUDENT ENGAGEMENT AND LEARNING

There is growing interest in undergraduate research, given its benefits to students, faculty members, and the institution. For higher education scholars, faculty, and administrators, this book logically synthesizes the literature to demonstrate its impact on facilitation of learning and engagement and to chart a course for expanding and improving these opportunities. This book provides a comprehensive overview of undergraduate research as a "high-impact practice" in postsecondary education, from its theoretical underpinnings and research-base, to student participation and faculty incentives. This important resource offers analysis of the current state of undergraduate research, explores challenges and unresolved questions affecting undergraduate research, and provides implications for research and practice.

Joseph L. Murray is an Associate Professor of Education and the Director of the College Student Personnel Program at Bucknell University, Pennsylvania, USA.

UNDERGRADUATE RESEARCH FOR STUDENT ENGAGEMENT AND LEARNING

Joseph L. Murray

NEW YORK AND LONDON

First published 2018
by Routledge
711 Third Avenue, New York, NY 10017

and by Routledge
2 Park Square, Milton Park, Abingdon, Oxon, OX14 4RN

Routledge is an imprint of the Taylor & Francis Group, an informa business

Library of Congress Cataloging-in-Publication Data
A catalog record for this book has been requested

ISBN: 978-1-138-91202-1 (hbk)
ISBN: 978-1-138-91205-2 (pbk)
ISBN: 978-1-315-69215-9 (ebk)

Typeset in Bembo
by Deanta Global Publishing Services, Chennai, India

CONTENTS

FOREWORD

Jillian Kinzie

ASSOCIATE DIRECTOR, CENTER FOR POSTSECONDARY RESEARCH, INDIANA UNIVERSITY

Undergraduate research provides precious opportunities for students to explore their intellectual curiosity. The impressive titles of some undergraduate research projects illustrate the substance of this work: "Column Study of Bio-Electric Remediation of Nitrate and Perchlorate in Groundwater Systems," "Sexual Assault, Domestic Violence, and Intimate Partner Violence among Latina Students," "Using the Data Envelopment Analysis (DEA) Method to Determine the Safest and Worst States in Which to Drive," and "The Applications of Consequentialist and Categorical Moral Reasoning: Medea and Murder." Even more important, by doing undergraduate research, students gain intellectual independence and acquire practical research and work-related skills.

By all accounts, dating back at least to the early 1900s, undergraduate research is a valued and enduring educational practice in higher education. Identified in 1953 by the National Science Foundation (NSF) as a way to improve undergraduate education in the sciences and promoted as an officially recognized practice following the 1979 incorporation of the Council on Undergraduate Research (CUR), undergraduate research has expanded to more and more colleges and universities and has matured as a prized higher education practice. Scholarly attention on the effects of undergraduate research has also grown—with the literature revealing evidence of the practice's positive impacts on student learning outcomes, continuation to graduate school, and development of problem-solving skills. Recently, interest in expanding undergraduate research opportunities to more students has surged with evidence of the value of "high-impact practices" (HIPs)—which include undergraduate research—and their positive association with key educational outcomes such as deep learning and student success.

Given the venerable history of undergraduate research and the recent swell of interest in it as a HIP, Joseph Murray's volume, *Undergraduate Research for*

Student Engagement and Learning, offers a timely synthesis of the relevant literature. Through a unified presentation of the history, scholarship, practice, and outcomes of undergraduate research, the author provides a comprehensive introduction to the undergraduate research movement, a detailed reference for scholars studying undergraduate research, and an essential resource for academic leaders striving to establish and improve undergraduate research.

Much is known now about undergraduate research, and this book effectively brings it all together. Chapters in Parts I–III—thoughtfully organized around descriptions of the concept, the rationale, and the conditions for undergraduate research—demonstrate the deep historical and theoretical base, the rich evidence about educational outcomes, and the proven organizational supports for undergraduate research. These knowns are important to document. The growth of the practice depends on clear definitions, specification of intended outcomes, and evidence of the effectiveness of these experiences for students and faculty.

This book comprehensively demonstrates that while undergraduate research rests on a solid foundation, a host of challenges and unresolved questions remain concerning the future of undergraduate research and the goals to expand the practice to more students and disciplines, to support greater faculty involvement, and to respond to the changing economics of higher education. The final two parts of the book discuss these issues and focus on implications for research and practice. Indeed, the framings of the issues and challenges for the practice of and scholarship in undergraduate research, which I highlight here, are the book's key contributions.

The first salient issue for undergraduate research is providing more such opportunities to more students. Although increasing numbers of colleges and universities have established undergraduate research opportunities over the last 40 years, these opportunities are still rather exclusive. Data on participation collected by the *National Survey of Student Engagement (NSSE)* show less than a quarter of students reporting work with a faculty member on a research project. Research experiences in community colleges are even rarer. In chapter 6, while noting wide disparities across the disciplines in the patterns of student and faculty participation in undergraduate research, the author affirms that new models for scholarship and creative activity have produced fertile ground for undergraduate research across the disciplines. Also noted are the promise of investments to infuse more community-based research into the undergraduate two- and four-year sector curriculum as well as faculty development initiatives to increase comfort levels among community college faculty in mentoring undergraduate researchers.

Even more important to the goal of expanding undergraduate research opportunities is ensuring equity. While efforts have been made to increase the participation of historically underrepresented students in these experiences, gaps persist by gender, race/ethnicity, and first-generation status. Chapter 8 addresses this critical topic directly, discussing the causes of the inequities and the promise of targeted approaches to increase participation from underrepresented student populations, including precollege outreach, structured mentoring relationships, and culturally inclusive instructional practices. Ultimately, discussions about undergraduate research must address matters of inclusion.

The current emphasis on assuring quality and learning outcomes is also addressed in this book. As colleges and universities create undergraduate research experiences, they should specify the intended outcomes explicitly, design experiences that lead to mastery, and gather evidence for assessing quality and learning gains. Assessment and research on outcomes is necessary for demonstrating evidence of value and for ensuring that—in their zeal to create undergraduate research experiences—institutions do not lose sight of what makes these experiences educationally meaningful.

In this era of accountability and pressure to produce "career-ready" graduates, knowing what and how undergraduate research contributes to employment outcomes is essential. Fortunately, employers value research skills. Hart Research Associates (2013) found that 83% of business and non-profit leaders said better-prepared students "develop research questions in their field and evidence-based analyses" and that 79% said a good preparation for workplace success is completing a major project demonstrating acquired knowledge and skills. These outcomes and other educational impacts of undergraduate research are well documented in chapter 4. A continuing key challenge for undergraduate research programs, however, is enabling students to explicitly communicate and demonstrate these outcomes to prospective employers and informing employers of the benefits conveyed through undergraduate research.

The final issue I highlight here regarding practice and scholarship in undergraduate research is support of faculty involvement. Mentoring and substantive feedback from faculty are among the hallmarks of effective undergraduate research, and yet these place heavy demands on faculty time and workload. Chapters 1, 3, and 7 address the need to support those faculty already active in undergraduate research and to create an environment to increase faculty involvement in undergraduate research through department cultures, tenure and promotion policies, faculty workload and compensation practices, and patterns of resource allocation. The crux of the future of undergraduate research is this. If we are to realize the true promise of undergraduate research, we must recognize that the time faculty spend mentoring undergraduates in research experiences is teaching, and this time must be integrated into the faculty member's total workload.

Undergraduate research conveys benefits to students, faculty members, and the institution. For scholars and practitioners of undergraduate research, this book logically synthesizes the literature to demonstrate these benefits and to chart a course for expanding and improving these experiences.

Reflecting on the impressive research project titles at the beginning of this foreword, I am encouraged by undergraduate students' research prowess. But wouldn't it be wonderful if more of them had the opportunity to pursue independent research; to work closely on their endeavor with faculty, peers, and other researchers; and, as early as practical in their education, to ignite their passion for new knowledge?

Reference

Hart Research Associates (2013). *It takes more than a major: Employer priorities for college learning and student success.* Washington, DC: Association of American Colleges and Universities.

PREFACE

Over the past three decades, I have been privileged to serve a wide variety of postsecondary educational institutions in a number of different capacities. Having been trained as a student affairs professional and employed as such for nearly a third of my career, I was afforded an extraordinary professional opportunity in the fall of 1994, when I joined the faculty of Bucknell University, a primarily residential liberal arts institution that serves mainly a traditional aged undergraduate student population. It was here that I began to fully appreciate the potential impact of theoretically based educational practices on the social, emotional, and intellectual development of young people entering the adult world.

While developmental theory has long served as a foundation for student affairs programs and services, it is only recently that its principles have been brought to bear on the practice of undergraduate teaching. A key factor in this broadened influence is the work of various student affairs luminaries who have built an empirical foundation for *student engagement* and communicated its benefits to a more general academic audience (Astin, 1984, 1993; Kuh, Kinzie, Schuh, Whitt, & Associates, 2005; Tinto, 1993). Such efforts have gained support from the Association of American Colleges and Universities (AAC&U), which has worked to actively promote adoption of *high-impact practices* grounded in principles of student engagement (Brownell & Swaner, 2010; Kuh, 2008; Kuh & O'Donnell, 2013). Concurrently, *constructive developmentalist* scholars have advanced an integrative view of student development that lends itself well to application across both academic and student affairs contexts (Baxter Magolda, 1992, 1999, 2000, 2004a, 2004b; Kegan, 1982, 1994).

Efforts to promote student engagement, meaning the investment of students' time and energy in activities linked to success in college, are valued for both their educational benefits and their positive impact on student retention (Astin, 1993;

Kuh, 2008; Kuh et al., 2005; Tinto, 1993). The combination of recruitment and retention has long been recognized as central to a comprehensive enrollment management strategy. However, success within this realm has also been understood to include efforts to "shape the class" (Hossler, 2015, p. 6). Today, such efforts are often focused on maximizing the educational benefits of human diversity, an aspiration that only begins with recruitment of a diverse student body (Hurtado, Milem, Clayton-Pedersen, & Allen, 1999). Here, too, the leadership of AAC&U has been evident, most notably in its Making Excellence Inclusive initiative, which emphasizes the removal of barriers to academic success for all students (Bauman, Bustillos, Bensimon, Brown, & Bartee, 2005; Milem, Chang, & Antonio, 2005; Williams, Berger, & McClendon, 2005). As colleges and universities have grown in their commitments to equity and access, engagement of diverse learners in the lives of their campuses has become a recurrent theme in the literature as well (Quaye & Harper, 2015).

Informed by a multifaceted educational agenda, adoption of high-impact practices has come to be regarded as a key strategy for enhancing the undergraduate experience of all students. Such practices include: (1) *first-year seminars and experiences,* (2) *common intellectual experiences,* (3) *learning communities,* (4) *writing-intensive courses,* (5) *collaborative assignments and projects,* (6) *undergraduate research,* (7) *diversity and global learning,* (8) *service-learning and community-based learning,* (9) *internships,* (10) *capstone courses and projects* (Kuh, 2008), and (11) *ePortfolios* (Center for Engaged Learning, 2016). While each of these practices offers students an excellent opportunity for engaged learning, undergraduate research is unique in concurrently advancing the scholarly productivity of faculty mentors. Whereas the competing demands of teaching and research have long been viewed as a source of tension for faculty (Boyer, 1987, 1990; Fairweather, 1996; Fukami, 1997; Schuster & Finkelstein, 2006), this complementarity of function is not insignificant.

Even beyond the weight of the evidence presented in the scholarly literature, I have seen first-hand the benefits of undergraduate research for students and faculty alike. Over the past 20 plus years, I have had occasion to engage in collaborative inquiry with numerous undergraduate students, under the auspices of the Bucknell Program for Undergraduate Research, an institutionally sponsored summer research fellowship program. I have also initiated course-based undergraduate research, supervised undergraduate independent studies and honors theses, and served on our Honors Council and Institutional Review Board (IRB). This work has yielded multiple publications and presentations with undergraduate student co-authors and has contributed greatly to my professional development as both a teacher and a scholar. More recently, I have had the privilege of serving as a Councilor for the newly established Education Division of the Council on Undergraduate Research (CUR), partnering with colleagues from across the nation to advance both our discipline and the pedagogy of engaged learning.

As a staunch advocate of undergraduate research, I have long perceived a need for broader dissemination of information on its potential to improve the state of American higher education. Because much of the literature to date has been published directly by CUR, its audience has consisted primarily of those who are already familiar with undergraduate research and are sufficiently committed to its advancement to hold membership in an organization established for that purpose, an assumption that is often reflected in the content of the publications themselves.

This book was written to provide a cogent, yet comprehensive, synthesis of the relevant literature. As such, it offers a unified introduction to undergraduate research for those with little or no prior experience with the practice or understanding of its underlying rationale. However, the book is also firmly grounded in the literature of higher education as a field of study, situating undergraduate research within the broader constellation of recognized collegiate pedagogies. Though scholarly in its orientation, the book is not intended to be solely of interest to academic researchers. At its core, it represents what Boyer (1990) termed the *scholarship of integration*, a branch of inquiry in which large and sometimes seemingly disparate bodies of prior scholarship are synthesized in ways that bring new meaning to earlier findings and communicate broad theoretical principles to specialists and non-specialists alike. The dual nature of the audiences toward which such works are addressed is of particular significance to the topic of undergraduate research, which is both a theoretical construct to be studied and a pedagogical approach to be implemented.

The book consists of 12 chapters, which are divided into five general parts, reflecting the emergence of several major themes within the relevant literature. The first part, *The Concept*, provides a basic introduction to what is meant by undergraduate research and draws distinctions among prevailing program models. The second part, *The Rationale*, explores the theoretical foundations for undergraduate research and situates its emergence within the ongoing evolution of the American higher education system. A review of the empirical data on the educational outcomes of undergraduate research programs is then used to substantiate the alignment of such programs with the goals and purpose of higher education. The third part, *The Conditions*, offers an assessment of the current state of undergraduate research as an element of the contemporary undergraduate experience, as well as national and institutional conditions that support or inhibit its expansion. The fourth part, *The Issues*, presents a compendium of challenges and unresolved questions affecting undergraduate research. Topics addressed in this section include equity and access, disciplinary perspectives, and the impact of economic, social, and political conditions on the future of undergraduate research. In the closing part, *The Outlook*, major themes emerging in the literature are reviewed, with a focus on implications for research and practice.

Almost 15 years in the making, this book has been influenced by numerous individuals and groups, whose support I appreciatively acknowledge. First, I am indebted to the many undergraduate students with whom I have worked with on various research projects. Although I have learned much from each and every one of them, I am especially grateful to Sean Kirnan, who first suggested that I write a book on undergraduate research, and Carol Varano, who worked with me in developing an initial prospectus for what would ultimately become this book. Along the way, I received helpful feedback on various aspects of the book's content and format from professional colleagues, both at Bucknell and elsewhere. Among these individuals were Adrianna Kezar, Elizabeth Ambos, Lindsay Currie, and Sue Ellen Henry. I am also beholden to the book's editor, Heather Jarrow, whose timeliness, attention to detail, and insightful recommendations greatly enhanced the quality of the finished product and were critical in bringing it to press. I would also like to thank the members of Bucknell's Faculty Development Committee, whose approval of my 2016–17 sabbatical proposal paved the way for completion of the project. Finally, I would like to thank my family for the support that they have provided to me over these many years. In addition to the ongoing encouragement that I have received from my brothers, Jim and John Murray, and my sisters-in-law, Karen Lynn and Taya Murray, I would be especially remiss in not mentioning the support and generosity of my sister and brother-in-law, Mary and Bill Martin, whose lakeside cottage offered the perfect setting for me to channel my inner Thoreau.

PART I

The Concept

1

AN OVERVIEW OF
UNDERGRADUATE RESEARCH

Over the past three decades, interest in undergraduate research has grown dramatically. The appeal of this pedagogical approach is understandable, as it allows academics to more fully integrate their roles as teachers, scholars, and community members, while exposing their students to rich educational opportunities. Growing awareness of the impact of student engagement on retention and academic success, across widely varied populations, has also heightened awareness of the potential for undergraduate research to serve as a vehicle for promoting an agenda of excellence and inclusion. As interest in undergraduate research has grown, the resultant dialogue has come to extend beyond the individual campus, reflecting the fact that preparation of young scholars for lives of inquiry holds national and international significance, both within the academy and elsewhere.

Defining Undergraduate Research

One challenge in framing discussions of research is the establishment of a common understanding of the term, particularly as it relates to multiple disciplines. Applying a decidedly broad definition, Lichter (1995) described research as "a set of activities leading to new knowledge that, in turn, is presented for critical review and assessment by scholarly leaders in the discipline" (p. 125). The breadth of this definition allows for its application to the investigation of topics in any field. Hence, it serves as an appropriate initial conceptualization for use in discussion of undergraduate research, a phenomenon that has increasingly captured the attention of academics across a wide range of disciplines.

Although Lichter's (1995) definition provides a starting point for developing a shared understanding of undergraduate research, it is by no means complete.

According to Strassburger (1995), undergraduate research must involve "students working in partnership with faculty in discipline-based inquiries" (p. 120). This criterion marks an important distinction between undergraduate research and other forms of scholarship in which faculty might engage, in that undergraduate research is not simply directed toward the advancement of knowledge within the discipline, but is also intended to provide an educational experience for the student researcher (Hakim, 2000). Malachowski (2012) characterized this distinction as a contrast between *product-oriented* scholarship, in which the contribution to the discipline is paramount, and *process-oriented* scholarship, in which the benefits of the research experience are of higher priority.

While undergraduate research differs from other investigative activities in which faculty might participate, insofar as discovery is not its sole function, it also differs from other learning activities in which students might participate, insofar as education is not its sole function either. Emphasizing the significance of the actual work product, the Council on Undergraduate Research (CUR) (2016a) has defined undergraduate research as "an inquiry or investigation conducted by an undergraduate student that makes an original intellectual or creative contribution to the discipline." Lopatto (2010) cautioned against any effort to divorce the educational functions of undergraduate research from the goal of contributing to the scholarship of the discipline, arguing that the two are inextricably linked, such that one cannot exist without the other.

Further clarifying the goals of undergraduate research, Elgren and Hensel (2006) cited three key outcomes: (1) promotion of student learning, (2) encouragement of faculty research productivity, and (3) advancement of knowledge within the discipline. In structuring undergraduate research programs, any of these functions may constitute a legitimate consideration. In examining variation in program emphases, Beckman and Hensel (2009) advanced a multifaceted view, which took into account such factors as targeted populations, program goals, organizational structures, and disciplinary foci.

Based on recurrent themes emerging in the professional literature, it would seem that undergraduate research can be properly understood as a unitive approach to teaching and scholarship, in which faculty members work with undergraduate students to facilitate their learning, through the production of original scientific or creative works, which are ultimately shared with the academic community and evaluated according to the prevailing standards of the relevant disciplines. Undergraduate research programs can be further understood as systematic initiatives that promote such activity in a coordinated fashion within one or more collegiate institutions.

Variations in Undergraduate Research Models

On individual campuses, various opportunities exist for students to participate in undergraduate research. These opportunities differ among themselves with respect to a number of factors, including student and faculty roles and provisions for credit, compensation, and exposure.

Forms of Student and Faculty Participation

Although undergraduate research generally involves contributions by both students and faculty members, the nature of these contributions and the relationship between the two parties can vary widely. Therefore, one basis upon which to classify undergraduate research models is according to the roles of the student and the faculty mentor in the research project. Previous authors have drawn a distinction between activities, including research, in which students assume primary responsibility for their own learning versus similar activities in which decision-making authority rests primarily in the hands of faculty members (McDorman, 2004; Weimer, 2002). Others have identified a third and more egalitarian model of the student-faculty relationship, in which learning itself is viewed as a shared endeavor (Cook-Sather, Bovill, & Felten, 2014; Fink, 2003; Kezar, 1999). Addressing undergraduate research in particular, Beckman and Hensel (2009) differentiated between projects that reflect primarily the vision of the student and those in which the faculty mentor exerts greater influence. Drawing a similar distinction, Levy (2011) further differentiated between projects that involve primarily *inquiry for learning* and those that focus more on *inquiry for knowledge-building*.

Consistent with the prior literature, three orientations toward undergraduate research will be examined in the remaining chapters of this book. In the interest of clarity and consistency, the terms used in reference to these three orientations are *student-directed*, *faculty-directed*, and *collaborative*.

The Student-Directed Model

Student-directed research involves projects in which undergraduate students are the principal investigators. Typically, the student investigates a research problem that he or she has identified. This type of research is often largely driven by students' own curiosity. While even student-directed research requires the guidance of a faculty member, this guidance typically comes in the form of support and consultation rather than close monitoring. Multhaup et al. (2010) referred to this model as the *consultant model*, to reflect the nondirective stance taken by the faculty advisor. Student-directed research is especially well suited to fields in which creativity is emphasized and equipment costs are minimal (Temple, Sibley, & Orr, 2010). This type of project has been credited with broadening the scholarly interests of faculty mentors, whose own lines of research tend to be more narrowly focused. It has been noted that institutional funding is especially important to the support of student-directed research, because projects of this nature tend not to comport with criteria commonly used by external funding agencies to prioritize grant proposals (Gazdik & Powell, 2012).

The Faculty-Directed Model

In faculty-directed research, the faculty member is the principal investigator. Students participating in faculty-directed projects typically assume the role of research assistants, supporting faculty members in the execution of studies designed by the faculty members themselves. It is not uncommon for this type of research to be carried out by teams of students, under the direction of a single faculty member, though more narrowly defined subtopics may be assigned to individual students within the team (Temple et al., 2010). Laursen, Hunter, Seymour, Thiry, and Melton (2010) used the term *faculty-led* to describe this model. Referring to this approach as the *traditional model*, Multhaup et al. (2010) described it as "the most conventional way that undergraduates gain research experience" (p. 21).

The Collaborative Model

The collaborative model closely parallels what Multhaup et al. (2010) have termed the *joint-creation model*, an approach to undergraduate research in which both the student and the faculty member leave their intellectual marks on the project. In collaborative research, the undergraduate student and the faculty member become partners, and both contribute substantially to the research project.

All three of these models for undergraduate research provide opportunities for both faculty members and students to learn and grow. However, they vary in the relative emphasis placed on the research interests of the two parties and their respective roles in the investigative process. In general, the collaborative model appears to most fully represent the ideals of undergraduate research, as articulated in the second section of this book. However, any of these models might be appropriate for inclusion in a comprehensive undergraduate research program.

Structural Provisions for Undergraduate Research

Just as there are numerous models for the roles of students and faculty members in undergraduate research, there are numerous ways in which research opportunities can be incorporated into the undergraduate experience. Three common provisions are course assignments, independent studies or theses, and fellowships.

Course Assignments

Course-based research activities can range from experiments conducted within the classroom or laboratory during regular class sessions to semester-long projects that students carry out either individually or in teams. Laursen et al. (2010) distinguished this model of undergraduate research from what they have termed the *apprenticeship model*, the latter being characterized by more intensive and sustained interaction with a faculty mentor or other experienced investigator. Although course-based research assignments are generally of limited scale, they can be used effectively to introduce students to basic elements of research and scholarly writing, and can enhance the overall quality of the classroom experience (Bean, 2011). A major benefit of course-based research is that it provides opportunities for students of widely varied skill levels to strengthen their research proficiency over time, rather than limiting research opportunities to only the most accomplished students (Martinetti, Leynes, Medvecky, Benson, & Paul, 2009).

Course-based research activities have a long history, particularly in the natural sciences (Tannenbaum, 2006), and there appears to be growing momentum for systematic efforts to incorporate research experiences into the undergraduate curriculum (Elgren & Hensel, 2006). The dedication of three thematic issues of the *Council on Undergraduate Research Quarterly* to this general topic serves as evidence of this trend (DeCosmo, 2016; Gould, 2016; McConnaughay & Rueckert, 2006). Together, these issues included reports of innovative practices in the teaching of biology, chemistry, geology, economics, education, engineering, mathematics, music history, psychology/neuroscience, and social work, all directed toward ensuring that students gain experience in research within their undergraduate degree programs. A fourth issue of the *Quarterly* more specifically highlighted curricular provisions for research outside the major (LaPlant, 2013a). CUR has also published a bound collection of essays, dealing with over 50 campus-based curricular initiatives designed to promote undergraduate students' engagement in creative or investigative activities in the humanities, social sciences, natural sciences, and engineering (Karukstis & Elgren, 2007).

In examining the characteristics of course-based research, Griffiths (2004) focused on three factors: (1) the breadth with which research is incorporated into the course, (2) the depth of its infusion, and (3) the direction of the relationship between teaching and research within the course. With these three factors taken into account, he identified four general models for the integration of research and classroom teaching: (1) *research-led* teaching, in which research findings are emphasized within the course content; (2) *research-oriented* teaching, in which the process of inquiry is emphasized within the course content; (3) *research-based* teaching, in which students' direct engagement in the process of inquiry is a primary method of instruction; and (4) *research-informed* teaching, in which empirical findings on the processes of teaching and learning are used to guide the pedagogical decisions of the instructor. Building upon this framework, Healey (2005) combined the first three orientations with a fourth approach, which he termed *research-tutored* instruction. Under the *research-tutored* model, students engage in processes of writing and discussion as a means of learning. Healey (2005) organized the four models into a two-dimensional classification scheme, based on their relative emphases on content versus process and the role of the teacher versus that of the student.

The research-oriented and research-based models are especially relevant to undergraduate research, as traditionally understood, insofar as they directly engage students in the acquisition and application of research skills. As enthusiasm for undergraduate research has expanded beyond the scientific disciplines, the research-tutored model has also gained significance (McDorman, 2004; Rogers, 2003). In actual practice, elements of multiple models can be integrated into a single course. In particular, the research-oriented and research-based models are frequently fused together in courses where students engage in research activities while learning about research as a subject (Murray, 2014; Posselt & Black, 2007; Rogers, 2010).

The decision to adopt an inquiry-based curriculum raises questions as to how best to organize research experiences for undergraduate students (Tannenbaum, 2006). In considering various patterns of organization, two characteristics of the curriculum must be taken into account: (1) the degree to which research experiences are distributed across the full four years, and (2) the degree to which they build cumulatively one upon another. On a very basic level, a research-intensive curriculum must include multiple opportunities for students to participate in research activity. Several authors have described individual or linked courses, across a variety of disciplines, in which students have completed entire research projects and prepared oral or written presentations of their work within a single academic term (Bender, 2010; Firmage, Tietenberg, & Cole, 2005; Golphin & Smith, 2007), as well as programs of study that have been comprised of several such courses (Brown & Yurekli, 2007). Others have presented curricula in which sequences of research-related courses have culminated in completion of senior theses, projects, or presentations (Awong-Taylor et al., 2016; Birkhead & Stanton, 2011; Hedley & Schneider, 2009; Shanahan, 2011; Sukumaran et al., 2006; Temple et al., 2010).

A popular feature of many research-intensive curricula is the capstone course. Capstone courses are designed to provide students with opportunities to synthesize insights gleaned from previous coursework and to apply theoretical understandings to problems or issues within or across disciplines. Such courses typically incorporate major projects, papers, or presentations (Clear, Goldweber, Young, Leidig, & Scott, 2001; Hicok, 2009; Hirsch, Lazarus, Wisler, Minde, & Cerasini, 2013; Munroe, 2016; Sukumaran et al., 2006; Wittner, 2007). Although culminating experiences of this nature can also be undertaken outside the context of structured courses (Kuh, 2008), the discipline-based capstone course remains the predominant model for such experiences (Hauhart & Grahe, 2015). A recent thematic issue of the *Quarterly* offered examples of how capstone experiences can be incorporated into curricula across a wide variety of disciplines (LaPlant, 2014).

Although capstone courses are usually taken during the senior year, Williams and Johnson (2007) presented an alternative model in which the capstone course was taken during the spring of the junior year, as a prelude to independent research during the senior year. In a variation on the capstone course, Harvey Mudd College, which specializes in science, technology, engineering, and mathematics (STEM) related fields, requires each student to complete at least one upper level integrative course, but with greater flexibility in the timing of enrollment and with course goals that are uniquely reflective of the institution's STEM mission (Karukstis, 2007a).

While capstone courses offer distinctive opportunities for synthesis and application of disciplinary content, it would be a mistake to assume that direct participation in research activity cannot occur well in advance of the senior year. Indeed, there is growing interest in the promotion of early exposure to undergraduate research, as highlighted in a special issue of the *Quarterly* devoted to the topic (Rueckert, 2008). Looking beyond the first-year student experience, Wilson and Crowe (2010) emphasized the need for continued attention to appropriate research opportunities during the sophomore year as well.

In general, it would appear that the most effective curricular strategy is one that promotes students' understanding of research and their ability to conduct research through a progressive immersion in the research process (Brownell & Swaner, 2010; Jenkins, Breen, Lindsay, & Brew, 2003). The Research Skill Development (RSD) framework was devised as a curricular model for promoting students' acquisition of research skills in a systematic and progressive fashion. Under this model, courses are structured and sequenced to promote students' advancement through five increasing levels of autonomy as researchers. At each level, attention is given to six facets of the research process and corresponding research skills. The goal of the program is for students to become proficient in defining research problems, choosing appropriate research methodologies, analyzing data, organizing information, applying research findings, and responsibly communicating results (Willison & O'Regan, 2007).

Independent Studies and Theses

In a definition drawn from the gifted education literature, Johnsen and Goree (2005) described independent study as:

> a planned research process that (a) is self-directed; (b) is similar to one used by a practicing professional or is authentic to the discipline; (c) is facilitated and monitored by the teacher; and (d) focuses on lifelike problems that go beyond the regular class setting.
>
> *(pp. 5–6)*

In an influential earlier work on the subject, focusing specifically on higher education, Dressel and Thompson (1973) advanced an understanding of independent study as both a pedagogical strategy to be used with students and a competency to be developed within them.

Whereas a collegiate independent study requires a relatively high level of sophistication on the part of the student, it is usually not conducted until the junior or senior year (Rotenberg, 2005). At some institutions, students in every major are required to complete a senior independent study. At other institutions, completing an independent study is optional or left to the discretion of the departmental faculty (Tannenbaum, 2006). The independent study typically takes the form of student-directed research. Though a faculty member oversees the project, an independent study allows students to determine their own research topics and work through the entire research process with minimal direction (Dressel & Thompson, 1973). Independent studies provide opportunities for students to engage in research on a larger scale than would be typical in a classroom situation and to venture into areas of research not addressed in the regular curriculum (Friedman, 1986).

Several authors have advocated the use of contracts as a tool for structuring individualized learning experiences in general (Austin, 1986; Friedman, 1986; Rotenberg, 2005) and for setting the terms of undergraduate research in particular (Fox, 2010; Groover, 2014; Mabrouk, 2003). Such devices clearly lend themselves well to use in the planning and execution of independent studies. In keeping with the nature and purpose of the independent study, a process of negotiation that begins with submission of a proposal by the student can be an attractive alternative to an instructor-generated contract and has been shown to be effective in lending structure to creative projects (Posnick, 2014).

One specific form of independent research that has become a mark of distinction for a number of institutions (Gray & Schermer, 2011), and a key component of honors programs on many more campuses (Anderson, Lyons, & Weiner, 2014), is the senior thesis. Under this model, throughout the senior year, the student conducts an investigation of a topic that is approved by a faculty advisor. The end result, usually a lengthy paper, is then presented to the advisor and a team of faculty members who critique the student's work (Austin, 1986). Additionally, the student is sometimes required to defend the thesis orally in front of a faculty panel. This rigorous evaluation process challenges the student to grow intellectually. By its nature, the thesis engages students in writing, problem-solving, self-reflection, original thought, and public presentation of their work (Anderson et al., 2014).

According to Austin (1986), the educational benefits of the thesis can be further enhanced through participation in a research seminar, either before undertaking the project or while it is underway. One of the benefits of a concurrent seminar is the reassurance that it offers students, as they attempt to cope with the inevitable anxiety associated with undertaking a project of such magnitude for the first time (Hedley & Schneider, 2009). The senior thesis can also be combined with earlier experiences of independent study, to mark the culmination of an undergraduate degree program that is rich in inquiry (Bettison-Varga, 2006; Chiang, 2007).

Fellowships

Undergraduate research fellowships provide students with remuneration for their scholarly work. Fellowship research can be student-directed, faculty-directed, or collaborative (Cook & McCauley, 2003; McGee, 2003), and students can be compensated in a variety of ways. For example, students can participate in summer research programs where they receive stipends and housing on campus for the duration of their research (Cook & McCauley, 2003; McGee, 2003; Noice, 2003; Turner, 2005) or they can serve as research assistants and receive hourly wages to work for faculty members (Turrens, 2003; Wozniak, 2011). Within the admissions process, merit-based financial awards are sometimes granted to outstandingly qualified incoming students for subsequent service in faculty members' laboratories (Shrier, 2007), collaboration with faculty members in summer research (Elgren, Billiter, & Paris, 2007; Rocheleau, Muschio, Malazita, Petrovich, & Mohan, 2013), or other types of supervised research activity (Wozniak, 2011). Closely related to fellowships are research scholarships, which help defray the cost of tuition for the semesters in which students work on research (Blockus, 2003; Randall & Collins, 2011; Turner, 2005), and grants, which cover various other expenses associated with students' research (McGee, 2003; Turner, 2005; Turrens, 2003; Whatley & Miller, 2001).

Summer fellowships are especially popular, because they allow undergraduate students and their faculty mentors to devote their undivided attention to research in a way that is not possible amidst the competing demands of the regular academic year (Boone, 2003; Temple et al., 2010; Turrens, 2003; Visick, 2006). Because the summer is a time when many students must work to meet their financial obligations, the stipends that are offered to summer research fellows are critical to many students' ability to participate in these programs (Turrens, 2003).

An additional benefit of the summer program format is the opportunity to cultivate a student culture that is built around the shared experience of academic inquiry. It is for this reason that participants are often encouraged, or even required, to live on campus during their summer research experiences (Boone, 2003). Many institutions also work to promote a sense of community among summer research fellows through social, cultural, and academic programs on campus (Blockus, 2003; McGee, 2003; Quinones & Marsteller, 2005; Turner, 2005; Turrens, 2003).

In contrast to the more inclusive definition presented here, Lopatto (2010) characterized the role of the *research fellow* as limited only to those students who are intensively immersed in research activity on a full-time basis, typically during the summer months and often with substantial autonomy. He distinguished this role from those of the *employee* and the *apprentice*. As conceived by Lopatto, employees are typically paid an hourly wage to perform laboratory maintenance or other tasks in support of faculty research, but with no direct involvement in the design of the study or interpretation of the findings. In contrast, apprentices more typically work for fixed stipends or for academic credit and make substantive contributions to their research projects, though often under the close supervision of their faculty mentors.

Although the broader definition of fellowship will be used through the remainder of this book, Lopatto's (2010) distinction is an important one, insofar as the three roles that he cited represent a developmental sequence through which paid undergraduate researchers should ideally pass over the course of their experience. Framing the progression in these terms can enable research mentors to structure their protégées' assignments in ways that systematically facilitate their continuous growth in autonomy.

Dissemination of Undergraduate Research Findings

An important aspect of undergraduate research is the dissemination of findings. In the words of Temple et al. (2010), "scholarship not communicated is essentially scholarship not done" (p. 12). When work on a project is complete, faculty mentors have the opportunity to present their results to peers in their fields. Undergraduates, likewise, have an array of opportunities to present their work, both at the institutional level and beyond. Through institutional and outside support, undergraduates can present their findings at professional meetings and conferences or in scholarly publications (Blockus, 2003; Hawkins, Leone, & Jarvis-Mejia, 2011; Turner, 2005; Whatley & Miller, 2001). In addition to the principal outlets of their disciplines, undergraduate researchers have the option of disseminating their work through conferences and journals established specifically for undergraduate students (Hakim, 2000; Kinkead, 2003).

Even apart from national and regional venues, undergraduates at many colleges and universities have opportunities to present their work at institutionally sponsored conferences and symposia. Through oral and poster presentations, students share their results with peers, faculty members, and administrators across all disciplines (Hakim, 2000). Such events have been successfully implemented at widely varied institutions (Brush, Cox, Harris, & Torda, 2010; Hoffman, Fletcher, & Dwyer, 2009; Kitchens, Dolan, Hinshaw, & Johnson, 2010; Shokair, 2002). Both institution-wide and program-specific events have been used to successfully highlight undergraduate student scholarship (Kinkead, 2010).

In addition to enhancing students' self-confidence, on-campus conferences and symposia help to convey the high academic standards that institutions hold for their students (Kuh et al., 2005). By opening the events up to various external constituencies, colleges and universities can showcase the intellectual life of their campuses on a wider scale as well (Hoffman et al., 2009). Lebanon Valley College, for example, elevated its undergraduate research conference to the level of a regional event by inviting participants from approximately 20 other institutions within about a 120-mile radius of its campus (Kitchens et al., 2010). A similar event at the University of South Carolina Upstate has evolved from an institutional undergraduate research showcase into one that is truly regional in scope, drawing financial support from area businesses and participation from approximately 12 postsecondary institutions and numerous high schools (van Delden, 2012).

Institutional publications, including journals devoted specifically to undergraduate research, also provide opportunities for students to showcase their work (Hakim, 2000). A recent monograph on the subject included profiles of numerous such publications, representing a variety of academic disciplines and institutional types (Hart, 2012a). Jenkins (2012) succinctly summarized the rationale for such publications, stating that:

> the value of undergraduate research journals lies in: (a) supporting students' entry and participation into a (discipline-based) research community; (b) the intellectual value to students in writing and rewriting in a public forum; (c) the benefit to students in being seen as producers of knowledge; and (d) the benefits to students, departments, and institutions of making student research public.
>
> *(p. 5)*

The review process for undergraduate research journals often mirrors that of other scholarly publications, providing students with an authentic experience of writing for an academic audience and receiving constructive feedback on their work (Turner, 2005). At some institutions, students also perform editorial functions in the publication of undergraduate research journals (Shokair, 2002; Whatley & Miller, 2001). In combination with conferences and symposia, such publications enable students to sharpen their skills in both oral and written communication, a benefit that can also be attained through the publication of conference proceedings (Turner, 2005).

In making the case for undergraduate research journals, Hart (2012b) positioned them as a necessary supplement to the existing periodical literature, noting that publishing opportunities within traditional outlets are insufficient to accommodate the growing body of research carried out by undergraduate students. Dellinger and Walkington (2012) offered further elaboration on how institutionally sponsored undergraduate research journals could enhance the curricular offerings of a particular institution, while also providing supplementary learning opportunities outside of class. A further benefit of producing such publications on campus is the resultant collection of artifacts, which can be used for purposes of institutional outcomes assessment (Karkowski, Hutchinson, & Howell, 2012).

Institutionalizing Undergraduate Research

While pockets of undergraduate research activity are undoubtedly present on nearly all campuses, and are certainly worthwhile, a carefully coordinated campus-wide undergraduate research program can increase further the opportunities that exist for all students and faculty members. With this benefit in mind, growing attention has been directed toward the institutionalization of undergraduate research, meaning the establishment of such activity as a central element of the educational enterprise, permeating all departmental and disciplinary boundaries. While such efforts have, thus far, been concentrated primarily at the level of the individual campus, there appears to be growing momentum for institutionalization across entire systems and consortia as well (Malachowski, Osborn, Karukstis, & Ambos, 2015).

A longtime advocate of institutionalization, Malachowski (2003) emphasized the need to support those faculty members who are already active in undergraduate research. Among the conditions that he cited as influential in creating a supportive environment on campus were departmental cultures, tenure and promotion policies, faculty workload and compensation, patterns of resource allocation, and student skill levels relative to the demands of faculty research. Citing many of these same factors, Hakim (2000) classified pertinent issues into four broad categories, based on whether they related to faculty, students, the curriculum, or the campus climate. In particular, he emphasized the need for faculty development efforts designed to promote interest in undergraduate research, along with parallel incentives and support for student researchers themselves. He also stressed the importance of strong administrative leadership and high visibility for undergraduate research, as well as effective use of benchmarking to assess the progress of efforts to create comprehensive undergraduate research programs. As other authors have recognized, the creation of an organizational culture that is supportive of undergraduate research can sometimes require nothing short of a full-scale institutional transformation (Lopatto, 2010; Malachowski & Webster, 2008).

On a very basic level, institutionalization of undergraduate research can be advanced through incorporation of relevant goals into statements of organizational purpose and alignment of program objectives with existing institutional goal statements (Kinkead, 2010; Spears, 2009; Winningham, Templeton, Dutton, & Scheck, 2009). Institutional case histories have illustrated how strategic planning documents can be used to secure a place for undergraduate research in institutions that have changed their statuses from liberal arts colleges to comprehensive universities (Levesque & Wise, 2001) and vice versa (Pierce, 2001). Such evidence has also affirmed the role that accreditation can play in advancing an institutional commitment to undergraduate research (Etaugh & Liberty, 2001; Hirsch et al., 2013).

Among the most significant factors in the institutionalization of undergraduate research is the importance that faculty members assign to such activity, as their attitudes have been shown to closely correspond to rates of student participation (Kuh, 2008). There are numerous ways in which the value of undergraduate research can be impressed upon faculty and support given to those who heed the call (Jenkins & Healey, 2015). References to research mentorship in job listings and in pre-employment interviews can send a strong message to faculty candidates, a message that can be reinforced through the faculty review process and the allocation of institutional funds to support mentorship activities on the job (Chmielewski, 2007; Jarvis, Shaughnessy, Chase, & Barney, 2011; LaPlant, 2011a). Compensation for involvement in undergraduate research can take many forms, including stipends (Elgren et al., 2007), travel resources, course reductions (Barthell et al., 2013), sabbatical funding, and acceleration of sabbatical eligibility (Walsh, 2007a).

Establishment of undergraduate research as a credit-bearing activity also holds the potential to increase faculty motivation to participate, if factored into the calculation of teaching loads (Chiang, 2007; Mickley, 2007). Walczak and Richey (2016) illustrated how a directed study course, offered in a group format, could be used effectively to achieve this end. Faculty members can likewise be encouraged to develop new research-intensive courses, or to revise existing courses so as to make them more research-intensive, through the use of curriculum development grants (Singer, 2007; Thornton, Beinstein-Miller, Gandha, & deWinstanley, 2004).

Informational campaigns must also be undertaken to ensure that faculty members are aware of the opportunities and resources that are available to them (Goodman, 2006) and understand the potential benefits of integrating research into undergraduate education (Castley, 2006). Kinkead (2010) advocated the application of basic marketing principles to the dissemination of information on undergraduate research within the campus community and offered numerous examples of successful marketing strategies. Peer mentoring is another strategy by which a culture of undergraduate research can be built within an institution, as faculty members who have developed an understanding of accepted principles and practices share their expertise with colleagues. Several national initiatives serve to illustrate how this strategy can be employed even beyond the boundaries of a single campus (Karukstis, 2010; Thorsheim, LaCost, & Narum, 2010).

The creation of a campus environment in which undergraduate research is celebrated stands as one of the most important factors in institutionalization of undergraduate research. One of the most common means of affirming the value of such activity within the campus community is through the types of conferences and symposia described previously (Kinkead, 2003). Other forms of recognition may include awards convocations or banquets (Hakim, 2000) and special honors at graduation (Whatley & Miller, 2001). Bulletin boards and display cases can also be used to highlight undergraduate research and creative work (Chmielewski, 2007). Interestingly, even showcasing faculty scholarship appears to be an effective way of increasing student interest in collaborating with faculty on research and parental support for such activity (Nichols & Lyon, 2013).

The establishment of an institutional committee charged with promoting undergraduate research activity can help generate new forms of celebration and, in itself, speaks to the value of undergraduate research within the institution. Therefore, appointment of such a committee can be an important step toward institutionalization of undergraduate research (Turner, 2005). In assembling such a committee, it is generally advisable to seek broad representation of multiple institutional units and to incorporate existing programs into any overarching initiatives that might be proposed (Spears, 2009; Winningham et al., 2009). Segura-Totten (2012) offered a step-by-step process for the development of an action plan for institutionalization of undergraduate research, making use of a broadly representative committee structure. In addition to producing a roadmap for expansion of undergraduate research, this process yields assessment matrices that allow for ongoing monitoring of progress.

As colleges and universities have begun to successfully institutionalize undergraduate research on their campuses, conversations have turned to the ultimate goal of making the production of original scholarship an inherent element of the undergraduate experience for all students. The phrase, "undergraduate research for all," has become a rallying cry among proponents of full inclusivity, and its selection as the theme of an issue of the *Quarterly* (Stocks, 2011a) suggests that this call has not fallen on deaf ears. Within the broader context of its Liberal Education and America's Promise (LEAP) initiative, the Association of American Colleges and Universities (AAC&U) recently set forth an innovative template for undergraduate liberal education in the 21st Century. Under this new paradigm, known as the LEAP Challenge, each student is required to produce a *signature work*, described as "a significant project—extending across an entire semester or more—that represents the student's own best work on a question or problem that matters to the student and to society" (Schneider, 2015, p. 6).

Individual institutions have employed a variety of strategies to broaden participation in undergraduate research, including enactment of new curricular requirements, expansion of financial support, and infusion of research into existing civic engagement activities (Hensel, 2011a). However, the feasibility of universal participation in undergraduate research across all institutional settings remains open to question (Stocks, 2011b). One strategy for alleviating the strain that strict research requirements can place on institutional resources is to articulate multiple project formats that are tailored to the academic and professional goals of students and that do not demand equal levels of faculty involvement (Dolan, 2011).

Additionally, course-based research has been advanced as a less resource-intensive alternative to more tutorially based forms of undergraduate research, such as independent studies, theses, and summer fellowships (Awong-Taylor et al., 2016; Mateja, 2011). There is reason to believe that the efficiency and effectiveness of this approach can be further enhanced through the availability of graduate students to serve as consultants on course-based projects (Pukkila, Arnold, Li, & Bickford, 2013). There is also some precedent for employment of undergraduate peer mentors to serve in a similar capacity, a staffing model that appears to contribute to the scholarly development of the peer mentor, in addition to increasing instructional support for the students enrolled in the course (Carr et al., 2013).

While recognizing the logistical challenges associated with mandatory undergraduate research in the major, Malachowski and Dwyer (2011) have argued that curricular requirements are one of the most powerful means by which we communicate to students the essential knowledge and competencies of their disciplines. Offering justification for its inclusion as a vital component of both professional and disciplinary based bachelor's degree programs, Hensel (2011a) observed that "undergraduate research provides both the intellectual development that is the hallmark of a liberal arts education and excellent preparation for entering the workforce" (p. 4).

Conclusion

Institutionalization of undergraduate research and the call for full participation are only the most recent steps in an evolutionary process that has transformed undergraduate research from a sound teaching practice employed by a relatively small number of academics into a major trend within American higher education. This trend is a product of emerging priorities within the academy and the broader culture, as well as contemporary understandings of the educational process and the relationship of the student to the teacher, the institution, the community, and the discipline. Each of these aspects of undergraduate research, its history, and its future direction will be explored further in the remaining chapters of this book.

PART II

The Rationale

2

A THEORETICAL FOUNDATION FOR UNDERGRADUATE RESEARCH

The growing interest in undergraduate research within American higher education has been linked in the academic literature to an even broader trend toward the adoption of active and collaborative pedagogies (Kinkead, 2003), which in turn is grounded in constructivist learning theory (Hu, Scheuch, Schwartz, Gayles, & Li, 2008), traditionally defined by its underlying premise that learning occurs through a process of discovery and transformation of information by the learner (Slavin, 2015). While constructivist learning theory offers ample support upfront for students' engagement in original research and creative activities, the past 30 years have brought a greater fusion of developmental and pedagogical perspectives on learning, which has resituated constructivist learning theory within a broader school of thought that offers an even more compelling case for undergraduate research than does constructivist learning theory alone.

The Constructive Developmentalist Perspective

American higher education has been influenced in recent years by dramatically changing views of the learning process, as exemplified by an ascending branch of educational theory known as *constructive developmentalism*. This term, initially coined by Kegan (1982), is currently understood to mean a:

> view of learning [that] incorporates two major concepts: (1) that students construct knowledge by organizing and making meaning of their experiences, and (2) that this construction takes place in the context of their evolving assumptions about knowledge itself and students' roles in creating it.
>
> *(Baxter Magolda, 1999, p. 6)*

The term is well chosen in that this point of view is informed by both constructivist learning theory and cognitive structural theory, the branch of developmental theory that deals with changes in "how people think, reason, and make meaning of their experiences" (Patton, Renn, Guido, & Quaye, 2016, p. 315). Kegan (1994) himself characterized constructive developmentalism as having its roots in both the constructivist and the developmentalist traditions.

Perhaps no theory more fully exemplifies the melding of epistemology and developmental psychology than does Kegan's (1994) own theory of meaning-making and self-authorship. According to this theory, the principles by which individuals organize their understandings of themselves, others, and the world around them become increasingly complex over time. Thus, cognitive development consists of a passage through progressively more advanced patterns of thought, termed *orders of consciousness*. An important aspect of this theory is the distinction between *object* and *subject*. Whereas the former consists of "those elements of our knowing or organizing that we can reflect on, handle, look at, be responsible for, relate to each other, take control of, internalize, assimilate, or otherwise operate upon" (p. 32), the latter includes "those elements of our knowing or organizing that we are identified with, tied to, fused with, or embedded in" (p. 32). While the predominant organizing principle associated with a particular stage of development can only be experienced as subject, advancement to a more mature pattern of understanding enables the individual to reflect upon this principle from a more detached perspective that transforms it from subject into object. Thus, "each successive principle subsumes or encompasses the prior principle" (p. 33), such that the world view of the individual becomes progressively more complex and inclusive at each iteration.

Among the cognitive structural theories of development, Perry's (1968/1999) conceptualization of the intellectual and ethical growth process has been especially influential within the constructive developmentalist school of thought. Focusing particularly on the influence of authority on the world view of the individual, this theory characterizes cognitive development as a process of advancement through three major patterns of reasoning: *dualism*, *multiplicity*, and *relativism*. Dualism is a pattern of thought in which truth is seen as absolute and faith is placed in authorities to provide correct answers. In multiplicity, it is recognized that authorities may not have all the answers, and that ultimately the truth may be unknowable. Consequently, when faced with uncertainty, differing beliefs often come to be seen as equally valid. Relativism is characterized by a realization that questions of right and wrong may be influenced by contextual variables, but that not all judgments are equally valid. Thus, while uncertainty is tolerated, even matters of opinion or conjecture are subject to critical examination. Progression into relativism ultimately sets the stage for mature value judgments and identity commitments, giving rise to a developmental state that Perry has termed *commitment in relativism*.

Building upon the work of Perry and others, Belenky, Clinchy, Goldberger, and Tarule (1986), Baxter Magolda (1992), and King and Kitchener (1994) have all crafted constructive developmentalist theories in which cognitive maturation is marked by growth in tolerance for ambiguity and independence of thought. Each of these theories, in its own right, has had a major influence on current understandings of the teaching and learning process. The work of Belenky et al. (1986) and Baxter Magolda (1992), in particular, has been valued highly for the light it has shed on women's thought processes and their unique experiences as students in American colleges and universities. This aspect of their work will be discussed further in chapter 8.

Baxter Magolda's more recent work has moved beyond her initial focus on cognitive development, toward a more integrated view of higher education's impact on students. Elaborating on the concept of self-authorship, meaning a "capacity to internally define a coherent belief system and identity that coordinates mutual relations with others" (2004a, p. 8), Baxter Magolda (2004b) has characterized the process as one of passage from reliance on externally imposed definitions toward an assumption of personal control over one's life and world view. This shift toward self-empowerment parallels her previous findings on students' growth in independence as learners (Baxter Magolda, 1992), but is more fully encompassing insofar as it incorporates three separate dimensions of development: (1) the *epistemological* dimension, which is concerned with how one constructs knowledge; (2) the *intrapersonal* dimension, which is concerned with one's sense of individual identity; and (3) the *interpersonal* dimension, which is concerned with one's capacity for mature relationships with others (Baxter Magolda, 2004a, 2004b).

This conceptualization of self-authorship is noteworthy insofar as the intrapersonal and interpersonal dimensions relate to aspects of development explored previously by scholars whose work is more firmly embedded in the psychosocial branch of developmental theory (Chickering & Reisser, 1993; Erikson, 1968; Josselson, 1987, 1996; Marcia, 1966). According to Patton et al. (2016), "psychosocial theorists examine the *content* of development; that is, the important issues people face as their lives progress, such as how to define themselves and their relationships with others, and what to do with their lives" (p. 287). The integration of psychosocial perspectives into constructive developmentalism reinforces a holistic view of student learning and attention to both content and process in college teaching.

The Pedagogy of Active Learning

The shift to a constructive developmentalist perspective on learning has had a direct impact on the practice of teaching. No longer viewed as a process in which the student passively absorbs knowledge imparted by the instructor, today's higher education emphasizes the active participation of learners in a process that is dynamic, complex, and collaborative. *Active learning*, as this general instructional orientation has come to be known, has its roots in constructivist learning theory and has gained further traction from the diversity and craving for excitement that characterize today's students (Silberman, 1996). In opposition to the more traditional model, Conrad and Dunek (2012) have argued that there is a need for citizens and workers who can independently acquire the knowledge and skills necessary to adapt to rapidly changing conditions. Constructivist learning theory has spawned several specific pedagogical approaches that have come to be widely embraced in higher education and that easily encompass opportunities for undergraduate research. These approaches include experiential learning, discovery learning, service-learning, and collaborative learning.

Experiential Learning

According to Cantor (1995), "experiential education refers to learning activities that engage the learner directly in the phenomena being studied" (p. 1). This instructional approach, while not new, appears to have become more prevalent in recent years, in part because of growing awareness of constructivist learning theory and cognitive developmental theory. Additionally, it is believed to be especially well suited to the demands currently placed on American higher education, including the need to accommodate the learning styles of diverse students and to prepare workers and citizens who are good collaborators and who are skilled in problem-solving (Cantor, 1995).

Building upon the earlier work of Dewey (1938/1963) and others, Kolb (1984) set forth a theory of experiential learning that has been especially influential in higher education. According to this theory, experiential learning typically follows a cycle in which four distinct modes of learning are employed. The first of these approaches, *concrete experience*, involves drawing conclusions from direct encounters with environmental stimuli through the use of one's senses. The second approach, *reflective observation*, consists of an internal processing of information in the environment, without any direct manipulation of external stimuli. The third approach, *abstract conceptualization*, is a process by which general understandings can be drawn from experiences, through symbolic representation. Finally, *active experimentation* is a process in which the learner gains new insight by acting directly upon his or her environment.

One of the principal benefits of this theory is its use in distinguishing among the preferred learning styles of various students. Drawing two separate dichotomies among the four modes of learning (concrete experience versus abstract conceptualization; reflective observation versus active experimentation), Kolb (1984) identified four distinct learning styles, each characterized by a different combination of preferred modes: (1) *convergent* (abstract conceptualization and active experimentation), (2) *divergent* (concrete experience and reflective observation), (3) *assimilative* (abstract conceptualization and reflective observation), and (4) *accommodative* (concrete experience and active experimentation).

Beyond its demand for students' active engagement in the learning process, which would clearly favor undergraduate research, Kolb's (1984) theory has also heightened awareness of the need for accommodating the varied learning styles of a diverse student population. Whereas undergraduate research projects are often tailored to the interests of individual students, such projects lend themselves well to applications of the typological aspect of this theory.

Discovery Learning

Discovery learning has been defined as "a constructivist approach to teaching in which students are encouraged to discover principles for themselves" (Slavin, 2015, p. 437). A noted proponent of this approach, Bruner (1961/1973) contrasted it with more traditional forms of instruction. Characterizing traditional instruction as an *expository* approach, meaning that the teacher presents content to the learner in a manner of the teacher's own choosing, he explained that discovery learning is *hypothetical* in nature, allowing the learner to play an active role in defining the course of the learning process. Bruner (1960) favored this approach as a means of attending to four conditions of the educational situation that influence its conduciveness to student learning: (1) a focus on the primary structures of the discipline, (2) an appropriate match between the complexity of the content and the student's stage of cognitive development, (3) cultivation of students' intuition, and (4) stimulation of students' intellectual curiosity and motivation to learn.

The process of student discovery can be facilitated, using a technique known as *inquiry learning*, which has been defined as an "approach in which the teacher presents a puzzling situation and students solve the problem by gathering data and testing their conclusions" (Woolfolk, 2017, p. G-5). Relating inquiry learning, also known as *inquiry-based learning*, specifically to undergraduate research, and drawing upon both her own findings and those of previous authors, Spronken-Smith (2010) further distinguished between two *framings* of this approach: (1) *information-oriented*, which is focused on personal discovery of previously existing knowledge, and (2) *discovery-oriented*, which is focused on generation of new knowledge. She also distinguished between three *modes* of application: (1) *structured*, in which both the research question and method of inquiry are prescribed by the instructor; (2) *guided*, in which the question is posed by the instructor, but the method of inquiry is determined by the students; and (3) *open*, in which both the question and the method of inquiry are determined by the students. Emphasizing the need for critical reflection as an element of inquiry-based learning, Howitt and Wilson (2016) illustrated how structured journaling could be used to promote complex reasoning within undergraduate research experiences.

Another form of discovery learning, known as *problem-based learning*, involves application of the basic strategies of inquiry to the solution of realistic problems that are personally meaningful to the learner (Woolfolk, 2017). Describing problem-based learning as "one of the most important developments in contemporary higher education," McKeachie and Svinicki (2006, p. 221) observed that this approach "is based on the assumptions that human beings evolved as individuals who are motivated to solve problems, and that problem solvers will seek and learn whatever knowledge is needed for successful problem solving" (p. 222).

Relating undergraduate research to problem-based learning, Tritton (2002) observed that "at its core, research is about problem-solving, and no matter what their calling in life, be it business, law, medicine, the arts, public service, or education, people will be called upon to solve problems" (p. 1). Applied undergraduate research is especially well suited to educational efforts based on King and Kitchener's (1994) work, as their primary focus was on students' responses to *ill-structured problems*, meaning those for which one clear solution is not evident. Newman, Daniels, and Faulkner (2003) advocated the use of such problems as a focus of undergraduate research. White (2007) also recommended the use of problem-based learning in undergraduate research, but favored more clearly defined problems than those described by King and Kitchener (1994).

Service-Learning

Among the major pedagogical trends afoot in American higher education today is the growth of service-learning programs, which combine community service with experiential learning. This development is noteworthy because it brings collegiate institutions and their students into collaborative and mutually beneficial partnerships with community agencies. This mutuality of benefit, often termed *reciprocity*, is seen as critical to the long-term success of such efforts (Jacoby, 2015). In its absence, such programs can potentially become exploitative toward either the participating students or the local citizens whom they serve, thereby damaging the burgeoning relationships between academic institutions and their surrounding communities.

Another distinguishing feature of service-learning programs is the provision of opportunities for *reflection* on the service experience by the participating students. Indeed, it is this aspect of the process that transforms the service activity into one that is also educational in nature (Jacoby, 2015). Ash and Clayton (2004) have advocated the use of inquiry to facilitate students' reflection on their service activities, an approach that they have termed *guided integrative reflection*.

While certain conditions are common to all forms of service-learning, philosophical orientations toward the process have been found to vary. One important distinction is the contrast between the *philanthropic* and *civic* orientations. While the former emphasizes acts of charity in behalf of individuals, the latter emphasizes social change that alleviates problems at the systemic level (Battistoni, 1997). In actual practice, most service-learning initiatives can perhaps be more accurately classified along a continuum between the purely philanthropic and the purely civic (Speck, 2001). Reflecting an apparent ascendancy of the civic orientation, there has been a trend toward the creation of service-learning opportunities in partnership with government entities, a form of public engagement that Rice and Redlawsk (2009) have termed *civic service*.

The evolution and expansion of service-learning have been accompanied by growing interest in community-based research, which serves societal needs through the scholarly activities of university faculty (Schneider, 2005; Strand, Marullo, Cutforth, Stoecker, & Donohue, 2003). It was perhaps inevitable, therefore, that engagement of undergraduate students in community-based research on matters of local concern would emerge as a natural extension of the complementary trends toward community-based research and service-learning. Paul (2003) used the term *community-based undergraduate research* to describe "research that is developed and conducted collaboratively by college and university faculty, undergraduate students, and community representatives in service of community-identified needs" (p. 180). Projects of this nature have been incorporated into academic courses, part-time research assistantships (Carter, Fox, Priest, & McBride, 2002), and summer or year-round internships or fellowships (Blauth & Schrum, 2005; Dehn, 2009; Rocheleau et al., 2013; Walsh, 2007b).

Under any of these models, community-based undergraduate research provides students with unique opportunities to apply their research skills to projects that reflect the priorities of their extended communities (Cooke & Thorme, 2011). Brown and Morrison (2009), for example, recounted how undergraduate research was used to inform several urban development initiatives in one southern city. Student investigators in another community were instrumental in the restoration of a local cemetery and refinement of public records (Gesink, 2010). Community-based undergraduate research has also been incorporated into a broad institutional initiative at Northern Arizona University, in which issues of sustainability are addressed through multiple curricular and co-curricular programs (Parnell, Berutich, Henn, & Koressel, 2014).

In analyzing philosophical perspectives particular to community-based research, Stoecker (2003) reaffirmed contrasts between previously articulated views of service-learning as emphasizing either *charity* or *social justice* and drew further distinctions between two established orientations toward research. While the first research orientation, *action research*, emphasizes the conduct of investigations in authentic settings to produce findings with practical utility, it does not seek to change the existing social order. In contrast, *participatory research* is conducted with the explicit goal of eradicating injustices within the current power structure. Participatory research and social justice service-learning combine to produce *radical* community-based research, which contrasts with the more common *mainstream* form that is comprised of action research and charity service-learning. It should be noted that Stoecker's (2003) use of this terminology did not carry a pejorative connotation toward either approach.

Within the academic literature, a strong case has been made for community-based undergraduate research. Paul (2006) cited its utility in advancing two desirable outcomes of undergraduate education: (1) a greater understanding and appreciation of research methods, and (2) a sense of social responsibility and engagement with one's community. Oates (2001) viewed it as a pedagogically sound strategy, in light of its active, collaborative, and individualized nature, as well as the high standards that it sets for both student and faculty participants. Finally, the integration of community-based undergraduate research into international education programs has shown great promise in advancing the goals of self-awareness and cross-cultural understanding that such programs have long sought to foster (Barkin, 2016; Best, DeJongh, Barton, Brown, & Barney, 2007; Glass-Coffin & Balagna, 2005; Sears & Yoder, 2014).

Collaborative Learning

In a departure from more traditional pedagogies, which have tended to cultivate individualistic orientations toward academic work, American higher education has increasingly come to embrace teaching methods that promote interdependence and mutual support among learners (Bruffee, 1999). Collaborative learning is an approach to education that purposefully draws upon the interpersonal dynamics of small groups of students to promote learning, through the contributions of all group members to the completion of shared activities (Barkley, Cross, & Major, 2005; Love & Love, 1995). An underlying assumption is that individuals learn through their interaction with one another, and that interpersonal dynamics are therefore central to the teaching and learning process (Gerlach, 1994; Lattuca & Creamer, 2005). The rationale for this approach is rooted in constructivism, insofar as educational activities are designed to directly engage group members in their own learning (Barkley et al., 2005; Love & Love, 1995). Consistent with the constructive developmentalist emphasis on holistic education (Baxter Magolda, 2000), collaborative learning simultaneously addresses the social, emotional, and cognitive needs of participating students (Love & Love, 1995).

Although the terms are sometimes used interchangeably, several authors have differentiated between collaborative learning and the related concept of cooperative learning, noting that the latter is typically characterized by more stringent mechanisms of accountability and a greater investment of authority in the instructor (Bruffee, 1995; Flannery, 1994). Among the leading proponents of cooperative learning are Johnson, Johnson, and Smith (1991), who identified five conditions that can be directly promoted to optimize student learning in small groups: (1) *positive interdependence*, (2) *face-to-face promotive interaction*, (3) *individual accountability and personal responsibility*, (4) *social skills*, and (5) *group processing*. Bean (2011) offered further guidance specifically on the use of small group work, within the context of the undergraduate classroom.

Beyond the theoretical rationale for group-based learning activities, their popularity appears to be due in part to growing demands from employers for graduates who are able to work collaboratively and to communicate effectively with others (Barkley et al., 2005). It has been further argued that today's world is one in which we confront large-scale problems that cannot be solved without cooperation across national boundaries. Interactive pedagogies are believed to foster the type of complex interpersonal skills that will enable future generations of leaders to respond to these challenges (Johnson et al., 1991). Accordingly, collaborative teaching techniques are often used in combination with problem-based learning (Fink, 2003).

In undergraduate research circles, there appears to be growing interest in the creation of structured leadership roles in learning groups and direct cultivation of group facilitation skills in individual students. Under emerging models, small groups of students participate in activities that are led by peers who are trained to serve as mentors (Detweiler-Bedell & Detweiler-Bedell, 2007; Mahlab, 2010). In discussing the benefits of peer mentorship, Paul (2010a) highlighted its role both in advancing understanding and in humanizing the learning environment, noting that "peer mentors provide care and comfort to students new to the experience of undergraduate research, and new to the higher orders of learning such experiences offer" (p. 2).

Collaborative learning and undergraduate research are clearly complementary forms of pedagogy. By design, the process of undergraduate research involves interaction between the undergraduate researcher and the faculty mentor, and, in many instances, groups of undergraduate students also work together on research teams. On a broader level, Tagg (2003) observed that "no work is more inherently and unavoidably collaborative than academic research" (p. 250). Rejecting the myth of the independent scholar, who toils in solitude within the Ivory Tower, he noted that an academic discipline is comprised of many individuals who simultaneously engage in related work and who communicate with one another in a common language, creating patterns of mutual influence within the field. This fundamental characteristic of the research process lends support to the application of collaborative learning techniques to the conduct of undergraduate research.

Conclusion

This chapter presented a theoretical rationale for undergraduate research that is grounded in constructive developmentalism, an ascending school of thought that draws upon the constructivist branch of learning theory, together with the cognitive-structural and psychosocial branches of developmental theory. This integration of theoretical perspectives results in an approach to teaching that is focused on the promotion of identity formation, growth in cognitive complexity, and mastery of disciplinary content, through processes of active learning and personal reflection. Both the outcomes and methods advanced by constructive developmentalism have been found to align with common practices in undergraduate research. In particular, undergraduate research consistently exemplifies the pedagogy of active learning.

3

UNDERGRADUATE RESEARCH AND THE EVOLVING CULTURE OF THE ACADEMY

In addition to the theoretically based arguments in favor of students' participation in scientific and creative activities, which were discussed in the previous chapter, changing conditions within the culture of American higher education have lent support to the proliferation of undergraduate research programs. In a popular monograph on the subject, Kinkead (2003) discussed the emergence of an "undergraduate research imperative" (p. 7), fueled in part by concern for both the state of science education in the U.S. and the seeming disconnect between the research culture of the modern university and the traditional mission of undergraduate education. In a subsequent report, Hu, Scheuch, et al. (2008) linked the rise of undergraduate research to an increased prioritization of students' engagement in the life of their campuses and their socialization into the academic community. Other factors that appear to have contributed to the advancement of undergraduate research include an ongoing redefinition of the student-faculty relationship, a deepening commitment to the integration of learning opportunities into students' out-of-class lives, and a renewed interest in the cultivation of ethically responsible behavior among the leaders of tomorrow.

A Commitment to Education in Science, Mathematics, and Technology

In making the case for undergraduate research, Karukstis (2007b) related efforts in this area to our national interest in preparing students for careers in science and technology amidst global competition. The argument is a familiar one, as public consciousness of the need for strong science education in the U.S. is widely held to have reached its zenith with the 1957 launch of the Soviet Union's *Sputnik* space satellite and the threat that the mission posed to perceptions of American scientific and technological supremacy (Divine, 1993). Riding a wave of continued public support, colleges and universities substantially improved their science programs and facilities during the 1960s, often with funding from the National Science Foundation (NSF) and other sources (Crampton, 2001). In the years since then, concern for the competitive advantages associated with cutting-edge science education programs has shown varying degrees of recurrent ascendancy, often timed to fluctuations in scientific interest among America's youth.

A critical juncture in the advancement of undergraduate research came in the mid-1980s, when American colleges and universities experienced a precipitous decline in the number of undergraduate students majoring in the natural sciences, amidst continuing economic and military competition worldwide. Recognizing the challenges attendant to this condition, the presidents of 48 private liberal arts colleges, under the leadership of Oberlin College's Frederick Starr, convened in an effort to identify strategies for advancing science education within primarily undergraduate institutions (PUIs) (Crampton, 2001). The collective strength that the group members drew from their association was undoubtedly instrumental in securing increased funding for undergraduate science education from NSF, which in turn placed the onus on undergraduate institutions to formulate research proposals that were worthy of public support. The Oberlin Group (2016), as this elite network of institutions has come to be known, has since expanded its membership to include 80 campuses, which together have built a distinguished record of success in securing NSF funding for research involving undergraduates (Slocum & Scholl, 2013).

There is some evidence to suggest that we have now entered a new era of heightened awareness of the need for science education. Scientific literacy among the young appears to have waned in past decades, raising concern within the scientific community (Kinkead, 2003). American teens' scores on measures of both scientific and mathematical literacy have lagged behind those of students in many other nations (Mateja, 2006). Citing the economic implications of global competition within the scientific and technological arenas, a coalition of leading business organizations was formed in 2005, with the goal of doubling the number of undergraduate degrees conferred by American colleges and universities in STEM-related fields over the decade that followed (Tapping America's Potential, 2008). During this same period and prompted by similar concerns, the National Academy of Sciences, National Academy of Engineering, and Institute of Medicine (2007a, 2010) formed a committee that from its inception had the ear of Congress, thereby positioning it well to advocate on behalf of science education at the national level.

Increased understanding of the link between science education and the nation's economic fortunes brought swift enactment of more supportive government policies. One key piece of legislation, the America COMPETES Act, was initially signed into law in 2007 and reauthorized in 2011 with bipartisan support. This law was especially noteworthy insofar as it directly stipulated a role for various federal agencies in the advancement of undergraduate research and encouragement of partnerships between research universities and PUIs (Hensel, 2011b). In light of our nation's ongoing transition to a knowledge-based economy, it would seem that undergraduate research holds the potential to increase greatly our ability to compete within a global market (Coleman, 2005; Mateja, 2006).

Concurrent with growing concern for the preparation of scientists, changes in both the state of technology and social priorities of the nation have helped to broaden the aims of education in STEM disciplines. Whereas, historically, proponents of science education have placed a high priority on cultivation of scientific talent in the extraordinarily gifted few, who have been groomed for graduate education and careers in scientific research, advances in technology have now changed the ways in which all Americans live, such that a higher standard of scientific and technological literacy among the masses must be met (Daves, 2002; Nelson, 2002). This trend, coupled with a growing concern for social equity, discourages an elitist approach to science education and creates a demand for greater access to research experiences in college. Based on its potential contributions to both scientific literacy and preparation for scientific leadership roles, undergraduate research has been recognized as playing a central role in advancing the science education mission of today's collegiate institutions (Taraban, 2008).

Integration of Teaching, Research, and Service

The tripartite mission of the contemporary American university, with its emphasis on teaching, research, and service, reflects the influence of two contrasting European academic traditions, as well as the characteristically American values that have shaped nearly all of our national institutions for over two centuries. A review of the history of American higher education reveals a recurring tension that has grown out of the competing demands placed upon the academy at various points in time.

Originally modeled on the residential colleges of England, the earliest colonial colleges were established primarily as teaching institutions. Education was broadly conceived to include the cultivation of the mind, body, and spirit, and the *in loco parentis* doctrine, under which professors were understood to function in the place of their students' parents, enjoyed widespread support. However, with the growing influence of the German research universities in the mid-19th Century, faculty became increasingly preoccupied with the generation of new scientific discoveries, and less focused on the preservation of culture through the socialization of young people. Meanwhile, passage of the Morrill Land Grant Act of 1862, coupled with the growth of state-supported systems of higher education, further advanced the notion that academic institutions were to function in the public interest (Beere, Votruba, & Wells, 2011; Cohen & Kisker, 2010; Ward, 2003). Thus, an enterprise that was once accountable to a narrowly defined clientele with clear and coherent needs came to face the demands of multiple constituencies whose interests would not always be seen as compatible.

In particular, by the close of the 20th Century, the competing demands of teaching and research had come to be seen by many as fundamentally irreconcilable (Barnett, 1992). During this time, critics of higher education painted a portrait of an academic culture in which the pursuit of institutional prestige, coupled with an increased emphasis on professionalization and specialization, had led to faculty reward structures that placed an inordinate emphasis on research productivity, often at the expense of creative teaching (Cuban, 1999; Sykes, 1988; Wilshire, 1990).

In contrast to many authors of this era, who issued blanket condemnations of the academic profession, Boyer (1987) used credible national data to fashion a more sympathetic image of a professoriate largely committed to excellent teaching but unable to attend simultaneously to the immediate needs of undergraduate students and the growing demands of the academic world as a whole. This characterization has since been corroborated in other studies, which have shown that teaching is not only the primary activity of most faculty members in the U.S., but often their preferred activity as well (Jackson & Guerrant, 2012; Schuster & Finkelstein, 2006). While consistent with other works in its recognition of the competing demands placed upon faculty members, Boyer's (1987) report was more hopeful insofar as it held open the possibility of receptivity to change among rank and file academics.

In a subsequent report, Boyer (1990) offered a model for reconciling the competing demands placed upon American university professors. In contrast to other authors, who framed the issue as one of balance, either at the individual (Fukami, 1997) or systemic (Fairweather, 1996) level, Boyer (1990) sought to integrate teaching and research, as well as service, within a broad conceptualization of scholarship that incorporated four major realms of activity: (1) *discovery*, (2) *integration*, (3) *application*, and (4) *teaching*. By design, this system of classification was less rigid than the traditional scheme, in that the four realms of activity were recognized as "separate, yet overlapping, functions" (Boyer, 1990, p. 16). The model was further distinguished by its seemingly willful omission of any hierarchical ordering of function, either explicit or implicit, and its demand that all activities be approached from a perspective that is scholarly in nature.

In a follow-up report that was initiated by Boyer, but that was published only after his death, a team of his research associates elaborated further on the forms of scholarship annunciated in his prior work. Framed as a discussion of faculty evaluation, their commentary focused on the necessity of documentary evidence as a means of substantiating scholarly achievement across all realms of activity. They maintained that scholarly projects—whether in the realm of discovery, integration, application, or teaching—should be characterized by six basic elements: (1) *clear goals*, (2) *adequate preparation*, (3) *appropriate methods*, (4) *significant results*, (5) *effective presentation*, and (6) *reflective critique* (Glassick, Huber, & Maeroff, 1997).

Calling to mind Gladwell's concept of the "tipping point," Rice (2002) posited that Boyer's work represented "a critical turning point in what is fundamentally valued in the scholarly work of faculty members" (p. 8). In the aforementioned posthumous report, Boyer's associates cited a national survey of chief academic officers, which revealed that 78% of the respondents' institutions had broadened their definitions of scholarship during the five-year period ending in 1994 (Glassick et al., 1997). In a subsequent survey of chief academic officers, O'Meara (2005) found that 68% of institutions had initiated reforms to advance a more expansive view of faculty scholarship within the ten years immediately prior to their being queried.

Boyer's (1987, 1990) work helped create fertile ground for undergraduate research, by broadening the accepted parameters of faculty scholarship and by affirming the centrality of undergraduate education to the mission of American higher education. In a report by the Boyer Commission on Educating Undergraduates in Research Universities (1998), undergraduate research was explicitly recommended as a means by which undergraduate education might assume a more central role within the nation's research universities. The Commission held that the nature of the research university was such that it had a special duty to prepare students in the skills of inquiry. The Commission called upon the nation's research universities to "make research-based learning the standard" (p. 15) through internships, mentoring relationships, and student participation in the research process.

More recent titles reflect continued interest in the integration of teaching and research, as well as recognition of Boyer's (1990) model as a viable alternative to more traditional views of these functions (Brew, 2006; Huber, 2004; O'Meara & Rice, 2005). Focusing specifically on undergraduate research as a means of unifying the roles of teacher and scholar, Lopatto (2010) made the case that students can benefit from exposure to role models who manifest congruence in their professional lives. Coleman (2005) reaffirmed the value of undergraduate research within the research university, citing its potential to reinforce the broader research mission of the institution. Hedley and Schneider (2009) discussed the concept of a *research college*, a type of institution that emphasizes the primacy of undergraduate teaching in its mission, yet demands that members of its faculty also distinguish themselves as scholars. Such institutions have emerged as natural breeding grounds for innovation in undergraduate research and other practices that advance an integrative vision of the faculty role.

Building a culture of undergraduate research on American college and university campuses necessitates reconsideration of institutional policies that reinforce a compartmentalization of faculty responsibilities. Ronnenberg and Sadowski (2011) highlighted ways in which undergraduate research can simultaneously engage faculty in teaching, research, and service functions, and called upon institutions to create more porous boundaries between the three areas of practice within their tenure and promotion policies. Echoing calls for reform of the tenure and promotion process, Schultheis, Farrell, and Paul (2011) observed that "the very work of revising tenure and promotion policy to recognize and reward undergraduate research is an important opportunity to advance the significance, quality, and extent of undergraduate research on campus" (p. 26). Focusing on procedures for curricular revision, Neary (2014) illustrated further how institutional protocols could be used to encourage infusion of research into teaching, with attention to broader social impacts as well.

Promoting Student Engagement

Over the past three decades, teachers and administrators across all segments of American higher education have begun to place a higher priority on increasing students' levels of participation in educationally purposeful activities in college. Kuh et al. (2005) have cited two specific aspects of *student engagement* that play an important role in successful college outcomes: (1) "the amount of time and effort students put into their studies and other activities that lead to the experiences and outcomes that constitute student success," and (2) "the ways the institution allocates resources and organizes learning opportunities and services to induce students to participate in and benefit from such activities" (p. 9).

Student engagement has its roots in Astin's (1984) concept of *involvement*, which he defined as "the amount of physical and psychological energy that the student devotes to the academic experience" (p. 297). Involvement has both quantitative and qualitative dimensions, in that it is influenced by both the amount of time that students invest in their education and the depth of their engagement in this process. Furthermore, it includes both in-class and out-of-class interaction with the college environment and those who populate it. Interaction with faculty members is especially important, in the context of overall student involvement, because it affects students' satisfaction with other aspects of the undergraduate experience as well. According to Astin (1984), "students who interact frequently with faculty members are more likely than other students to express satisfaction with all aspects of their institutional experience, including student friendships, variety of courses, intellectual environment, and even administration of the institution" (p. 304).

Also related to student engagement is Tinto's (1993) concept of *integration*, which is a basic sense of belonging that students develop within their social and academic environments. Integration includes both a feeling of compatibility with the institution and formation of personal bonds with other members of the campus community. In situations where integration is lacking, students often withdraw from their institutions, rather than remaining to complete their degrees. Student-faculty interaction is an important factor in integration, particularly when it occurs informally, outside the context of the classroom, and when students feel they are the beneficiaries of special attention.

The notion that interaction with faculty has an educational impact upon students is consistent with a number of findings reported in the scholarly literature. According to Astin's (1993) own research, such interaction is positively associated with a variety of student personality outcomes, including interest in scholarship, social activism, artistic endeavors, and leadership. His research also indicated that talking and visiting with faculty members, together with other forms of student-faculty interaction, were associated with a wide range of intellectual and academic outcomes, including disciplinary knowledge, critical thinking skills, analytical and problem-solving abilities, competence in public speaking, readiness for graduate or professional school, and professional knowledge. Based on an extensive review of the research, focused specifically on out-of-class interaction with faculty, Kuh, Douglas, Lund, and Ramin-Gyurnek (1994) concluded that such interaction was positively related to persistence in higher education, complexity of thought, understanding and application of knowledge, human awareness, and social and emotional competence. In a similarly comprehensive review of the research literature, Pascarella and Terenzini (1991) drew like conclusions in regard to students' intellectual development but found only mixed support for a relationship between student-faculty interaction and student persistence. In a review of subsequent studies, the authors found positive relationships between student-faculty interaction and cognitive, moral, and vocational development, as well as educational attainment (Pascarella & Terenzini, 2005). In the third installment of this series, an expanded team of researchers found a relationship between student-faculty interaction and gains in critical thinking skills, which was evident in contexts that included undergraduate research (Mayhew, Rockenbach, Bowman, Seifert, & Wolniak, with Pascarella & Terenzini, 2016).

In an effort to identify institutional characteristics associated with high levels of student involvement, Kuh, Schuh, Whitt, and Associates (1991) undertook a major investigation of 14 so-called *Involving Colleges*, a widely varied cross-section of institutions that shared a distinguished record of promoting student involvement. Their research revealed six characteristics that were commonly observed among the various institutions: (1) clarity of institutional purpose, (2) promotion of student responsibility and initiative, (3) a focus on all aspects of students' lives on campus, (4) existence of numerous sub-communities and social environments of a personal scale, (5) institutional affirmation that students and their learning were valued, and (6) cultivation of loyalty and a sense of the institution's uniqueness.

In a subsequent project, entitled *Documenting Effective Educational Practice (DEEP)*, Kuh et al. (2005) studied 20 exemplary institutions, with a focus on specific practices that were conducive to student engagement and achievement. In discussing important characteristics of the institutions, the authors directly cited support for undergraduate research, as well as provisions for senior projects and undergraduate research symposia. In commenting on the significance of undergraduate research to student engagement, the authors offered the following observations:

> It is hard to imagine a richer educational setting for student-faculty interaction than working side by side with a faculty member on a research project.

Students not only observe an expert at work, but they also contribute to that work by applying in-class learning to the research project. And because many such projects extend beyond a single academic term, they provide students and faculty with many opportunities to discuss topics related and unrelated to the research.

(p. 214)

The promotion of student engagement has frequently been recognized as requiring a broad institutional effort that touches all aspects of undergraduate students' lives. Love and Love (1995) emphasized the need for both faculty and student affairs staff to actively immerse students in the lives of their campuses. Kuh et al. (1994) favored collaboration among members of the faculty and staff to transform the entire undergraduate experience into "a seamless web of learning across the classroom and out-of-class settings" (pp. vii–viii).

Supported by research on student engagement, learning communities, which draw groups of students into intensive and sustained educational activities pertaining to topics of shared interest, have become increasingly common on college and university campuses (Jessup-Anger, 2015). Such initiatives naturally lend themselves to partnerships between faculty and student affairs staff, in advancement of a more integrated and educationally purposeful undergraduate experience (Smith & Williams, 2007). Mickley (2007) proposed the establishment of residential learning communities specifically for students engaged in collaborative research with faculty. Others have described undergraduate learning communities built on research activity within individual academic departments (Kight, Gaynor, & Adams, 2006; Reinen, Grosfils, Gaines, & Hazlett, 2006). In general, Shapiro and Levine (1999) noted that learning communities are uniquely conducive to undergraduate research insofar as they facilitate collaboration and the integration of disciplinary perspectives.

The Professor as Mentor

An examination of the evolving role of the professor reveals a shift in emphasis from traditional notions of instruction to the emerging function of mentoring (Reinarz & White, 2001). Using the metaphor of a journey, Daloz (1999) portrayed the role of the mentor as that of a trusted traveling companion, who enhances the educational experience of the protégé, while sharing as a partner in the learning process. He identified three main functions of the mentor: (1) to *support*, (2) to *challenge*, and (3) to *provide vision*. Whereas the mentor's support serves to strengthen the protégé's sense of security in the present situation, the challenge that the mentor provides to the protégé creates an incentive to grow beyond current boundaries, and the vision offered by the mentor gives direction to this creative energy. Additionally, the mentor must sometimes assume the role of an advocate, by representing the interests of the protégé to third parties. Nakamura,

Shernoff, and Hooker (2009) emphasized, however, that a narrowly defined role in supporting the career of another is not properly characterized as mentoring in the absence of a broader and more long-term relationship. They contended that more limited involvement of this nature is more appropriately termed *sponsorship*.

Focusing specifically on the student-faculty relationship in higher education, W. B. Johnson (2007) identified six important aspects of mentoring: (1) promoting student success and maturation through informal interaction outside of class; (2) providing students with guidance on academic and career-related matters; (3) lending emotional support to students, especially during the early stages of their college enrollment; (4) encouraging students' identity exploration and clarification of their goals and purposes in life; (5) coaching students on how to prepare for their careers; and (6) assuming a limited role as a transitional parent figure during students' enrollment in college. Nakamura et al. (2009) further stressed the significance of academic mentoring in preserving the accumulated wisdom of a discipline from one generation to the next.

In a popular model drawn from the organizational literature, Kram (1985) emphasized the transitory nature of the mentoring relationship, identifying four stages through which such relationships typically pass. Because the protégé grows in independence at each stage, the relationship cannot ultimately survive unless it is eventually redefined to reflect the two parties' more equal status as friends or colleagues. In studying mentorship within the context of a research team, Creamer (2005) found affirmation of this characterization of the mentoring relationship as one that evolves from a "master-apprentice model" toward a "coequal relationship" (p. 38). Speaking specifically of undergraduate research settings, Swift (2012) advocated mentoring relationships in which responsibility for the investigative process is gradually transferred from the mentor to the protégé, such that "as students grow into skilled researchers, they become *their own* best teachers" (p. 19).

This natural course of the mentoring relationship is consistent with calls for a more even balance of power between teachers and learners (Fink, 2003; Kezar, 1999) and a recasting of the teacher into the role of a facilitator of students' own work of learning (Weimer, 2002). In making the case for a more egalitarian power structure, Kezar (1999) envisioned teachers as "active co-learners," who "attempt to share their expertise without eclipsing the students' beginning attempts to develop their own ideas" (p. 28).

The mentoring relationship has been repeatedly cited in the literature as a fundamental element of the undergraduate research experience (Hakim, 2000; Kinkead, 2003; Temple et al., 2010). However, it appears that specific expectations of the mentor may vary somewhat within this context (Yaffe, Bender, & Sechrest, 2012). While some authors have emphasized the need for supportive undergraduate research mentorship (Bruno, Thomas, James, & Frazier, 2011), others have encouraged mentors to balance challenge and support in their work with undergraduate researchers (Brownell & Swaner, 2010). Based on surveys of both undergraduate researchers and faculty mentors, Shellito, Shea, Weissmann,

Mueller-Solger, and Davis (2001) identified three broadly conceived functions of the undergraduate research mentor: (1) "managing time and resources," (2) "establishing relationships with students," and (3) "offering continued student guidance" (p. 461).

Although mentoring is most commonly conceived to occur within the context of one-on-one relationships, Parks (2011) has advanced the concept of *mentoring communities,* which are group environments in which multiple relationships provide support to individuals, while simultaneously challenging them to grow. Originally introduced as a means of promoting young adults' personal development, the mentoring community has emerged as a promising model for learning communities of all types. Relating the concept specifically to undergraduate research, Lopatto (2010) discussed the research team as a unique mentoring context and urged faculty to draw upon leadership theory to inform their work with students.

A Focus on Ethics

The shift toward a mentoring model of the faculty role, with its emphasis on the development of the whole student, would seem to offer some solace to critics who have suggested that the primacy of empiricism in the modern research university has at times undermined the cultivation of character and a sense of moral purpose (Kronman, 2007; Parks, 2011). The notion that a singular focus on the pursuit of verifiable truth can desensitize one to the moral dimension of life gained credence from several highly publicized ethical breaches, arising from the rapidly expanding research culture of the 20th Century. Paradoxically, public awareness of such episodes ultimately gave rise to increased stringency in standards of research ethics (Macfarlane, 2009), such that the conduct of academic research today offers a uniquely rich opportunity for the cultivation of ethical judgment in undergraduates, when carried out under the guidance of a conscientious and caring mentor (Merkel & Baker, 2002). Attesting to the priority placed on ethical considerations in undergraduate research, three feature issues of the *Quarterly* have been devoted to the topic since the opening of the new millennium (DeCosmo & Gould, 2015; Stocks, 2010; Wenzel, 2001a).

Although each undergraduate research project is unique, certain broad categories of ethical concern have been found to emerge with some frequency. Research, in general, poses ethical dilemmas at three distinct phases of the investigative process: (1) planning, (2) conduct, and (3) reporting (Steneck, 2007). From the perspective of the faculty mentor, undergraduate research, in particular, is further complicated by ethical principles that apply to the student-faculty relationship for the full duration of this process (Markie, 1994; Rocheleau & Speck, 2007).

Steneck (2007) identified three broad categories of issues that commonly emerge in the planning stage of research: (1) *protection of human subjects,* (2) *the welfare of laboratory animals,* and (3) *conflicts of interest.* In its landmark publication,

The Belmont Report, the National Commission for the Protection of Human Subjects of Biomedical and Behavioral Research (1978) articulated the rights of research participants, based on three general principles: (1) *respect for persons*, (2) *beneficence*, and (3) *justice*. The federal government has also issued a set of nine principles for minimizing harm to laboratory animals in studies undertaken as an alternative to research on human subjects. In regard to conflicts of interest, three general categories have been identified in the relevant literature: (1) *financial conflicts*, (2) *conflicts of commitment*, and (3) *personal and intellectual conflicts* (Steneck, 2007).

The principal concern at the conduct phase of an investigation is the management of data, which includes collection, storage, and sharing. Ethical issues emerging in this process include ownership of data, accuracy and precision in the collection and recording of data, and security and confidentiality in the preservation of data. During the conduct stage, it is also important to clearly establish the respective roles and responsibilities of the principal investigator and members of the research team. This is especially important in undergraduate research and other situations where a mentor-trainee relationship exists (Shachter, 2007; Steneck, 2007).

As noted in the opening chapter of this book, the sharing of findings is a key element of the investigative process. Thus, neither the research project itself, nor the ethical responsibilities that accompany it, can end with the collection and analysis of data. Although the integrity of a publication depends on the good faith of both authors and reviewers (Steneck, 2007), the duties of the former are generally of more direct consequence to faculty mentors. Focusing specifically on the context of undergraduate research, Shachter (2007) succinctly summarized the researcher's duties as including "assigning appropriate credit, citing work appropriately, refraining from repetitive or fragmentary publications, and providing a sufficient description of methods" (p. 213). Among the specific obligations subsumed under this general description are appropriate assignment of authorship and complete and accurate reporting of findings (Steneck, 2007).

Looking beyond faculty members' own commitment to both their students' ethical development and the responsible conduct of research, it is clear that social, political, legal, and financial considerations have all played a part in the growing emphasis on research ethics. In particular, attention to protection of human subjects and laboratory animals, as well as reduction of research misconduct, gained a significant boost from three key federal statutes that were signed into law in the latter half of the 20th Century: (1) the 1966 Animal Welfare Act, (2) the 1974 National Research Act, and (3) the 1985 Health Research Extension Act. Under the authority of this legislation, various funding agencies housed in the executive branch of the federal government ultimately established administrative policies that demanded more strict oversight of research ethics at institutions receiving federal funding. Perhaps most notably, Institutional Review Boards (IRBs) and Institutional Animal Care and Use Committees (IACUCs), which are charged with overseeing the conduct of research on human subjects and laboratory animals respectively, are now mandatory at all institutions where federally sponsored research is conducted (Steneck, 2007).

This development has added a new dimension to the undergraduate research experience of students and faculty at many PUIs. Although the transition to a more structured system of oversight has posed new challenges to leaders on many campuses (Cunningham, Gaffield, Halpern, & Rackoff, 2001; Dehn, 2010; Freed & Farnsworth, 2001), the requirement that undergraduate researchers secure IRB or IACUC approval before undertaking their studies has likewise provided many teachable moments for budding research ethicists. Consistent with constructive developmentalist principles, the cognitive skills that are cultivated through the application of ethical principles to tangible research problems offer the promise of promoting systems of moral reasoning that are complex, coherent, and comprehensive.

Preparing the Next Generation of Scholars

As any profession looks toward the future, recruitment and enculturation of new members is a matter of concern. Within the academic world, this process begins with education. According to Shaw (2004), "education plays the dual role of both gatekeeper and track-setter" (p. 8), meaning that the requirements for successful completion of various levels of education serve as screens through which aspiring academics must pass, and the experiences and associations that accrue over the course of this process can determine the paths that their careers might take. Education also provides the primary context in which aspiring academics forge their professional identities (Colbeck, 2008). The significance of education to the formation of academic careers raises yet another potential benefit of undergraduate students' participation in the creation of original scholarship. Undergraduate research can serve as a means by which to launch young people on academic and other investigative career tracks.

At first blush, recruitment of future academics may seem a low priority, insofar as higher education has long experienced an oversupply of career aspirants, relative to the rate at which job openings have occurred. The academic labor market has been repeatedly characterized as a "strong buyer's market" (Schuster & Finkelstein, 2006, p. 165; Shaw, 2004, p. 8). Uncertainty of future job prospects has been a common source of anxiety among graduate students for several decades (Gappa, Austin, & Trice, 2007), and doctoral graduates have been frequently disappointed in their immediate employment options upon completion of their degrees (Nerad, Aanerud, & Cerny, 2004). In fact, some have even questioned whether the nation's universities have acted responsibly in conferring doctoral degrees upon far more graduates than the academy itself can absorb (Zusman, 2005).

For years, concerned scholars have responded to such objections by pointing toward the need for the professoriate to remain vigilant in competing with other fields for the strongest talent available, even when faced with no shortage of individuals seeking to join its ranks (Bowen & Schuster, 1986). With the passage of time, such concerns have proven to be well founded, in light of the very real formidability of the competition for talent that other sectors of the economy have begun to pose (Gappa et al., 2007). Employers across multiple industries have begun to take notice of the value of research experience, often favoring candidates who would bring such background to work in corporate settings (Brakke, Crowe, & Karukstis, 2009). Although graduate education has historically been viewed primarily as preparation for entry into the professoriate, it has been observed that large numbers of newly minted Ph.D.s have begun to find their way into the commercial sector (Zusman, 2005), and that cooperation between the nation's universities and business entities has blurred the line between the academic and non-academic worlds (Leggon, 2001).

Growing demands for research skills within the non-academic sector have also brought calls for reform of doctoral education, focused on preparation of graduates for a broader range of career opportunities, both within higher education and elsewhere (Austin & Wulff, 2004; Nerad et al., 2004). In a review of doctoral education across multiple academic fields, Golde and Walker (2006) and their associates framed the role of the doctoral graduate as that of a *steward of the discipline*. In elaborating upon this role, Golde (2006) argued that such scholars:

> should be capable of *generating* new knowledge and defending knowledge claims against challenges and criticism, *conserving* the most important ideas and findings that are a legacy of past and current work, and *transforming* knowledge that has been generated and conserved by explaining it and connecting it to ideas from other fields.
>
> *(p. 10)*

In a subsequent report, Walker, Golde, Jones, Bueschel, and Hutchings (2008) reaffirmed this vision, and emphasized that the role of the scholar transcends occupational categories. In the words of the authors, "the work of scholarship is not a function of setting but of purpose and commitment" (p. 8). This vision of graduate education casts issues of professional regeneration into a new light, insofar as the preservation and future vitality of the disciplines provide a compelling rationale for the recruitment and preparation of young scholars, independent of conditions in the job market.

The benefits of undergraduate research in preparing future scholars are largely attributable to the student's interaction with the faculty mentor. Through collaborative research, faculty members have the opportunity to share their enthusiasm for and insight on their fields with undergraduate students. In so doing, they provide a service to the field, by helping to attract talented researchers into their areas of inquiry (Jarvis et al., 2011). Students benefit from both the cultivation of intellectual skills and socialization into the cultures of their disciplines and the broader academic community (Temple et al., 2010). Through this process, faculty members benefit as well, by generating a larger group of fellow researchers with whom to collaborate in the future. By attracting students into careers in teaching and research, faculty members develop a larger support system for future projects (Hakim, 2000). Thus, the process of socialization that occurs in an undergraduate research setting is one that benefits the student, the faculty mentor, the discipline, and the academic community as a whole.

Conclusion

This chapter provided an overview of emerging priorities of the academy that have aligned to bolster the rationale for undergraduate research programs and to generate support for their implementation. The cultural factors that have given rise to undergraduate research reflect changes in the values and goals of American higher education and in the roles envisioned for both students and faculty members in the pursuit of these ideals. The underlying cultural shift has manifested itself in both the content of the undergraduate curriculum and the social structures of the overall campus environment. The close alignment of the philosophical foundations of undergraduate research with the emerging ideals of the academy offers hope of a promising future for undergraduate research programs.

4

THE EDUCATIONAL IMPACT OF UNDERGRADUATE RESEARCH PROGRAMS

As indicated in the previous two chapters, the philosophical foundation for undergraduate research programs has been well articulated in the professional literature. Proponents of undergraduate research have identified a number of desirable outcomes that might reasonably be expected to follow from students' participation in the process of collaborative inquiry with faculty mentors. Increasingly, scholars have begun to turn their attention to verification of these purported benefits. A growing number of studies, some national in scope and others focused more narrowly on institutional programs, have begun to provide an evidentiary basis for conclusions concerning the educational value of undergraduate research. This chapter provides an overview of the research literature, including an examination of the implications and limitations of available findings.

Research Activity as a Program Outcome

Whereas much of the national conversation on undergraduate research has focused on comprehensive institutional efforts to increase student and faculty participation in collaborative scholarship (Hakim, 2000; Malachowski, 2003), it should perhaps come as no surprise that one branch of assessment that has emerged in the relevant literature has centered on the impact of such initiatives on actual rates of participation. Authors have used such objective criteria as rates of peer-reviewed publication or presentation, grant-writing, participation in summer research activities, continuation of related research activities beyond the duration of the formal program, and completion of honors and independent or supervised projects to demonstrate that institutional or regional undergraduate research programs stimulate students' interest in producing original scholarship and faculty members' support for such endeavors (Caldwell, 2007; Conway et al., 2012; Haik & Bullen, 2011; Hoke & Gentile, 2008; Pawlow & Retzlaff, 2012; Schammel et al., 2008; Ward & Dixon, 2008). Students' participation in conferences and publication of their work have also been used to demonstrate the success of research-oriented courses, curricula, and special projects in promoting skills and interest in research (Birkhead & Stanton, 2011; Malachowski & Dwyer, 2011; Martinetti et al., 2009; Overath, Zhang, & Hatherill, 2016; Sims, Le, Emery, & Smith, 2012; Troischt, Koopmann, O'Donoghue, Odekon, & Haynes, 2016). Comparative data on rates of subsequent research activity among participants versus non-participants have been cited in support of both curricular and co-curricular research initiatives targeting lower division students from disadvantaged backgrounds (DeAngelo & Hasson, 2009; Olson-McBride, Hassemer, & Hoepner, 2016).

Such promising findings notwithstanding, this body of research must be placed in its proper perspective. One limitation in many of these studies is the absence or non-equivalency of control groups. On a more basic level, one might also question the underlying assumption that participation in undergraduate research, as an end in itself, offers sufficient justification for the investment of resources in what is sometimes a costly undertaking. In the words of Childress (2015), "the existence and elegance and strength of our [undergraduate research] activities, admirable as they may be, are not the outcomes" (p. 6). When the question of outcomes is raised, it is generally in the interest of establishing a link between participation in undergraduate research and the development of competencies that are used for the common good. It would seem, therefore, that studies of educational outcomes associated with participation would potentially be of greater interest than those focused on rates of participation alone.

Cognitive and Affective Outcomes of Undergraduate Research

In applying Bloom's influential taxonomy to the process of educational assessment, a distinction has traditionally been drawn between outcomes of a *cognitive* nature and those that fall within the *affective* domain. While the former involve mastery of "intellectual tasks," the latter "emphasize a feeling line, an emotion, or a degree of acceptance or rejection" (Bloom, Hastings, & Madaus, 1971, p. 39). This distinction is evident within the higher education literature (Astin, 1993) and has been applied specifically to the assessment of outcomes associated with undergraduate research (Hu, Scheuch, et al., 2008). In a factor analysis of benefits to undergraduate research participants, as identified by a national sample of psychology faculty, Landrum and Nelsen (2002) differentiated between "technical skills and abilities" and "interpersonal benefits" (p. 18). Using similar methods to analyze benefits identified by research program alumni, Bauer and Bennett (2003) drew somewhat finer distinctions among four categories of skill, yet the basic distinction between those outcomes that were personal in nature and those that were more purely academic was again evident in their classification scheme. A review of the full body of literature on the educational impact of undergraduate research reveals a common interest in both cognitive and affective outcomes.

Cognitive Outcomes

Over the past two decades, a growing number of researchers have sought to document the intellectual gains associated with participation in undergraduate research. By far, the most common method of data collection used in these investigations has been self-reporting by students. Faculty perceptions have also been used as a means of gauging cognitive outcomes. In a relatively small number of studies, more objective measures have been used as well.

Student Perceptions of Intellectual Growth

Given higher education's widespread reliance on student course evaluations as a means of assessing the quality of classroom instruction, perhaps it is to be expected that their use would become prominent in the outcomes assessment literature, particularly where the research opportunities under investigation have occurred within the context of undergraduate courses. Studies of courses across a variety of subject areas have suggested that research opportunities within the undergraduate curriculum are well received by participating students and are seen as contributing to their technical skills and understanding of research within the respective disciplines (Firmage et al., 2005; Jacob, 2008; Murray, 2014; Overath et al., 2016; Pukkila et al., 2013). Evaluations of an education course that incorporated a substantial research component revealed that collaboration with peers, in particular, was perceived to be facilitative of learning within a research context (Waite & Davis, 2006a, 2006b). An interdisciplinary capstone seminar in environmental studies at Middlebury College, which incorporated a community-based research component, was recognized by students as contributing to their knowledge of course content, understanding of public policy issues, ability to entertain multiple perspectives, and capacity for integrative thought (Munroe, 2016).

Beyond student course evaluations, self-reporting by students has been widely used in assessing outcomes of broader organizational initiatives to promote undergraduate scholarship. Undergraduate research programs, in general, have received favorable marks from former participants, who have typically credited their experiences with strengthening their understanding of research and preparing them for future scholarly endeavors (Conway et al., 2012; Edgcomb et al., 2010; Vieyra, Gilmore, & Timmerman, 2011; Wilson & Howitt, 2012). In addition to these benefits, participants have sometimes cited gains in communication (Noji, 2011), technical (Bauer & Bennett, 2008), critical thinking (Shokair, 2002), and problem-solving (Ward & Dixon, 2008) skills, as well as a more complete knowledge of the discipline (Pawlow & Retzlaff, 2012; Trosset, Lopatto, & Elgin, 2008).

Survey data presented by van Delden (2012) suggested that students' perceptions of the academic benefits associated with undergraduate research may be further enhanced through dissemination of their work.

Interaction with peers seems to be especially beneficial to students participating in undergraduate research programs. Group-based programs have been found to promote a deeper understanding of both research and group processes (Kephart, Villa, Gates, & Roach, 2008) and to supplement learning that occurs in other academic settings (Schroeder, 2008). Russell, Rivenburg, Creedon, Anderson, and Yager (2004) found that a peer-mentoring program developed to support undergraduate research was evaluated favorably by students who participated, whether as mentors or as protégées. The program was believed to effectively promote skills in research and communication, as well as a deeper understanding of disciplinary content.

In one of the first studies where preliminary and follow-up measures were used to gauge actual gains in students' perceived skill levels, Kardash (2000) administered questionnaires to undergraduate natural science interns in a research university setting. The study revealed significant gains in students' ratings of their skills in 13 out of 14 areas included in the evaluation. Drawing upon Kardash's (2000) work and using similar methodology, Erbes (2008) documented increases in students' self-reported skills in research design and execution, integration of ideas and information, and dissemination of results, among participants in a summer biology research program. More recent studies have made use of repeated measures to document gains in self-reported competencies among participants in a broad range of undergraduate research initiatives within a variety of academic disciplines (Awong-Taylor et al., 2016; Baynham, 2016; Carr et al., 2013; Cook & Kelly, 2013; Gary, de la Rubia, Brinkley, & Thompson, 2010; Plunkett, Saetermoe, & Quilici, 2014; Singer & Zimmerman, 2012; White, Ward, Agarwal, Bennett, & Varahramyan, 2013).

Few studies of either course-based undergraduate research or more broadly coordinated programs have included control groups, though there have been several exceptions. In an institutional study by Ishiyama (2002a), social science and humanities majors who had collaborated with faculty members on research scored higher on self-reported independent analytical reasoning than did those without such research experience. Brothers and Higgins (2008) found that community college students who participated in undergraduate research within a multi-institutional consortium reported educational gains that equaled or exceeded national averages on 21 domains of the *Survey of Undergraduate Research Experience (SURE)*, using norms based primarily on students at four-year institutions. In studying the self-reported impact of students' research experiences within undergraduate curricula in the natural sciences, Wilson and Howitt (2012) affirmed the benefits of such experiences, but found little difference in impact across degree programs based on the number of such experiences required. In comparing 44 participants in a comprehensive undergraduate research and mentoring program for students underrepresented in mental health fields against 55 non-participants, during the same period of time, Plunkett et al. (2014) found that the program participants rated themselves higher on both their research experiences and their knowledge and skill acquisition.

In Bauer and Bennett's (2003) institutional study, distinctions were drawn among three groups of alumni: (1) those who had participated in the institutional undergraduate research program, (2) those who had completed other forms of undergraduate research, and (3) those who had not engaged in research during their undergraduate enrollment. The authors found that perceived gains in research skills were significantly greater among those who had completed research than among those who had not and that such gains were greater among those who had participated in the undergraduate research program than among those whose research experiences occurred in other contexts. Program alumni also rated themselves significantly higher than non-research alumni in their development of intellectual curiosity, ability to access information independently, understanding of scientific concepts, and ability to analyze literature critically. A separate analysis of data pertaining specifically to engineering students at the same institution yielded nearly identical findings (Zydney, Bennett, Shahid, & Bauer, 2002a).

National and regional studies of program outcomes have generally revealed cognitive gains similar to those observed at the local level. A nationwide survey of former participants in undergraduate research programs sponsored by NSF revealed numerous facets of respondents' research skills and understanding that had been enhanced by their involvement in the NSF programs (Russell, 2008). More recently, Strand and Jansen (2013) reported on a study of outcomes associated with participation in a state-wide biomedical technology research program for undergraduates. Current students expressed appreciation for the opportunity to apply academic learning to problems encountered in authentic work settings. Alumni were able to shed further light on how skills gained through the program benefited them in their subsequent careers.

In addition to studies of specific institutions and programs, several more general surveys of undergraduate students' experiences with research have been reported in the professional literature. Mabrouk and Peters (2000), for example, conducted a web-based survey of former undergraduate researchers in biology and chemistry at institutions across the U.S. and Canada. The authors found that 98% of the respondents recommended undergraduate research to others. Participants rated the experience as beneficial in promoting a wide variety of cognitive competencies, especially technical and problem-solving skills. The opportunity to present one's work at a conference was cited as particularly beneficial to those who had experienced it. Gray and Schermer (2011) reported on a study of required senior research experiences at four liberal arts colleges. Participants in the study consistently indicated that their senior projects were the most challenging and educational components of their academic programs.

Lopatto (2003) reported on a survey of undergraduate researchers at four other liberal arts colleges, conducted soon after their research experiences. Among the most frequently cited benefits were enhanced credentials, familiarity with research methods of the discipline, in-depth knowledge of a particular topic, the ability to work independently, technical and problem-solving skills, and an understanding of "how scientists think" (p. 142). The results of a follow-up survey one year later indicated a high level of stability from one phase of the study to the next (Lopatto, 2002a), and analysis of concurrent qualitative findings by Seymour provided further corroboration of the results (Lopatto, 2002b). Details of the qualitative findings were subsequently put forth by Seymour, Hunter, Laursen, and DeAntoni (2004), and collection of follow-up data led to further interpretation by Hunter, Laursen, and Seymour (2007). Based upon his own earlier work and that of his colleagues, Lopatto (2008) constructed a new questionnaire and administered it to a national sample of undergraduate researchers from 41 diverse institutions, again finding that gains in research competencies and scientific reasoning were among the principal benefits reported. On a follow-up survey approximately one year later, responses were found to be quite stable. Both Lopatto (2010) and Laursen et al. (2010) have since incorporated their findings into more comprehensive examinations of the role of undergraduate research in the teaching of science, situating their work within the broader body of literature on the topic.

Based on an analysis of data collected from a sample of 5,557 undergraduate students at hundreds of institutions throughout the U.S., using the *College Student Experiences Questionnaire (CSEQ)*, Hu, Kuh, and Li (2008) found that levels of participation in research activities were positively correlated with self-reported gains in global measures of learning. However, the study yielded only mixed results on more specific learning outcomes. While levels of research activity were positively correlated with self-reported gains in vocational preparation, intellectual development, and knowledge of science and technology, they were negatively correlated with gains in general education. Additionally, the positive effects of undergraduate research on general education, intellectual development, and global outcome measures appeared to be limited to students of moderate to high academic achievement, as measured by grade point average.

In a separate analysis of data from the *National Survey of Student Engagement (NSSE)*, which was carried out as part of AAC&U's Liberal Education and America's Promise (LEAP) initiative, Kuh (2008) found that participation in undergraduate research, as well as participation in capstone courses and projects, was associated with self-reported gains in four "essential learning outcomes" (Kuh, 2010, p. vii) identified by AAC&U as goals of liberal education in the 21st Century. These findings led Kuh (2008) to identify both undergraduate research and capstone experiences as *high-impact educational practices*, a characterization that has since been reaffirmed in a related publication by Brownell and Swaner (2010). In a replication of the original analysis, using *NSSE* data collected five years later, Kuh's (2013) findings remained essentially unchanged.

Faculty Perspectives on Cognitive Outcomes

The use of self-reporting by students in much of the outcomes research poses a limitation, insofar as it presupposes that students' subjective impressions of their intellectual growth are a reliable indicator of their actual growth. In reality, even students' understanding of the questions posed to them in self-assessment instruments has sometimes been cast into doubt (Wilson, 2012). Several authors have attempted to place a check on potential distortion in students' perceptions by surveying faculty members and other observers, concerning their views of the benefits associated with undergraduate research.

Among the aforementioned institutional and program-based studies in which both students and faculty were queried, faculty perceptions largely mirrored those of their students (Erbes, 2008; Kardash, 2000; Noji, 2011; Russell et al., 2004). In Singer and Zimmerman's (2012) study of outcomes associated with participation in their institution's summer undergraduate research program, faculty mentors' ratings of their students' competencies showed significant gains on 24 of the 34 academic outcomes assessed. Although initial ratings assigned to students by their mentors tended to be lower than those the students assigned to themselves, this pattern was reversed in ratings given at the end of the program. Similarly, van Delden (2012) found that faculty perceptions of the educational benefits of sharing work in undergraduate research journals and symposia generally matched or exceeded those of participating students. Findings from Strand and Jansen's (2013) surveys of current and former undergraduate biomedical technology researchers were generally consistent with additional survey data collected from graduate students who served as team leaders, as well as informal feedback from inventors and project managers associated with the program. In a structured assessment of a summer research program in physics, which focused on teaching of innovation, Brandenberger (2013) made use of repeated observations by a faculty panel, who scored students at three intervals, based on 15 traits associated with innovation. Cognitive traits on which significant gains were observed included *skillfulness, creativity and imagination, divergent thinking, tolerance for ambiguity*, and *insightfulness*.

In addition to studies of specific programs and institutions, several broader faculty surveys shed further light on the contributions of undergraduate research to students' intellectual growth. Among the benefits cited by faculty members at the four selective liberal arts colleges in Lopatto's (2003) study were students' development of specialized knowledge in their topic areas, problem-solving skills, practical understanding of research, communication skills, understanding and appreciation of science, and familiarity with the literature and how to use it. In related research by Hunter et al. (2007), faculty cited gains in students' understanding and application of scientific principles with greater frequency than any other category of benefit associated with participation in undergraduate research. Landrum and Nelsen's (2002) national survey of psychology faculty focused on their perceptions of both the importance of various learning outcomes and their ability to promote these outcomes through undergraduate research assistantships. Among those cognitive outcomes cited as both important and attainable were critical thinking skills, knowledge of data collection procedures, and preparation for graduate studies.

Objectively Assessed Cognitive Outcomes

Although faculty members' affirmation of students' reported gains in intellectual competencies can enhance somewhat the credibility of such claims, surveys of both students' and faculty members' perceptions of change are ultimately subjective measures of outcomes that are purportedly matters of objective fact. In order to avoid this common limitation in college outcomes research, several investigators have made use of various objectively defined criteria to determine the impact of undergraduate research on the intellectual competencies of participating students.

Among the more commonly assessed cognitive outcomes reported in the literature is mastery of curricular content, an outcome that has traditionally been measured through the use of written examinations. In a study by Ishiyama (2002b), the *Major Field Aptitude Test (MFAT) Political Science II*, a standardized test of general disciplinary knowledge, was used to compare among political science graduates from a single university over a four-year period. With ACT scores used to control for initial aptitude, those who had collaborated with faculty members on research and presented their work at professional conferences while enrolled as undergraduates were found to score significantly higher on the *MFAT* than those who had no such experience. This result suggests that undergraduate research can indeed facilitate content mastery, at least within the overall context of the discipline. In a more recent study of 58 students at six institutions, comparisons of pre- and post-test scores showed a 28% increase in content mastery, following participation in two research modules on stream temperature (Simmons et al., 2016). Despite the narrower range of disciplinary content assessed in this study, the significance of the finding is noteworthy, in light of its multi-institutional scope and the more limited research exposure provided.

In several other studies, researchers have sought to determine the impact of participation in undergraduate research on students' overall academic performance. In one such study, Shields, Hewitt, and North (2010) found that participants in a STEM research program on campus during the summer prior to the first year of college attained higher cumulative college grade point averages than did a group of similarly qualified non-participants. In studying an institutional program for sophomores and juniors majoring in wildlife science, Kinkel and Henke (2006) found significantly greater gains in grade point average from the beginning of the junior year to the end of the senior year among program participants than among a comparable group of wildlife science majors who had not participated in the program. In comparison to overall institutional figures, Haik and Bullen (2011) reported higher first-year grade point averages among participants in a comprehensive research and mentoring program for low-income, first-generation, and underrepresented students in STEM-related fields.

While analyses of first-year grade point averages have generally shown favorable outcomes for undergraduate research participants, measures of long-term impact have been mixed. In a study by Wozniak (2011), in which grade point averages at graduation for students participating in a first-year fellowship program for talented students were compared against those of eligible students who had not participated in the program, the advantage to program participants fell short of statistical significance. However, in an analysis of student transcripts, in which credit hours earned for undergraduate research were correlated with final grade point average, with differences in SAT scores taken into account, Webber, Fechheimer, and Kleiber (2012) found that "statistical analyses of these data supported a relationship between [undergraduate research] and student success and a clear positive effect of extended engagement in [undergraduate research]" (p. 16). It would appear that perhaps a key distinction is between early research alone versus distributed research. Additionally, because the first-year fellowship program described by Wozniak (2011) was used to recruit highly talented students, ceiling effects might account for the narrower variation in final grade point average across the two groups.

As indicated in the second chapter of this book, one of the goals of higher education is to promote complexity in students' patterns of reasoning. Using both quantitative and qualitative methods, Waite and Davis (2006b) analyzed manifestations of critical thinking in students' oral and written comments associated with the design and execution of undergraduate research projects. The researchers discovered evidence of critical thinking in students' conversations within six collaborative group sessions, though specific facets of critical thinking varied in their prevalence over time. Additionally, students generally manifested a greater degree of critical thinking in their oral comments than in their written comments, suggesting that collaboration with peers may play a role in promoting critical thinking within the context of undergraduate research. More recently, Cheong and Willis (2015) compared students' responses to questionnaire items administered before and after their participation in field-based geographical research. Although changes were evident in responses to a number of items pertaining to students' views of knowledge in the social sciences, these changes did not consistently reflect predictable patterns of maturation, as described in chapter 2. One possible explanation for such inconsistencies would be that students had perhaps been prompted by their experiences to rethink their prior assumptions, but had not yet fully resolved the resultant dissonance.

In recent years, the use of portfolios has emerged as an increasingly popular form of authentic assessment in higher education. This method allows for educational outcomes to be documented through tangible work products created by the student (Banta, 2003; Zubizarreta, 2004). Although there appears to be growing interest in the use of portfolios to assess undergraduate research outcomes, as evidenced by NSF's financial investment in the development of an electronic portfolio system for this purpose (Wilson et al., 2009), such assessment has thus far remained scarce. In what appears to be one of the earliest reported uses of portfolios to measure undergraduate research outcomes, Eddins, Williams, Bushek, Porter, and Kineke (1997) found evidence of undergraduate researchers' acquisition of skills in communication, organization and planning, decision-making, problem-solving, and analytical reasoning. More recently, analysis of artifacts collected at multiple stages of pilot programs in accounting, biology, and political science at Florida Atlantic University was used to assess a proposed model for continuous scaffolding of undergraduate research within diverse disciplines. Over the course of all three programs, notable increases were attained in the percentage of student work rated as *exemplary* on various learning outcomes (Chamely-Wiik et al., 2014). Leek (2014) made use of multiple student assignments to assess mastery of learning goals associated with a short-term communication research program conducted in London by an American university. Using an adapted version of AAC&U's *Intercultural Knowledge and Competence* rubric, faculty ratings of student work yielded mean ratings of 2.7/3.0 on *knowledge of world views*, 2.4/3.0 on *data collection*, 2.3/3.0 on *knowledge of method* and *application of method*, and 2.1/3.0 on *connections* and *knowledge of the research cycle*.

Beyond the aforementioned studies, several researchers have used analysis of individual student work products to document learning outcomes. In one such analysis, Orr (2011) found evidence of incorporation of multiple disciplinary perspectives into nine out of ten projects completed in an international undergraduate research program in which interdisciplinarity was emphasized. A multifaceted rubric was used to structure faculty ratings of poster presentations by participants in a summer fellowship program in digital cultural heritage at Drexel University. Mean ratings on 13 aspects of the presentations ranged from 2.40/4.00 to 3.11/4.00, with a median of 2.68/4.00 and a grand mean of 2.74/4.00 (Rocheleau et al., 2013). In yet another study, a five-scale rubric was used to analyze students' final reports on course-based projects in research and technology, with an expectation that students would achieve a minimum score of 3.0/5.0 on each scale. Of the 581 students completing the course, 82% achieved this goal (Knezek, Morreale, Keddis, & James, 2015).

Affective Outcomes

The overwhelming majority of evidence on affective outcomes of undergraduate research has involved self-reporting by students. This pattern is consistent with traditional approaches to educational research, in which interviews and questionnaires have been commonly used to collect data on participants' attitudes, opinions, feelings, values, and intentions (Johnson & Christensen, 2000).

One area of potential interest to faculty members who are considering use of undergraduate research as a pedagogical tool is the impact of participation on students' attitudes toward the learning situation itself. In general, feedback from students on their research experiences has been favorable (Ahern-Rindell & Quackenbush, 2015; Grabowski, Heely, & Brindley, 2008; Hunter et al., 2007; Jacob, 2008; Mickley, 2007; Murray, 2014; Russell, 2008; Schroeder, 2008; Strand & Jansen, 2013; Troischt et al., 2016). Student evaluations of research-intensive undergraduate biology courses have indicated that students appreciate the hands-on nature of the learning process (Chaplin, Manske, & Cruise, 1998), as well as the quality of the interaction between students and faculty members (Towle, Hand, Kent, McKernan, & Lawson, 2003) and among students themselves (Jones & Bolyard, 2009). Hirsch et al. (2013) reported that students enrolled in a senior capstone course, in which focus group research was a major component, credited the research experience with enhancing their enjoyment of the course and viewed the skills developed through the activity as having utility beyond the course.

As collaborative learning becomes a more common element of undergraduate research, the quality of students' interaction with their peers becomes an important factor in their satisfaction with the research experience. Kephart et al. (2008) reported that members of research groups experienced a deepening commitment to one another's learning as a consequence of their participation. Barlow and Villarejo (2004) discovered that students who had engaged in research within the context of a comprehensive program for minorities in biology valued the opportunity to work as part of a research team and credited the experience with improving their time management skills and heightening their awareness of the relationship between the content of their science courses and their future careers as scientists. Students involved in a community college STEM research program frequently cited "team-work and leadership skills" (Noji, 2011, p. 19) as a major benefit of their participation.

It should be noted that not all student comments on undergraduate research have been unequivocally positive. Becker (2005) noted a pattern of dissatisfaction during the research process, followed by a retrospective recognition of its value. She attributed the initial displeasure to students' venturing beyond their "comfort zones" (p. 165) in their research projects. Kinkel and Henke (2006) found that students were generally satisfied with their undergraduate research experiences but were dissatisfied with the amount of time required to carry out their projects. Foertsch, Alexander, and Penberthy (2000) also reported concerns about the time commitments required of undergraduate researchers, but related these concerns more directly to the constricted timeframe of a summer research program. Sabatini (1997) found that time commitments were a matter of concern during the academic year as well, primarily due to the competing demands of traditional coursework. However, the students in his study also indicated that the demands of their research projects had led them to manage their time more effectively, consistent with more recent findings by Wilson and Howitt (2012).

Several authors have sought to determine whether or not the undergraduate research experience has an impact on students' attitudes toward their education beyond the course or program in which the research experience occurs. Bauer and Bennett (2003) found that undergraduate research program participation was associated with greater overall satisfaction with the undergraduate experience. Additionally, some participants in a more recent survey of psychology faculty credited the research process with enhancement of student-faculty relationships (Kierniesky, 2005). Social interaction with peers and supportive relationships with faculty members have, in turn, been cited by participants in a comprehensive research and mentoring program as contributing to their satisfaction and success in college (Ward & Dixon, 2008). Locks and Gregerman (2008) found that participants in a similar program tended to adopt a more proactive approach to problems encountered in college than did non-participants, and this proactive stance appeared to enhance the quality of their overall undergraduate experiences.

Another outcome of potential interest to educators is the student's attitude toward the academic discipline in which the research experience occurs. In one study by Schroeder (2008), participants directly credited their research experiences in electrical and computer engineering with increasing their interest in the field. Likewise, Russell's (2008) study of NSF-sponsored programs revealed that a majority of program alumni linked their participation in the programs to increases in their levels of interest in related careers.

The impact of undergraduate research experience on students' attitudes toward science, in particular, has been examined in multiple studies. Surveys of former participants in undergraduate STEM research have linked such experience to favorable attitudes toward science (Mabrouk & Peters, 2000), as well as interest in coursework, academic majors, and career opportunities in STEM-related fields (Awong-Taylor et al., 2016; Barlow & Villarejo, 2004; Hammond & Lalor, 2009; Overath et al., 2016; Troischt et al., 2016). Participation in STEM-related institutional undergraduate research programs has been found to be associated with both selection of related majors (Egger & Klemperer, 2011; Shields et al., 2010) and retention in such majors (Awong-Taylor et al., 2016; Felix & Zovinka, 2008) or curricula (Carter, 2011). Consistent with these findings, alumni surveys have also shown large percentages of former undergraduate researchers employed in STEM-related positions (Dowling & Hannigan, 2009; Russell, 2008; Troischt et al., 2016). While most studies have shown the influence of research experience on attitudes toward science to be affirmative, Kardash, Wallace, and Blockus (2008) found that 23% of undergraduate research program participants indicated that their experience had decreased their interest in pursuing research careers, compared with only 22% who said that it had increased their interest in such careers.

The impact of undergraduate research on students' attitudes toward science has implications beyond their decisions concerning entry into the field. Qualitative research by Seymour et al. (2004) and Hunter et al. (2007) revealed that undergraduate research was often seen as instrumental in cultivating students' emerging identities as scientists and their adoption of characteristic patterns of thought. Edgcomb et al. (2010) found that faculty ratings of student learning across multiple summer research programs within a single institution largely mirrored those of student participants, reflecting gains in "both hard and soft scientific skills" (p. 22) pertaining to research protocol and laboratory culture respectively. In Brandenberger's (2013) study of gains in physics students' traits associated with innovation, affective rubrics on which ratings by faculty observers increased significantly included *ambitious, self-reflecting, fully engaged, productive,* and *risk-taking.*

Feedback from students has also generally supported the conclusion that undergraduate research experience promotes interest in research itself (Foertsch et al., 2000; Jacob, 2008), as well as in research-related careers (Ward & Dixon, 2008). Students and faculty alike have recognized the value of undergraduate research as a means by which to gauge the degree of fit between the talents, interests, and temperament of the student and those demanded in a research career (Hunter et al., 2007). These earlier results notwithstanding, subsequent findings suggest a more nuanced link between undergraduate research experience and interest in the investigative process. In one of the few studies where a pre-test and post-test control group design was used to gauge actual changes in students' attitudes subsequent to research participation, Deicke, Gess, and RueB (2014) found that research experience, in itself, was not associated with increased interest levels. However, among those students who had participated in research, greater depth of engagement was associated with greater gains in interest.

Career development appears to be a major benefit of participation in undergraduate research. Surveys of both students (Bauer & Bennett, 2003; Campbell & Skoog, 2004; Kardash et al., 2008; Lopatto, 2002b; Seymour et al., 2004; Zydney et al., 2002a) and faculty members (Lopatto, 2003; Zydney et al., 2002b) have suggested that participation in undergraduate research can help students to clarify their career goals and future plans. Similarly, Shokair (2002) and Gary et al. (2010) found that some undergraduate research program alumni credited their experiences with helping them to feel more confident in their plans for the future. In other studies, former undergraduate researchers indicated that their experiences had directly influenced their career choices (Russell, 2008) or led to professional opportunities (Conway et al., 2012). Sims et al. (2012) found that business students who had engaged in optional research projects credited the experience with enhancing their professionalism and their ability to complete projects within a prescribed timeframe, in addition to broadening their professional networks.

Based on several studies, it appears that participation in undergraduate research can affect students' attitudes toward learning. Bauer and Bennett (2008) found evidence to suggest that involvement in undergraduate research was associated with both increased motivation to learn and increased "quality of effort" (p. 99) in students' learning activities. Lopatto (2008) found that former participants in undergraduate research reported becoming more active, independent, and intrinsically motivated learners as a result of their research experience. Waite and Davis (2006a) pointed toward multiple ways in which collaboration with peers appeared to enhance motivation among the undergraduate researchers in their study.

Whereas most undergraduate research involves some element of collaboration, its potential impact on students' ability to interact effectively with others is a topic worthy of investigation as well. Faculty observations have supported the conclusion that undergraduate research promotes effective teamwork (Bauer & Bennett, 2008; Zydney et al., 2002b). Former participants have also frequently credited their own experiences with enhancement of their understanding of the value of teamwork (Bauer & Bennett, 2008), as well as their interpersonal (Shokair, 2002; Ward & Dixon, 2008) and group process skills (Firmage et al., 2005; Kephart et al., 2008; Pierce, 2005). However, in one of the few studies in which a control group was used, Bauer and Bennett (2003) found no significant effect of undergraduate research participation on self-reported gains in personal and social skills. There is, nonetheless, some evidence to suggest a link between participation and self-reported gains in leadership skills (Bauer & Bennett, 2003; Eddins et al., 1997; Pierce, 2005).

The final aspect of students' affective development that has been examined in the literature is their emotional growth and well-being. In particular, the impact of participation in undergraduate research on students' levels of self-confidence, self-efficacy, and self-esteem has been studied by multiple authors. Surveys of former undergraduate researchers have documented students' perceptions of gains in self-confidence associated with their research experiences (Campbell & Skoog, 2004; Conway et al., 2012; Gary et al., 2010; Hammond & Lalor, 2009; Lopatto, 2008; Mabrouk & Peters, 2000; Seymour et al., 2004; Sims et al., 2012). White et al. (2013) offered further evidence of such gains, through comparisons of preliminary and follow-up questionnaire data. Kardash et al. (2008) found that increased self-efficacy was perceived to be a benefit of undergraduate research among participating students, but significantly more so among women than among men. Gains in self-esteem associated with participation in an undergraduate research program have been verified in longitudinal research using an equivalent control group design (Jonides, 1995). In a survey of faculty, gains in self-confidence were cited as a common benefit of students' participation in a community college STEM research program (Noji, 2011). Other attitudinal benefits of participation in undergraduate research that have been cited in the literature include an increased ability to adapt to change (Eddins et al., 1997) and greater openness to new ideas (Zydney et al., 2002b). In Leek's (2014) study of communications research in London, the two highest mean ratings of student outcomes were on openness and cultural self-awareness. However, given the international setting of the program, it cannot be assumed that the research experience itself was the primary contributor to these outcomes.

In contrast to other researchers, Hu, Kuh, and Li (2008) found a negative relationship between participation in undergraduate research and general growth in personal development. Acknowledging disappointment in this finding, the authors maintained nevertheless that the balance of evidence across multiple outcomes favored continuation of efforts to promote undergraduate research, albeit with an eye toward rectification of any shortcomings in existing programs.

Educational Attainment

The influence of various aspects of the undergraduate experience on students' educational attainment has been widely studied for many years, in part because of its significance to individual socioeconomic mobility (Feldman & Newcomb, 1969/1994; Mayhew et al., 2016; Pascarella & Terenzini, 1991, 2005). Not surprisingly, as opportunities for participation in undergraduate research have expanded, its particular impact on educational attainment has emerged as a topic of investigation. Pascarella and Terenzini (2005) have defined educational attainment generally as "the number of years of schooling completed or degrees earned" (p. 373). The body of research on educational attainment can be further divided into studies of undergraduate persistence and those dealing with graduate education.

Undergraduate Persistence

In addition to affecting the student's future economic opportunities, persistence to degree completion is generally in the institution's best interest, as a high rate of attrition can threaten its ability to survive (Tinto, 1993). According to Penn (1999), "low attrition/high retention is seen as a key indicator of institutional success" (p. 2). Therefore, the impact of participation in undergraduate research on student persistence is a matter of genuine consequence. Whereas institutional enrollment managers concern themselves with both the size and composition of the student body (Penn, 1999), studies of differential effects on various segments of the student population are of particular interest.

Thus far, the literature dealing with the impact of undergraduate research on student persistence has largely consisted of evaluative studies of comprehensive undergraduate research and mentoring programs that primarily target at-risk student populations. In one prominent study, involving the University of Michigan's Undergraduate Research Opportunity Program (UROP), the second-year attrition rate was found to be significantly lower for program participants than for members of an equivalent control group, though first-year attrition rates were not found to differ significantly. In this same study, the overall attrition rate for African-Americans was significantly lower among program participants than among non-participants, though no significant difference was detected among Caucasian students (Jonides, 1995; Nagda, Gregerman, Jonides, von Hippel, & Lerner, 1998). Further research on the program revealed a positive relationship between participation and degree completion among African-American and Hispanic females majoring in engineering (Gregerman, 2009).

Studies of similar programs have yielded impressive findings as well. Long-term graduation rates have consistently been found to be higher among program participants than among control group (Ishiyama, 2001), college (Keasley &

Johnson, 2009), or institutional (Flores, Darnell, & Renner, 2009) student populations. Comparable differences in interim retention rates have also been documented, using either control group (Ishiyama, 2001) or general institutional (Ward & Dixon, 2008) data. Focusing specifically on retention of first-generation and underrepresented STEM majors beyond the first year, Haik and Bullen (2011) found that participants in one program were retained in both the university and STEM majors at higher rates than was the general student population.

While these studies have shed some light on the potential impact of undergraduate research programs on retention, the investigations were not structured to ascertain the effect of research activity per se, independent of the various other provisions incorporated into the particular programs. In another study, dealing with a program that targeted minority students in the biological sciences, Barlow and Villarejo (2004) sought to assess the program's impact on attrition at multiple stages of enrollment and to gauge the independent effects of various program components. Relative to a comparison group on the same campus, with incoming differences controlled, program participants were found to be significantly more likely to successfully complete the required introductory mathematics and science course sequence and to graduate with a degree in biology. Because participation in research was optional within this particular program, it was possible to draw further comparisons between program participants who had engaged in research and those who had not. The results of the study indicated that researchers were significantly more likely than non-researchers to: (1) graduate from the university with a degree in any field, (2) graduate from the university with a degree in biology, and (3) graduate from the university with a degree in biology and a grade point average of 3.0 or higher. These findings withstood further analyses in which academic and possible motivational factors were controlled.

In addition to studies of comprehensive research and mentoring programs for targeted populations, the academic literature includes some information on the effects of non-targeted research initiatives and more narrowly structured programs on student retention. Studies of several institutional efforts to promote research activity early in students' undergraduate experiences have revealed higher retention rates among participants than among non-participants (Grabowski et al., 2008; Olson-McBride et al., 2016; Wozniak, 2011). Studies of research-intensive STEM curricula have shown promise of increasing student retention, among both underrepresented student populations and students in general (Awong-Taylor et al., 2016; Sukumaran et al., 2006). Kinkel and Henke (2006) reported that participants in a voluntary wildlife studies research program had a six-year graduation rate of 96%, compared with a rate of 60% for a control group. In Noji's (2011) study of a community college STEM research program, 34% of program participants continued on to four-year institutions, compared with a transfer rate of 6% for liberal arts majors who had not participated in the program.

Graduate Education

As stated in the previous chapter, one of the goals of undergraduate research programs is to ensure ongoing preparation of future generations of scholars. Therefore, in gauging the impact of such programs, promotion of students' interest in graduate education is an outcome of potentially great importance. Investigations of this outcome have generally fallen into three categories: (1) studies of program participants' degree aspirations while in college and soon thereafter; (2) studies of graduate school attendance patterns among program alumni; and (3) surveys of student and faculty perceptions of the influence of undergraduate research participation on degree aspirations and attainment.

As in the case of the undergraduate persistence research, most studies of students' degree aspirations have been program-specific, though a number of these studies have been national in scope. In Russell's (2008) study of recent college graduates, rates of doctoral degree aspirations and attainment were higher among NSF program alumni than among others and higher among those who had participated in either sponsored or non-sponsored undergraduate research than among those with no undergraduate research experience. This pattern held even among those who had not aspired to the doctorate prior to their enrollment in college. Other studies of programs that have enrolled students from multiple institutions have shown pre- to post-assessment gains in various aspects of participants' self-reported graduate degree aspirations (Brothers & Higgins, 2008; Dahlberg, Barnes, Rorrer, Powell, & Cairco, 2008; Higgins et al., 2011), which have been found to be significant when tested (Gonzalez-Espada & LaDue, 2006). In Hammond and Lalor's (2009) survey of engineering program alumni, over 60% of respondents directly credited their participation in the program with increasing their interest in pursuing graduate education in STEM or a related field.

More general studies of undergraduate researchers' degree aspirations have included several analyses of data from the Cooperative Institutional Research Program (CIRP), an ongoing national survey of American college students. In one such analysis, Walpole (1997) found that, among students of higher socioeconomic status, working with professors on research was predictive of higher grade point averages, which were in turn associated with more frequent plans to attend graduate school. Using the same methodology, but limiting the analysis to highly selective institutions, Walpole (1998) found that collaboration with faculty on research was associated with elevation of degree aspirations for all students and was predictive of immediate plans for graduate school attendance among students of lower socioeconomic status. In another analysis of CIRP data, Heath (1992) found that participation in undergraduate research, whether independent or in collaboration with faculty, was associated with higher degree aspirations for both African-American and White students.

Other national studies have also shown high levels of interest in graduate education among undergraduate researchers. Eighty-four percent of undergraduate researchers in Lopatto's (2008) survey of 41 colleges and universities expressed intent to pursue a graduate or professional degree, as did half of those in Seymour et al.'s (2004) study of four selective liberal arts colleges. Descriptive data from a national study of seniors majoring in physics revealed that 90% of respondents who planned to pursue graduate degrees in physics had participated in research as undergraduates, compared with only 76% of respondents overall (Mulvey & Nicholson, 2002).

Thus far, nearly all of the published research on actual graduate school attendance rates of former undergraduate researchers has been limited to specific programs and institutions, and much of it has been descriptive in nature. A sampling of institutional studies of summer undergraduate research program alumni showed graduate and professional school attendance rates ranging from 21% to 100%, with a mean of 62% (Caldwell, 2007; Dahlberg et al., 2008; Dowling & Hannigan, 2009; Hoke & Gentile, 2008). Graduate and professional school attendance rates for alumni of undergraduate research programs at the state and national levels have been found to hover more uniformly around the three-quarter mark (Conway et al., 2012; D'Souza, Dwyer, Allison, Miller, & Drohan, 2011; Foertsch et al., 2000), though Troischt et al. (2016) and Wilson (2009) both reported rates of about 60%.

In examining a comprehensive undergraduate research and mentoring program for disadvantaged students on one campus, Posselt and Black (2007) found a graduate school attendance rate of 70% among program alumni who had completed their undergraduate degrees. Based on their research involving a similar program that served primarily Latino students, Flores et al. (2009) reported a comparable figure of 50%. Because of the extensive mentoring and support services incorporated into some targeted undergraduate research programs for disadvantaged students, the isolated impact of research experience on students' prospects for graduate school attendance is difficult to ascertain. However, May, Cook, and Panu (2012) have devised a statistical model for predicting the individual influences of multiple factors on graduate school acceptance, which they plan to use in future research on the topic.

A growing number of investigators have sought to ascertain the influence of undergraduate research experience on patterns of graduate school attendance through the use of comparison group designs. Institutional studies have shown higher rates of graduate and professional school application, admission (Ishiyama, 2002b; Kinkel & Henke, 2006) and attendance among students who have participated in various undergraduate research activities than among comparable groups of students who have not (Barlow & Villarejo, 2004; Bauer & Bennett, 2003; Hathaway, Nagda, & Gregerman, 2002; Ishiyama, 2001; Zydney et al., 2002a). Similarly, Russell's (2008) national study of NSF-sponsored programs revealed that college graduates with research experience earned Ph.D.s at significantly higher rates than did those without such experience.

Opinion surveys of undergraduate researchers (Zydney et al., 2002a) and faculty members (Landrum & Nelsen, 2002) have suggested that participation in undergraduate research positively influences the decision to attend graduate school. Participants in undergraduate research have also indicated that their research experiences enabled them to make more clear and informed decisions about graduate education (Foertsch et al., 2000; Russell, 2008; Seymour et al., 2004) and prepared them to succeed in graduate or professional school (Campbell & Skoog, 2004). In a study of federally funded research programs for disadvantaged students, involving a national sample of program directors and an institutional sample of program participants, Nnadozie, Ishiyama, and Chon (2001) found that program directors and students alike saw the programs as supportive of participants' admission to graduate school.

The Benefit of the Mentoring Relationship

In surveys and interviews of both students (Barlow & Villarejo, 2004; Conway et al., 2012; Kardash et al., 2008; Sabatini, 1997; Seymour et al., 2004) and faculty members (Landrum & Nelsen, 2002), the mentoring relationship has been cited as one of the principal benefits of the undergraduate research experience. In Foertsch et al.'s (2000) study of minority undergraduate research programs, participants asserted that the mentoring relationship had the capacity to "make or break" (p. 118) the opportunities that the programs offered.

Several studies have provided further insight into the nature of the mentoring relationship, largely affirming Daloz's (1999) characterization of the mentor as an advisor, a motivator, and an advocate. Sims et al. (2012) recounted how undergraduate research experience had led to an elevation of faculty members' expectations of participating students, which in turn motivated them to achieve at a higher level. Career development has also been cited as an area in which research mentors have been particularly influential (Campbell & Skoog, 2004). In Zydney et al.'s (2002a) study of engineering alumni, those who had participated in undergraduate research were more likely to indicate that faculty members had been influential in their career choices and their decisions to attend graduate school than were those who had not participated. Wong (2004) found that participants in an undergraduate research program reported greater reliance on faculty members for academic or professional advice than did students on the same campus who had not participated in the program. Likewise, Hathaway et al. (2002) found that participants in undergraduate research used faculty members as references more frequently than did non-participants.

Several studies have revealed differences in perspectives on the mentoring relationship among the various parties involved in undergraduate research. In comparing faculty and student perspectives, Gafney (2005) found similarities in perceptions of the essential qualities of a mentor, but differences in the prioritization of these qualities. While students tended to place a higher priority on personal support, faculty members were more likely to emphasize professional initiation. Other authors have reported variation among undergraduate researchers in the priorities assigned to characteristics of their mentors, based on race (Ishiyama, 2007), gender (Mabrouk & Peters, 2000), and first-generation enrollment status (Mekolichick & Gibbs, 2012). Additionally, students working in smaller research groups have been found to place a higher priority on the supportive qualities of the mentor than those working in larger groups (Mabrouk & Peters, 2000), suggesting that management of the dynamics of the research group may be an important aspect of the mentoring role.

Conclusion

The past 15 years have brought dramatic growth in the body of empirical literature on educational outcomes of undergraduate research programs. In general, the studies that have been conducted have supported the extension of research opportunities to undergraduate students. Studies of productivity measures, such as publications and conference papers, attest to the power of undergraduate research programs to promote scholarly activity. Studies of cognitive outcomes suggest that undergraduate research can facilitate content mastery, research competency, critical thinking skills, and effective communication. Demonstrated attitudinal outcomes include satisfaction with instruction, interest in the discipline, clarity of educational and occupational goals, self-confidence, self-efficacy, self-esteem, open-mindedness, and adaptability. Based on available evidence, it also appears that participation in undergraduate research programs supports students' persistence to completion of their bachelor's degrees and their subsequent pursuit of graduate education. In addition to facilitating many of the aforementioned outcomes of undergraduate research, the relationship that is formed with the faculty mentor appears to be widely valued as an end in itself.

PART III
The Conditions

5

THE NATIONAL CLIMATE FOR UNDERGRADUATE RESEARCH

The potential benefits of undergraduate research for both the individual student and the academic community have contributed to an increased commitment to such activities at the national level. This expanding commitment manifests itself in a growing number of public and private initiatives to encourage scholarly activities among undergraduate students and the formation of organizational structures to facilitate this process.

Organizational Support for Undergraduate Research

One measure of the growing support for undergraduate research that exists at the national level is the emergence and expansion of organizations that explicitly embrace a mission of promoting undergraduate research. In addition to providing material support for undergraduate researchers and their faculty mentors, many of these organizations provide advocacy for supportive governmental policies and encourage dialogue among academics seeking to create hospitable climates for undergraduate research on their own campuses.

Professional Associations

Much of the support for undergraduate research has come from within the academy itself. Professors with an interest in undergraduate research, especially within the natural sciences, have joined forces to provide leadership in advancing a national effort to incorporate research opportunities into undergraduate education. Their efforts have led to the establishment of several influential professional associations.

Council on Undergraduate Research (CUR)

Widely regarded today as the voice of the undergraduate research community, the Council on Undergraduate Research (CUR) was first assembled in 1978 and adopted its first constitution and by-laws in 1980 (CUR, 2009). Today, the Council has as its stated mission "to support and promote high-quality undergraduate student-faculty collaborative research and scholarship" (CUR, 2015, December). CUR provides information and support to students and faculty members in their research endeavors and provides advocacy for undergraduate research at the national (CUR, 2016a; Karukstis, 2005a; Osborn, 2008) and international (Ambos, 2016; Hensel, 2011c) levels.

Additionally, CUR sponsors its own peer-reviewed journal(s), heretofore known as the *Council on Undergraduate Research Quarterly* and *CURQ on the Web*. The *Quarterly* was recently renamed *Scholarship and Practice in Undergraduate Research: The Journal of the Council on Undergraduate Research*, effective Fall, 2017 (E. L. Ambos & S. Larson, personal communication, March 6, 2017), reflecting its emphasis on undergraduate research as a topic of investigation and its stature as a scholarly journal.

To strengthen its efforts in support of undergraduate research, and to broaden its overall impact, CUR has formed strategic partnerships with a number of other educational and research organizations (Hensel, 2011c; Karukstis, 2007c). Under a series of NSF grants, CUR has trained thousands of faculty and administrators, representing over 200 colleges and universities, in strategies for institutionalizing undergraduate research on their campuses (Malachowski, Hensel, Ambos, Karukstis, & Osborn, 2014). Over the course of its history, CUR's individual membership has continued to grow, rising from just over 1,000 in 1989 (Halstead, 1997) to almost 7,000 in 2011. As of that date, its institutional membership had also surpassed 600 (Campbell, 2011), and five state systems of higher education held membership as well (Hensel, 2011c).

The acceleration of CUR's growth, in recent years, is undoubtedly due in part to its consolidation with another professional association, the National Conferences on Undergraduate Research (NCUR). NCUR was founded in 1987, to provide support for undergraduate scholarship within all areas of study and across all types of institutions (CUR, 2016b). Its primary activity has been sponsorship of an annual conference at which students from across the nation present their work. NCUR has also served as a professional network for faculty members and administrators seeking to engage undergraduate students in research activities on their own campuses and has provided conference sessions specifically for such individuals (CUR, 2016c).

In July, 2009, the governing boards of CUR and NCUR announced plans to consolidate their organizations under the CUR banner. Recognizing the growing similarities between the organizations, the board members concluded that such a merger would enable them to more efficiently serve the needs of the undergraduate research community (CUR, 2009, August; Husic, 2009a). Together, representatives of the two organizations identified multiple functions to support a joint mission of advocacy for undergraduate research and service to students, faculty, and institutions (Young & Nelson, 2010). In June, 2011, the merger of the two organizations was finalized (Campbell, 2011). In anticipation of the event, Hensel (2010) foresaw that the consolidation of the two associations would "bring together students, faculty, and institutions to support, promote, and enhance undergraduate research experiences" (p. 4).

National Collegiate Honors Council (NCHC)

Though not focused specifically on undergraduate research, the National Collegiate Honors Council (NCHC) has played an indirect role in the advancement of undergraduate research at the national level, through its work in support of undergraduate honors programs. Such programs provide gifted and talented students with a variety of academic enrichment opportunities, which often include undergraduate research (NCHC, 2013). In commenting on the potential for advancement of undergraduate research through honors programs, Fox (2010) observed that "the marriage of undergraduate research and honors seems obvious" (p. 162). While recognizing that both honors and undergraduate research programs "share the goal of engaging students in genuine research," Grobman (2011, p. 29) drew a distinction between them nonetheless, as she noted that undergraduate research programs are typically more inclusive, with respect to student characteristics, models of collaboration, and venues for dissemination of findings. NCHC was established in 1966 to provide advocacy for honors education and networking opportunities to those affiliated with honors programs. The organization is distinctive in that membership is open to undergraduate students, in addition to faculty, staff, and administrators (NCHC, 2015).

Association of American Colleges and Universities (AAC&U)

Another association that has contributed significantly to the advancement of undergraduate research, within the context of a broader organizational mission, is the Association of American Colleges and Universities (AAC&U). Founded in 1915, as the Association of American Colleges (AAC), the organization was initially comprised solely of liberal arts colleges, whether independent or affiliated with comprehensive universities. In 1995, it was renamed AAC&U, to reflect what had become a more inclusive membership. Although its institutional base has broadened since its founding, the Association's mission has remained steadfastly focused on the promotion of liberal learning (Tritelli, 2014). AAC&U has published a number of influential reports, as part of its Liberal Education and America's Promise (LEAP) initiative, which emphasizes the cultivation of skills in addressing complex problems through "evidence-based inquiry, analysis, and decision making" (Schneider, 2015, p. 6). Under this initiative, both undergraduate research and capstone experiences have been advanced as *high-impact practices* (Kuh, 2008; Kuh & O'Donnell, 2013).

In 2010, AAC&U entered into a formal partnership with another group that has been influential in promoting undergraduate research, known as Project Kaleidoscope (PKAL, 2016). Founded in 1989, this network of STEM educators is committed to the transformation of undergraduate education in the various disciplines represented by its membership (AAC&U, n.d.). The group uses the metaphor of the kaleidoscope to convey the multifaceted nature of pedagogical leadership, which it sees as incorporating four broad aims: (1) "advancing the field," (2) "ensuring the success of all students," (3) "enhancing institutional vitality," and (4) "advocating for science" (PKAL, 2000, p. 5). Today, PKAL serves as "AAC&U's STEM higher education reform center dedicated to empowering STEM faculty, including those from underrepresented groups, to graduate more students in STEM fields who are competitively trained and liberally educated" (AAC&U, n.d.).

Council for the Advancement of Standards in Higher Education (CAS)

One of the most recent organizations to step forward in shaping the course of undergraduate research programs is the Council for the Advancement of Standards in Higher Education (CAS). Founded in 1979 as the Council for the Advancement of Standards for Student Services/Development Programs, CAS is a consortium of professional associations dedicated to the articulation and dissemination of standards of professional practice in higher education administration. CAS today consists of almost 40 member organizations (CAS, 2016a) and has issued statements of professional standards in 45 areas of administrative practice (CAS, 2016b). Statements of professional standards are periodically reviewed and updated when necessary. In 2009, CAS introduced its first statement of professional standards for undergraduate research programs. The statement addresses such matters as program goals, staffing, legal and ethical issues, resources, and access to services (CAS, 2009). Although the subsequent publication of CUR's own *Characteristics of Excellence in Undergraduate Research (COEUR)* (Rowlett, Blockus, & Larson, 2012) has largely eclipsed the CAS document, the earlier effort was undeniably a noteworthy first step in establishing uniform standards of quality across institutional programs.

Government Agencies

As indicated in chapter 3, the promotion of education in science and technology has long been regarded as a critical national interest. It is not surprising, therefore, that much of the current support for undergraduate research has emerged under the authority of the federal government. Several agencies have been particularly influential in promoting a national agenda that includes research opportunities for America's undergraduate students.

National Science Foundation (NSF)

Among those governmental organizations that have been most active in the promotion of undergraduate research is the National Science Foundation (NSF), an independent federal agency, whose mission is "to promote the progress of science; to advance the national health, prosperity, and welfare; [and] to secure the national defense" (NSF, n.d.a). In 1987, NSF developed the Research Experience for Undergraduates (REU) program. Through this program, the Foundation provides awards that assist in the development of undergraduate research sites or that provide further funding for students to participate in existing NSF projects (Lanza, 1998). Students are given the opportunity, through REUs, to learn how research is carried out while contributing to research projects. These projects may be conducted during the summer, the academic year, or both (NSF, 2013).

The Foundation's Research in Undergraduate Institutions (RUI) program aims to promote faculty scholarship involving undergraduate students, to enhance the research culture of PUIs, and to promote the integration of teaching and research within such institutions. Through this program, funding is awarded to faculty members, on a competitive basis, to support their research endeavors (NSF, 2014). Comparative data across NSF programs suggest that RUI has indeed contributed to PUIs' success in securing research funding (Slocum & Scholl, 2013). In a related program, the Foundation makes Research Opportunity Awards (ROA) available to faculty members at PUIs, so that they can collaborate on scholarly projects with colleagues at other institutions (NSF, 2014). The Foundation's Experimental Program to Stimulate Competitive Research (EPSCoR), which "seeks to strengthen research and education in science and engineering in states that historically have not been leaders in winning federal research grants" (D'Souza et al., 2011, p. 41), has offered support for such partnerships as well.

Department of Energy (DOE)

The U.S. Department of Energy (DOE) offers undergraduate research opportunities through its Science Undergraduate Laboratory Internship (SULI) program. This program is conducted at 17 DOE laboratories throughout the nation and is designed to encourage students to pursue careers in STEM-related fields. The Department offers two 16-week sessions during the academic year and one ten-week session during the summer. Participants in the program engage directly in research at their designated sites, under the oversight of DOE scientists and engineers (U.S. Department of Energy, 2016).

National Institutes of Health (NIH)

The National Institutes of Health (NIH) is a federal agency, within the Department of Health and Human Services, that is comprised of 27 centers and institutes, which together serve as "the nation's medical research agency" (NIH, n.d.). In 1985, in response to a mandate from Congress, NIH initiated a program known as the Academic Research Enhancement Award (AREA), which provides support for behavioral and biomedical research at predominantly undergraduate non-research-oriented institutions. The purposes of the program are: (1) to enhance the research culture within such institutions, (2) to introduce students within such institutions, particularly those at the undergraduate level, to the process of biomedical research, and (3) to encourage outstanding research within this sector of American higher education. Although AREA grants can be used to cover a wide variety of expenses associated with selected projects, applicants are encouraged to budget for at least one undergraduate research appointment, so as to more fully accomplish the stated goals of the program (Chin, 2004). Another NIH program, the Institutional Development Award (IDeA) Networks of Biomedical Research Excellence (INBRE), has supported undergraduate research opportunities offered through partnerships of research universities with PUIs (Conway et al., 2012; D'Souza et al., 2011).

Department of Education

The U.S. Department of Education's Ronald E. McNair Postbaccalaureate Achievement Program was established to increase opportunities for graduate education and to diversify the nation's community of scholars. Through this program, funding is made available to collegiate institutions, to support local initiatives designed to prepare disadvantaged undergraduate students for entry into doctoral programs. Typical provisions of the program include both mentoring and research opportunities (U.S. Department of Education, 2011).

Private Foundations

Beyond the sources of support that exist within the public sector, private philanthropy has become an important contributor to the advancement of research opportunities for undergraduates. Such support is often granted to institutions or faculty members, who are given some measure of discretionary authority over the use of funds to support undergraduate research. In other instances, awards are provided directly to students. Foundations vary in the breadth of disciplines in which they support undergraduate research opportunities.

Alice and Leslie E. Lancy Foundation

Among the private foundations that have contributed to the advancement of undergraduate research nationally, the Alice and Leslie E. Lancy Foundation is distinctive in its dual focus on the roles of individual campuses and professional associations in the attainment of this goal. From 1999 to 2008, the Foundation partnered with NCUR to sponsor 26 institutionally based summer undergraduate research programs, focusing on interdisciplinary studies (Stocks & Gregerman, 2009). On the heels of this success, its support was vital to the consolidation of CUR and NCUR, as well as the subsequent revitalization of the reconfigured organization. In addition to its financial backing, CUR has benefited from Lancy's articulation of five strategic pillars, which have informed CUR's own organizational planning (Ambos & Rivera, 2015).

VentureWell

VentureWell is dedicated to bringing ideas of collegiate inventors to market. VentureWell administers a grant program that allows students to work together on 'E-Teams.' The program provides funding and coaching through a three-stage process, in which projects progress based on merit (VentureWell, 2016).

Research Corporation for Science Advancement (RCSA)

The Research Corporation for Science Advancement (RCSA) maintains a grant program, the Cottrell Scholar Awards (CSA), which supports the development of promising teacher-scholars in chemistry, physics, and astronomy. In order to be considered for a CSA, an applicant must present both a research plan and an educational plan. This stipulation helps to encourage work with undergraduate students on sponsored projects, as does the program's focus on faculty at both research universities and PUIs (RCSA, 2015).

Camille and Henry Dreyfus Foundation

The Camille and Henry Dreyfus Foundation promotes chemical research "as a means of improving human relations and circumstances throughout the world." The Foundation offers a number of grant opportunities, which support both undergraduate research and faculty development at PUIs (Camille & Henry Dreyfus Foundation, n.d.).

Howard Hughes Medical Institute (HHMI)

The Howard Hughes Medical Institute (HHMI) is committed to the improvement of science education at all levels of schooling (HHMI, 2016). Its higher education initiatives include an array of programs that make funding available to support undergraduate research. Historically, the Institute has maintained separate programs for comprehensive universities and undergraduate colleges. More recently, it has introduced targeted initiatives that focus instead on student populations that have traditionally been disadvantaged in the pursuit of scientific careers (HHMI, 2015).

American Chemical Society (ACS)

Founded in 1944 by seven major oil companies, the Petroleum Research Fund was reorganized in 2000 and placed under the oversight of the American Chemical Society (ACS), as the American Chemical Society Petroleum Research Fund (ACS PRF). The purpose of the Fund is to promote education and research, across multiple disciplines, with broad applicability to the petroleum field (ACS, 2016). ACS PRF offers a variety of grants to scientists and educators, and the educational aspect of its mission is taken seriously in the allocation of funding (Funke, 2000). In recent years, ACS PRF has also begun to take a more active role in supporting faculty grant-writing through training (Hollinsed, 2007).

Jackson Laboratory

The Jackson Laboratory seeks to promote human health through genetic research. Each summer, it conducts a fellowship program for high school and college students, at its main facility, in Bar Harbor. Each intern is paired with a mentor, who works individually with the student to plan and carry out a research project. Each intern receives a stipend and travel allowance, in addition to room and board. The organization also operates an unpaid internship program during the academic year, for which students often earn academic credit from their home institutions (Blockus & Wilson, 2012).

Leadership Alliance

The Leadership Alliance is a national consortium of over 30 academic institutions and other organizations, which provides training and mentoring to diverse undergraduate students, in order to prepare them for graduate education and careers in research (Leadership Alliance, 2016a). The primary mechanism used to advance the Alliance's mission is its Summer Research Early Identification Program (SR-EIP), which makes mentored research experiences at affiliated institutions available to eligible undergraduates from any accredited college or university in the nation. With the support of the Andrew W. Mellon Foundation, the Leadership Alliance Mellon Initiative (LAMI) has extended such opportunities specifically to students with doctoral aspirations in the humanities and social sciences (Leadership Alliance, 2016b).

Industry

Like the many non-profit organizations that are dedicated to the advancement of undergraduate research, many industrial corporations support academic research projects as well. Businesses provide many educational opportunities for students, including laboratory and plant tours, technical and career seminars, and funding of research projects. Companies also offer summer and cooperative employment that enables students to work on projects and to gain familiarity with advanced laboratory equipment (Burke, 1996). Through mutually beneficial collaborations with students and faculty, corporations receive valuable research results, the opinions and expertise of faculty members as consultants, and a new supply of trained undergraduates as future employees (Scott, 1996).

Several corporations, across a variety of industries, maintain ongoing relationships with individual colleges and universities to create research opportunities for undergraduates (Carney, 2006; Holman, 2006; Wade, Gragson, Wubah, & Nalley, 2000). Representatives of various industries have also been called upon to advise university scientists on the research needs of the broader scientific community (Yavelow, 2006). With seven corporate affiliates, the Jordan Valley Innovation Center at Missouri State University serves as an example of a university-led partnership to align the interests of multiple corporations with those of an academic institution and its surrounding region (Giedd & Baker, 2006). Similarly, Loyola Marymount University has partnered with both industrial corporations and municipal governments to provide authentic research experiences to undergraduate engineering students (Ramirez, McNicholas, Gilbert, Saez, & Siniawski, 2015).

Collaboration Across Institutions

In addition to gaining support from the commercial, non-profit, and governmental entities mentioned previously, faculty members engaged in research with undergraduate students often gain support from one another, through collaborative relationships that transcend institutional boundaries. Such relationships may exist either formally or informally, and may be formed by as few as two faculty members or by entire academic divisions. Regardless of the particular form that a collaborative relationship takes, the potential benefits are many.

At an NSF-sponsored summit, pertaining to undergraduate research in the chemical sciences, a group of educators cited a number of ways in which faculty members at PUIs, in particular, can benefit from such partnerships, by gaining access to facilities, equipment, and colleagues who share their specialized research interests and expertise (*Enhancing research*, 2003). Haase and Fisk (2008) recommended collaborative research specifically for untenured faculty members, who must struggle to move forward their programs of research while simultaneously adjusting to other demands of their positions.

Collaboration between faculty members at PUIs and colleagues at major research universities, in particular, has proven to be beneficial. In addition to alleviating many of the aforementioned concerns, collaboration with research university colleagues can provide faculty members from PUIs with access to support in grant-writing. For social scientists, access to large numbers of research participants is an additional benefit. Undergraduate students working with faculty on research projects can also benefit from exposure to the collaborative relationships that their mentors model through their association with colleagues from other types of institutions (Waddill & Einstein, 1996).

Cooperative relationships between teaching and research institutions are sometimes formed specifically for the purpose of promoting undergraduate research. Polack-Wahl and Squire (2003) recounted how one student at a small liberal arts college participated in an REU at a neighboring research university and then drew upon this experience as a foundation for a subsequent honors research project at his home institution. Hunnes and Dooley (2004) described a program through which students at another small liberal arts college spent ten weeks during the summer working in the biochemistry laboratory at a research university in their state.

Partnerships between institutions can take a variety of forms and often provide unique benefits to undergraduate researchers. Schammel et al. (2008) and Dehn (2009) recounted how partnerships were formed between universities and neighboring hospitals to provide students with clinical research opportunities that would not have been possible within the universities themselves. Academic and medical partnerships have also opened up opportunities for undergraduate research in biomedical technology (Strand & Jansen, 2013). With the growth of international education programs and the inclusion of field-based research components therein, the cultivation of partnerships with a variety of academic and non-academic organizations in the host country has become a critical component of program administration (Barkin, 2016).

One of the more popular models of collaboration is the formation of regional consortia, comprised of multiple PUIs, which share resources to advance undergraduate research opportunities across all participating institutions. A major benefit of this approach is its appeal to funding agencies. Through the formation of larger research groups that also represent multiple institutions, grant applicants can tap into a greater pool of matching funds and can more readily justify major expenditures, based on the shared demand for the proposed research support. Additionally, the richer pool of research talent that results from this type of collaboration enhances the scholarly credibility of the team, which in turn instills greater confidence in the worthiness of the proposal among potential benefactors (Shields, 2002).

A good example of this type of consortium is the Molecular Education and Research Consortium in Undergraduate Computational Chemistry (MERCURY), which was initially comprised of faculty and student researchers in computational chemistry at seven PUIs in Massachusetts, Connecticut, and upstate New York, and which has since expanded to the national level. Through NSF's Major Research Instrumentation (NSF-MRI) program, the Consortium obtained funding for two shared supercomputers and a systems administrator. Throughout the year, faculty and student researchers at the member institutions visit one another's campuses and communicate through e-mail. Additionally, the Consortium sponsors an annual undergraduate research conference, where students from throughout the nation present their findings in studies of computational chemistry (*Enhancing Research,* 2003; MERCURY, 2015; Parish, 2004; Shields, 2002).

In a similarly diverse alliance, the Arecibo Legacy Fast ALFA (ALFALFA) survey project has been described as a "19-institution collaboration founded to promote undergraduate research and faculty development within the context of an astronomical-survey project, discuss its efficacy, and summarize how this model may be applied to other large-scale research projects" (Troischt et al., 2016, p. 4). This partnership is comprised of a diverse group of institutions, representing all regions of the continental U.S. and Puerto Rico. Since 2007, the consortium has offered research opportunities for students through its Undergraduate ALFALFA Team (UAT), an NSF-funded initiative that originated on three campuses, before expanding to its current membership.

Operating on an international scale, the Ecological Research as Education Network (EREN) is comprised of 278 faculty and staff, affiliated with 210 institutions. In addition to 41 states and Puerto Rico, its membership is drawn from Canada, Mexico, the Bahamas, Colombia, Scotland, and Singapore. Established in 2010, under a grant from NSF's Research Coordination Networks—Undergraduate Biology Education Program, EREN's purpose is "to enhance undergraduate research in ecology at primarily undergraduate institutions (PUIs) by (1) providing networking and collaborative research opportunities for both faculty and students and (2) developing free educational resources" (Simmons et al., 2016, p. 12).

Forums for Dissemination of Findings

When a project is completed, faculty mentors have the opportunity to present their findings to peers in their fields. Undergraduates, likewise, have an array of opportunities to present their work, both locally and nationally. Through institutional and outside support, undergraduates can present their findings at professional meetings and conferences or in scholarly publications.

Undergraduate Research Conferences

As a major supporter of undergraduate research, CUR provides numerous opportunities for students to present their work. One of the pioneering initiatives to assist undergraduates in the presentation of their research results was the annual NCUR event, mentioned previously. Additionally, the Council sponsors annually *Posters on the Hill*, an event that showcases a select number of undergraduate students' research at the U.S. Capitol. Students display their posters and speak with their Senators and Representatives about their projects (CUR, 2016d). This program model has also been adopted at several state capitols (Havholm, 2012; Karukstis, 2005b; Kvale et al., 2012).

With the support of other organizations, undergraduates can present their research on the regional level as well. For example, an annual event in Oklahoma brings together student researchers from throughout that state for a day of dialogue modeled on traditional academic meetings (Cherry, 2001). Other student conferences, such as the aforementioned MERCURY event (Parish, 2004), provide opportunities for undergraduate researchers from across the nation to present their work to audiences within their specific disciplines. The emergence of such varied forums can help ensure that every undergraduate researcher has an opportunity to share his or her findings with an appropriate audience.

Undergraduate Research Journals

Another vehicle for showcasing undergraduates' research results is through publication. A number of journals are dedicated specifically to the publication of works by undergraduate students. The *Journal of Young Investigators* (*JYI*) is one such journal. This journal is peer-reviewed and provides students with the opportunity to perform the roles of author and editor (*JYI*, 2016). The *Undergraduate Research Journal for the Human Sciences* is an annual online publication of the Undergraduate Research Community (URC) of Kappa Omicron Nu, the national honor society for the human sciences. The goal of the journal is "to foster and reward the scholarly efforts of undergraduate human sciences students as well as to provide a valuable learning experience," through the publication of outstanding undergraduate student scholarship within the related disciplines (URC, 2016). Two additional publications, the *Journal of Student Research* (2016) and *Inquiries Journal* (2016), operate as online open access peer-reviewed journals and publish original work by graduate and undergraduate students across multiple disciplines.

Conclusion

As is evident from the information presented in this chapter, the national climate for undergraduate research is supportive and continues to grow increasingly so. Grassroots organizations within American higher education provide faculty mentors and other undergraduate research advocates with mechanisms to promote interest in this form of pedagogy and to increase opportunities for student participation. These groups have been supported in this endeavor by a variety of other public and private organizations that have generously funded undergraduate research activities. Colleges and universities, as well as individual academics, have also grown increasingly resourceful in their collaborative efforts to support undergraduate research. A key element of the fertile ground for undergraduate research that now exists at the national level is the broad array of conferences and publications that provide suitable outlets for the scholarly work of undergraduates. Collectively, the various factors outlined here offer hope of a very promising future for undergraduate research.

6

PATTERNS OF STUDENT AND FACULTY PARTICIPATION IN UNDERGRADUATE RESEARCH

As indicated in previous chapters of this book, interest in undergraduate research is clearly building within American higher education. The rationale for this pedagogy has been well articulated in the professional literature and there exists a growing base of support for expansion of undergraduate research opportunities at the national level. This chapter will examine the current state of undergraduate research, as it exists in practice. The chapter will include an overview of current rates of participation in undergraduate research, differential patterns of participation across institutional types and disciplines, and various other aspects of student and faculty involvement in the process.

The Overall Prevalence of Undergraduate Research

Although there appear to have been few comprehensive national studies of undergraduate student participation in research activities, a number of more limited studies together provide some basis for assessing the current state of undergraduate research. While some of these studies have dealt with multiple disciplines or institutions, others have focused more narrowly on patterns of research activity within specific fields of study or on specific campuses.

The Boyer Commission Study

In one of the most influential studies addressing the prevalence of undergraduate research thus far, the Boyer Commission (2001) assessed conditions for undergraduate education in the nation's research universities, three years after issuing a series of recommendations to such institutions, which included a call for more frequent involvement of undergraduate students in research (Boyer Commission,

1998). In the follow-up study, the Commission found that all of the institutions surveyed offered opportunities for undergraduate students to engage in research and creative activities, but participation rates tended to be low, with only 16% of institutions indicating that all or most of their students availed themselves of these opportunities, compared with 48% that indicated one-quarter or fewer of their students did so. Only 8% of institutions required that all undergraduates participate in some form of research or creative activity, though a complete absence of such requirements was also rare, with only 14% of institutions adopting this stance. Between these two extremes was a range of policies that imposed requirements only on honors students or other specific groups.

An obvious limitation of the Boyer Commission (2001) study was its exclusive focus on research universities. According to the Commission's own figures, research universities accounted for only 3% of all higher education institutions and 6% of all bachelor's degree-granting institutions in the nation at the time of its initial report (Boyer Commission, 1998). Therefore, the findings reported in the follow-up study would not necessarily reflect the overall level of undergraduate research activity nationally.

The NSF Study

A more recent survey, commissioned by NSF, included a nationally representative sample of 22- to 35-year-olds, each of whom had earned at least a bachelor's degree in a field designated as "science, technology, engineering, or mathematics (STEM)" or "social, behavioral, or economic science (SBES)" (Russell, 2008, p. 53). The sample included approximately 3,400 (52%) STEM graduates and 3,200 (48%) SBES graduates. A total of 53% of the STEM graduates surveyed and 52% of their SBES counterparts indicated that they had engaged in active research as undergraduates. This included 7% of STEM graduates and 5% of SBES graduates who engaged in research sponsored by NSF, NASA, or NIH. Among both STEM and SBES graduates, researchers tended to have higher undergraduate grade point averages than did non-researchers and were also much more likely to have held doctoral degree aspirations in advance of their enrollment in college (Russell, 2008).

The NSF study (Russell, 2008) was in one respect more comprehensive than the Boyer Commission (2001) study, insofar as it included graduates from a wider variety of four-year institutions. However, a major limitation of the study was its relatively narrow focus on STEM and SBES disciplines to the exclusion of the humanities and a number of professional fields.

The CSEQ Studies

The *College Student Experiences Questionnaire (CSEQ) Assessment Program* was a national initiative for the study of undergraduate students' educational experiences in college, which operated continuously for 35 years, initially based at the

University of California, Los Angeles (UCLA) and subsequently transferred to Indiana University. The principal instruments used in the collection of data were the *CSEQ* and the *College Student Expectations Questionnaire (CSXQ)*. Prior to discontinuation of the project in 2014, the *CSEQ* was administered to over 400,000 students at more than 500 institutions, and the *CSXQ* was administered to over 120,000 students at more than 100 institutions (CSEQ Assessment Program, 2007) [sic]. The longitudinal nature of the data enabled investigators to examine shifting patterns of involvement in various learning activities over time, in addition to gaining an in-depth understanding of rates of participation at a given point in time.

Using various samples from the overall data set, investigators found a general increase in students' levels of participation in research with faculty, beginning around the mid- 1990s, as well as an overall increase in the frequency of their engagement in a variety of specific behaviors related to the conduct of research (Hu, Kuh, & Gayles, 2007). Students with higher academic achievement, as measured by grade point average, were found to participate in undergraduate research with greater frequency than those with lower achievement (Hu, Kuh, & Li, 2008).

The NSSE Studies

The *National Survey of Student Engagement (NSSE)* is an ongoing project that deals with students' experiences in college, focusing specifically on activities and conditions that have been shown to be associated with student learning. Like the *CSEQ* before it, the *NSSE* is conducted out of the Indiana University Center for Postsecondary Research, but incorporates data on students from hundreds of institutions throughout the U.S. The instrument used in the survey queries students directly on five categories of information: (1) "student behaviors," (2) "institutional actions and requirements," (3) "reactions to college," (4) "student background information," and (5) "student learning and development" (Kuh, 2009, p. 11).

Using data from the 2005 *NSSE*, Hu, Scheuch et al. (2008) found that 4.2% of first-year students and 21.8% of seniors surveyed had participated in some form of research activity with faculty members. Working with data from the 2007 survey, Kuh (2008) found that 19% of graduating seniors had worked with faculty on research and 32% had participated in capstone experiences. Similarly, Wilson (2012) found that 20.3% of seniors completing the 2010 survey had worked with faculty on research. Replicating his previous analysis, using data from the 2012 survey, Kuh (2013) found participation rates largely unchanged, with 20% of seniors having collaborated with faculty on research and 33% having completed senior capstone experiences.

Variation across Institutional Classifications

There is reason to believe that institutions might differ according to type in their levels of support for undergraduate research. In a *U.S. News & World Report*

(Archambault, 2008) survey of college and university administrators and other educational experts, in which 33 institutions were identified as offering outstanding opportunities for undergraduate students to participate in research and creative activities, only three categories of institutions were so identified: (1) national universities, which accounted for 64% of the identified institutions; (2) liberal arts colleges, which comprised 33% of the list; and (3) master's level universities, which made up the remaining 3% of this select group of institutions. One-third of the colleges and universities on the list were public institutions and the remainder were private non-profits. It should be noted that such surveys measure only reputation, which can be affected by institutional visibility, a factor that might account for the large number of national universities on the list. Even so, reputation serves as one marker of an institution's leadership role in the undergraduate research community, a role that currently appears to fall primarily to those that conform to a fairly narrowly defined institutional profile.

An analysis conducted in the course of writing this book, using data that were publicly available online from the Council on Undergraduate Research (CUR) (n.d.) and the Carnegie Foundation for the Advancement of Teaching (2006a), revealed that research universities accounted for 8% of those colleges and universities that were institutional members of CUR in 2006. Other doctoral universities, termed *doctoral/research universities* by the Carnegie Foundation (2006b), comprised an additional 6% of CUR's institutional membership. In contrast, each of these categories represented only a 3% share of the nation's collegiate institutions, as reported by the Boyer Commission (1998). Baccalaureate colleges were similarly overrepresented in CUR, making up 36% of the institutional membership, while the Boyer Commission's figures placed them at 18% of higher education institutions nationally. Even more striking was the fact that master's colleges and universities made up 48% of CUR member institutions, but only 15% of the nation's colleges and universities. Perhaps the most remarkable finding was that specialized institutions and associate's colleges, which respectively accounted for 20% and 41% of the nation's higher education institutions, together comprised only 1% of the institutional membership of CUR.

More recent data, reported by Hensel (2011a), place the institutional membership of CUR at 46.5% public institutions and 53.5% private institutions. Additionally, community colleges now account for 1.5% of the institutional membership and minority serving institutions account for 5.6%. In a separate analysis of data on institutions holding enhanced membership in the organization, Hensel (2010) found that 68% had enrollments under 5,000, 15% had enrollments of 5,000 to 10,000, and 16% had enrollments over 10,000, though no information was reported on institutional classifications.

To the extent that CUR serves as a visible embodiment of faculty who are champions of undergraduate research, the absence of a substantial two-year and community college presence in the organization raises questions about the research opportunities available to students in this large segment of American higher education. In a survey of academic administrators at community colleges, Perez (2003) found that only about 15% of the respondents' institutions offered opportunities for students to engage in research under the tutelage of faculty members. Of those respondents whose institutions did not offer undergraduate research opportunities, 80% believed that such opportunities fell outside the scope of their institutional missions. Lack of institutional funds and facilities, cited by 28% and 18% of these respondents respectively, were also seen as factors inhibiting the advancement of undergraduate research in community colleges. Offering a surprisingly optimistic interpretation of the findings, Perez (2003) noted that any undergraduate research activity in a community college setting might be seen as encouraging insofar as it defies the widely held assumption that student research can be conducted only by graduate students and advanced undergraduates.

In further discussion, Perez (2003) elaborated on the work of a group of northeastern community colleges, known as the Beacon Associate Colleges, which had joined together to organize an annual undergraduate research conference. Gaglione (2005) cited several successful efforts at two-year colleges as evidence of the potential for undergraduate research to increase retention and transfer rates, but characterized such isolated endeavors as an "underground existence" (p. 1613). Other authors have illustrated how undergraduate research can be carried out to good effect within two-year colleges, despite constraints of time, resources, and patterns of enrollment (Brandt & Hayes, 2012; Brown, Higgins, & Coggins, 2007; Slezak, 2007). Citing multiple examples of successful initiatives, Guertin and Cerveny (2012) offered practical advice on the design and implementation of undergraduate research programs within this unique institutional context, following a simple step-by-step format.

One strategy for increasing research opportunities for two-year college students is through professional alliances. Jacob (2008) explained how undergraduate research has been incorporated into the biology curriculum of a two-year college affiliated with a private university. Other authors have offered examples of even broader partnerships between two-year and four-year institutions (Bender, 2007; Brothers & Higgins, 2008; Craney & Dea, 2003; Gasparich, 2009; Higgins et al., 2011; Ingram, 2009; Pearson et al., 2009; Watkins, 2009), and among multiple two-year institutions (Hewlett, 2009), which have increased opportunities for community college students to participate in scientific research. Coggins (2009) described how one community college used multiple partnerships with local and regional employers to expand undergraduate research opportunities for its students. Brown and Tyner (2009) described another community college's comprehensive strategy for institutionalizing undergraduate research, which incorporated opportunities both on campus and at neighboring four-year institutions. Even in the absence of formal partnerships, four-year institutions can broaden access to undergraduate research opportunities by opening up their programs to students from neighboring two-year institutions, as one major research university has done (Gregerman, 2009).

It would seem that a key factor in creating opportunities for community college students to participate in undergraduate research is increasing awareness of its value among community college faculty and inspiring them to engage collaboratively with their own students. Thorsheim et al. (2010) described an NSF-sponsored national faculty development initiative, carried out in partnership with Project Kaleidoscope, which aimed to increase community college faculty members' levels of comfort in mentoring undergraduate researchers. Using a pre- and post-test control group design, incorporating surveys of both students and faculty, the researchers found that participation in this program was associated with a significant increase in faculty members' levels of comfort with undergraduate research mentorship, which in turn was accompanied by significantly greater gains in their students' sense of research competency.

Despite the near invisibility of two-year colleges among the institutional membership of CUR, the leadership of the organization has recognized the value of undergraduate research to students enrolled in two-year technical and transfer programs. Not long ago, the Council secured an NSF grant, together with the National Council of Instructional Administrators (NCIA), an affiliate of the American Association of Community Colleges, to assess current opportunities for undergraduate research within two-year programs and to explore strategies for expansion of such opportunities (Cejda & Hensel, 2008; Karukstis, 2007c). The formation of this partnership, coupled with the continued emergence of independent undergraduate research initiatives within the nation's two-year colleges, holds the potential to advance undergraduate research opportunities for two-year college students far beyond their current levels.

The partnership between NCIA and CUR has already resulted in publication of a monograph on undergraduate research experiences for community college students, under the joint editorship of the organizations' respective executive leaders (Cejda & Hensel, 2009). This publication includes a summary of findings from a national study of current conditions for undergraduate research in community colleges. The investigation yielded evidence of both basic and applied research involving undergraduate students at community colleges, much of which was incorporated into the curriculum. Faculty development and curricular reform were advocated as strategies for expansion of such efforts, based on institutional case study data. A follow-up publication, under the same editorship, highlighted models of successful undergraduate research at community colleges across the nation (Hensel & Cjeda, 2014).

Although, historically, there have been few direct comparisons of undergraduate research participation rates across institutional categories, the emergence of several large national databases on the undergraduate experience has begun to yield some interesting findings. For example, a comparative analysis of *CSEQ* data revealed that students enrolled in doctoral universities and liberal arts colleges participated in undergraduate research with greater frequency than did those enrolled in research universities. In discussing possible reasons for such discrepancies, the authors cited higher student to faculty ratios and competition with graduate students for faculty attention as factors that might prevent undergraduate students from working with faculty on scholarly activities within research university settings (Hu et al., 2007). For over a decade, the percentage of *NSSE* respondents who have reported working with faculty on research has consistently been higher at liberal arts colleges than at other types of institutions (Hu, Scheuch, et al., 2008; Kuh, 2008, 2013; Wilson, 2012). Higher rates of participation have also been observed at more selective institutions (Hu, Scheuch, et al., 2008; Kuh, 2008, 3013), as well as private institutions (Hu, Scheuch, et al., 2008; Kuh, 2008), though the latter gap has closed over time (Kuh, 2013).

Although the NSF-sponsored study of STEM and SBES graduates revealed a narrow range of variation among institutional categories, the rate of participation in undergraduate research among STEM graduates was found to be lower at master's level institutions than at baccalaureate colleges and doctoral/research-extensive universities. Among both STEM and SBES graduates, rates of participation in sponsored research were lowest at master's level institutions and highest at doctoral/research-extensive universities. Graduates who had previously attended two-year colleges were no less likely than others to have engaged in research as undergraduates (Russell, 2008). However, it is not clear what percentage of these respondents had actually engaged in research before transferring to their four-year institutions.

More recent studies of NSF programs have yielded mixed findings. In a survey of Research Experiences for Undergraduates (REU) sites, Beninson, Koski, Villa, Faram, and O'Connor (2011) found that a majority of participating students were recruited from non-Ph.D.-granting institutions, consistent with the intent of the program. A subsequent analysis of data on institutional affiliations of principal investigators awarded grants administered by the Directorate for Biological Sciences revealed comparable success rates for PUI versus non-PUI affiliated applicants, though awards to the latter tended to be more generous (Slocum & Scholl, 2013). A separate analysis of data on grants administered by the Directorate for Social, Behavioral, and Economic Sciences showed that a clear majority of recipients in each of the five disciplines examined were affiliated with institutions classified as "very high" in research activity (Kopko, Edwards, Krause, & McGonigle, 2016, p. 7).

Variation across Disciplines

Beyond the overall rate of participation in undergraduate research, it is important to examine differences among the disciplines in their engagement of students in active inquiry. In the Boyer Commission (2001) study, participation rates were found to differ widely across the disciplines. On the high end, 62% of institutional respondents indicated that at least half of their laboratory science students participated in research, and 44% reported such rates of participation among engineering students.

In contrast, the corresponding figures for the arts, social sciences, and humanities were 36%, 25%, and 21% respectively. Even within the more limited range of disciplines included in the NSF-sponsored survey of STEM and SBES graduates, sharp contrasts were noted, with participation rates ranging from 28% to 74% among STEM disciplines and 38% to 63% among SBES disciplines (Russell, 2008).

More recent analyses of NSSE and CSEQ data have also revealed discrepancies across the disciplines. NSSE data collected from the senior class of 2005 revealed far higher rates of self-reported participation in research with faculty among students majoring in the biological and physical sciences than among those majoring in other fields. Participation rates were lowest among students majoring in business and education (Hu, Scheuch, et al., 2008). This overall pattern changed little in the 2012 survey, with the biological and physical sciences again showing the highest rates of participation. Business and education again showed lower rates of participation than did other fields, with only undecided students ranking lower (Kuh, 2013). In their longitudinal analysis of CSEQ data, Hu et al. (2007) found a sharp decline in the rate of undergraduate research participation among humanities majors in general liberal arts colleges, beginning in 1998, in contrast to a continuing upward trajectory among students in all other institutional and disciplinary categories.

Analyses conducted at the institutional level have generally shown results similar to those obtained from national studies. Even in programs that have been completely open to students in all disciplines, rates of participation have consistently been much higher among STEM majors than among those majoring in the humanities and social sciences (Goodman, 2006; Grabowski et al., 2008; Nyhus, Cole, Firmage, & Yeterian, 2002; Wilson, Cramer, & Smith, 2004). In an analysis of institutional NSSE data, collected from first-year students and graduating seniors, Cunningham and Murray (2002) found differences by major in both expectations and experiences of undergraduate research, with science and engineering majors favored at each stage.

While most studies have shown uneven participation in undergraduate research across the disciplines, some exceptions have been found at the institutional level. For example, Belkhir et al. (2002) reported on an undergraduate research event in which 39% of participants were drawn from the natural sciences, mathematics, and computer science; 44% were drawn from the social sciences and humanities; and 17% were drawn from education. Misceo and O'Hare (2002) described a similar event in which 80% of academic departments on campus were represented. In one institutional grant program, 40% of funded projects were in the humanities, 38% in the natural sciences, and 22% in the social sciences (Hicok, 2009). Caldwell (2007) recounted details of a summer research program in which 16 disciplines were represented, though 54% of projects were in the natural sciences.

The literature also includes documented instances in which patterns of participation in institutional undergraduate research programs have shifted toward greater inclusion. Pukkila, DeCosmo, Swick, and Arnold (2007), for example, found that implementation of a summer program specifically for students in the humanities was accompanied by a nine-point increase in the percentage of campus undergraduate research symposium participants representing the arts, humanities, and discursive social sciences over a three-year period. Osgood, Morris, and Rice (2009) recounted how a 43 percentage point spread in undergraduate research program participation rates across the humanities, social sciences, and natural sciences divisions of a small liberal arts college was narrowed to 10 percentage points, and the relative standing of the divisions reversed, within a period of three years. Relating this success to policies and procedures for administering the program, the authors cited the need for broad institutional support, effective communication, uniformly high standards of quality, and inclusive selection criteria.

Concern for undergraduate research across the disciplines has emerged as a recurrent theme in the professional literature. The dialogue generated on this topic has been fruitful in advancing understanding of the issue and exploration of potential solutions. The nature of the problem, its root causes, and possible ways of addressing it will be discussed in greater detail in chapter 9 of this book.

The Nature and Circumstances of Student and Faculty Participation in Undergraduate Research

As indicated in the opening chapter of this book, undergraduate research can generally be classified into three different categories: (1) student-directed, (2) faculty-directed, and (3) collaborative. One way of estimating the prevalence of each model is by studying the origins of undergraduate research topics and the roles of students and faculty mentors in initiating research projects. In a study by Lopatto (2006), over half of undergraduate researchers in the natural sciences indicated that their faculty mentors had assigned them to their projects, compared with only a third of undergraduate researchers in the humanities and social sciences, suggesting that the faculty-directed model may be more prevalent in the natural sciences than elsewhere.

Students' levels of communication with their faculty mentors over the course of their projects can provide yet another basis for determining their roles in the research process, insofar as communication levels would predictably be lowest in student-directed research and highest in collaborative research. On this aspect of undergraduate research, Lopatto (2006) again found variation across the disciplines. The number of hours per week that students spent in direct contact with their mentors in the natural sciences, mathematics, and computer science ranged from six to 15, compared with eight in the social sciences and three in the humanities. However, Mabrouk and Peters's (2000) survey of undergraduate researchers in chemistry and biology revealed that daily supervision was frequently delegated to postdoctoral and graduate students, who were responsible for overseeing the work of 12% and 14% of the respondents respectively. Additionally, 8% of the respondents indicated that they were not supervised on a daily basis at all.

Lopatto (2006) also found that 58% of students in the humanities and social sciences worked alone in conducting their research, compared with only 20% in the natural sciences. Mabrouk and Peters (2000) found further evidence of the collaborative nature of scientific inquiry in their survey of chemistry and biology students, though they found that the size of research groups was generally small. Fifty-seven percent of their respondents worked in groups with one to five members, 23% worked in groups of five [sic] to ten members, and 19% worked in groups of more than ten members. Collaboration among undergraduates was common, with 85% of respondents working in laboratories with at least one other undergraduate and 60% with two or more.

In studying the supervisory styles of mentors, Lopatto (2006) found that faculty in the natural sciences typically followed an approach in which they demonstrated procedures to their students, who then replicated these procedures, as would be typical in faculty-directed research. In contrast, students in the humanities and social sciences more often devised their own procedures for carrying out their work, as would be typical in student-directed research. Despite these differences, a majority of students across all disciplines characterized their mentors as friendly, respectful, and collegial toward them.

Conclusion

To distill the overall findings on the current state of undergraduate research at the institutional level, it appears that opportunities for undergraduate research are common in theory, but rarely seized upon in practice. Only a small minority of institutions have achieved a state in which research is understood to be a normal part of the undergraduate experience. Moreover, such institutions are limited almost entirely to the four-year sector of American higher education. A similar divide can be found across the disciplines, with participation in undergraduate research far more common in engineering and the natural sciences than in the humanities and social sciences. Despite this gap, the literature includes accounts of specific instances in which institutions have successfully achieved balanced disciplinary participation in undergraduate research initiatives, calling into question the assumption that certain disciplines simply do not lend themselves to the pedagogy of undergraduate research.

7

INSTITUTIONAL SUPPORT FOR UNDERGRADUATE RESEARCH

The previous chapter provided an assessment of current levels of participation in undergraduate research, both generally and across disciplines and institutional classifications. This chapter will focus on the role of the institution in promoting student and faculty involvement in undergraduate research and the specific mechanisms that are most frequently employed in pursuing this goal. In particular, structural provisions for undergraduate research, forms of faculty support, and prevailing administrative configurations will be explored.

Structural Provisions for Undergraduate Research

In the opening chapter of this book, several common forms of undergraduate research were discussed, including course assignments, independent studies, senior theses, and fellowships. Institutionally sponsored conferences, symposia, and journals were also discussed as important vehicles for dissemination of undergraduate research. Here, the prevalence of various structural provisions for the conduct and dissemination of undergraduate research will be examined, based on various published reports and analysis of publicly available data.

Course Assignments

According to the Boyer Commission (2001), despite the lack of a common definition of inquiry-based learning, the nation's research universities have made considerable progress in promoting various forms of this pedagogy. When asked if their institutions actively encouraged and assisted faculty in adopting inquiry-based teaching methods, 64.8% of respondents answered affirmatively. Among those who did, over half indicated that such efforts had shown at least some impact. Approximately 43% of the institutions surveyed offered research methods courses to undergraduates, but only about 3% required that all students enroll in such courses. About 37% had research course requirements for students in honors or other special programs and about 32% had such requirements for other specific student populations.

In a more recent analysis of published degree requirements at the top 100 national universities in *U.S. News and World Report*'s 2006 rankings, Parker (2012) found wide variation across the disciplines of business, economics, political science, psychology, and sociology. The percentage of universities requiring that students complete a general research methods course as part of the academic major ranged from 5% for economics to 90% for sociology, with a mean of 43% and a median of 30%. The percentage requiring a quantitative methods course ranged from 15% for political science to 89% for economics, with a mean of 66% and a median of 79%.

Based on an analysis of findings from multiple studies of capstone experiences, Hauhart and Grahe (2015) determined that approximately three-quarters of colleges and universities incorporate some form of capstone into their curricula, with discipline-based courses as the most common model. Capstones were most common in institutions with full-time equivalent enrollments of 1,000 to 5,000 students. They were also more common in private institutions than in public institutions. Finally, doctoral level universities were less likely to offer capstones than were non-doctoral colleges and universities.

Independent Studies and Theses

Independent studies have clearly gained widespread acceptance in American higher education, particularly within colleges and universities that have demonstrated an institutional commitment to undergraduate research. A search of a *U.S. News & World Report* (2007) database, which contained information on 1,857 colleges and universities in the U.S. and its territories, revealed that 1,379 (72%) of these institutions offered independent studies. A review of the institutional websites of a 50% sample of CUR (n.d.) member institutions (n=197), conducted in preparation of this book, produced information confirming the availability of independent studies at 194 (98%). This included two institutions (1%)—both classified as baccalaureate colleges of arts and sciences—that required all undergraduate students to complete at least one independent study. Within institutions, there was some variation across disciplines in the availability of independent studies, and faculty members were typically given broad discretion to decline oversight of independent study projects.

Based on this review of CUR institutional member websites, it appears that senior theses have also found extensive favor, at least among colleges and universities that have established undergraduate research as an institutional priority. Of the 197 websites that were reviewed, 181 (92%) contained information confirming curricular provisions for senior theses. This included 15 (8%) institutions where undergraduate students were required to complete theses in all or most majors. Many of the other institutions also required senior theses within a more limited range of programs and majors. Thesis requirements were especially common in institutional and departmental honors programs.

While the availability of a thesis option cut across all institutional categories, the requirement of a senior thesis was more typical of institutions that specialized in undergraduate education. None of the doctoral or research universities included in this sample appeared to have broad undergraduate thesis requirements. In contrast, 14% of baccalaureate institutions required senior theses in all or most majors, regardless of whether their curricula were diversified or concentrated in the arts and sciences.

It should be noted that this review did not systematically assess variation across disciplines in curricular provisions for senior theses, nor did it address the frequency with which the thesis option was actually exercised. In his study of degree requirements in the social sciences at leading national universities, Parker (2012) found that the percentage of institutions requiring a thesis or a comparable research project in the major ranged from 0% for business to 10% for sociology, with both a mean and a median of 4%. A comparison to a sample of international institutions revealed a similar paucity of requirements among Australian, Canadian, and Spanish colleges and universities. In contrast, the percentage of Dutch, Norwegian, and Swedish institutions requiring a research project was much higher across all five majors, in some instances reaching 100%. It should be noted, however, that sampling techniques varied across the nations surveyed, such that the U.S. sample was limited to a narrower and more research-intensive class of institutions. Such institutions have traditionally placed less emphasis on undergraduate teaching, which might account in part for the pattern observed.

Fellowships

To date, most studies of undergraduate research fellowships have focused primarily on summer programs. In one such study, McKay and Lashlee (2007) reviewed the institutional websites of *U.S. News & World Report*'s top 30 liberal arts colleges to assess the prevalence of what they termed the "formal summer research program," defined as "a school-sponsored summer program that provides a limited number of student applicants with positions accompanied by a preset stipend and usually a housing allowance" (p. 132). Their study revealed that 80% of the institutions offered such a program. Another study, conducted by Noice (2003), consisted of an e-mail survey of CUR institutional members. The survey yielded information on 43 summer programs administered by 39 institutions. Of these programs, 21 (49%) were open to students across all disciplines, four (9%) were limited to a single discipline, and 18 (42%) were more generally restricted to mathematics and science.

There is some evidence to suggest that disciplinary inclusion in summer programs may have actually proven to be much narrower, had rates of participation been considered, as opposed to eligibility to participate. In an e-mail survey of 56 CUR member institutions, with primarily undergraduate enrollments, Einstein (2003) found that only 14 (25%) characterized their summer research students as representing all disciplines. The remainder described the participants in their summer programs as being drawn exclusively or mainly from science disciplines.

In a survey of individual CUR members, Blossey (as cited by Hakim, 2000) found that the average duration of summer undergraduate research programs was nine weeks. The survey revealed, further, that the expected time commitment over the course of the program averaged 35 hours per week. In a more recent study of 55 centralized offices of undergraduate research, Crowe and Sienerth (2006) found that "virtually all institutions offer summer student research opportunities for a specified length of time" (p. 57). Consistent with previous findings, the typical length of commitment was found to range from eight to ten weeks.

Although instances of summer fellowship stipends ranging from $500 (Crowe & Sienerth, 2006) to $5,500 have been reported, rates of $2,500 to $3,000 appear to be more typical (Noice, 2003). Academic year stipends have been found to range from $250 to $2,400 for private institutions and $350 to $2,500 for public institutions (Crowe & Sienerth, 2006). In a survey of 64 CUR member institutions, Bushey (as cited by Hakim, 2000) found that a majority provided at least partial housing subsidies to summer research program participants. Other common benefits include meal plans, travel funds, and supply allowances (Crowe & Sienerth, 2006; Noice, 2003).

Conferences and Symposia

In the Boyer Commission's (2001) study of the nation's research universities, it was found that over half of the institutions surveyed conducted public undergraduate research events on their campuses. In a more recent study of institutions with centralized undergraduate research offices, 83% were found to sponsor such events. Sponsorship was more common among private institutions than among public institutions, and within the public sector, it was more common among institutions with lower enrollments (Crowe & Sienerth, 2006).

In addition to the overall prevalence of such programs, several studies have addressed their most common characteristics. Surveys by Collett, Marks, and Vatnick (as cited by Hakim, 2000) revealed that 85% of undergraduate research events, at a wide variety of institutions, crossed all disciplinary boundaries in their scope. With histories running as deep as 23 years, on average the events had existed on their campuses for 6.8 years. The large majority of events were held annually, varying in length from two hours to three days. The typical format included both presentations and poster sessions, while some also included keynote speakers or faculty panel discussions. Annual budgets for the events ranged from

$100 to $50,000, but only 25% of the events were reported to have budgets of over $1,000. In further differentiation, Crowe and Sienerth (2006) found that budgets ranged from $500 to $25,000 for private institutions and from $250 to $25,000 for public institutions.

Journals

In the Boyer Commission's (2001) study of the nation's research universities, it was found that one in three institutions offered opportunities for undergraduate students to publish their research findings, in the form of either abstracts or full-length reports. What is not clear from the study is how many of the institutional publications were journals, as opposed to written programs produced in connection with undergraduate research conferences or symposia.

A more recent CUR publication featured a listing of 138 undergraduate research journals, of which 110 (80%) were sponsored by individual American colleges and universities. Of the institutionally sponsored publications, 72 (65%) accepted manuscripts from within the STEM disciplines, 65 (59%) from within the social sciences, 63 (57%) from within the humanities, and 42 (38%) from within one or more professional fields. These figures reflect the fact that 56 (51%) welcomed manuscripts from at least some disciplines drawn from two or more of the major categories. Of the 110 journals, 72 (65%) were published exclusively in an online format, compared with only ten (9%) that were distributed exclusively in print. An additional 28 (26%) were published in both print and online formats (Hart, 2012a).

Further analysis revealed that 62 (56%) of the journals' sponsoring institutions were public and 48 (44%) were private. Beyond this basic distinction, their classifications were as follows: research universities, 73 (66%); master's colleges and universities, 21 (19%); baccalaureate colleges, 14 (13%); associate's colleges, one (1%); and schools of engineering, one (1%) (Carnegie Foundation, 2010a, 2010b).

In their study of colleges and universities with centralized undergraduate research offices, Crowe and Sienerth (2006) found that 24 (43%) of the 55 institutions published their own undergraduate research journals. Financial support for these publications was found to vary widely, with annual budgets ranging from less than $1,000 to almost $20,000. The authors raised the possibility that such variation might be attributable to differences in format, with some journals distributed electronically and others in print.

Facilitation of Faculty Involvement in Undergraduate Research

Regardless of what structural provisions are established for undergraduate research within a college or university, institutionalization of this form of pedagogy is ultimately dependent on the commitment of faculty members to its implementation. Therefore, key factors in the institutional climate for undergraduate research include the degree to which incentives exist for faculty to become involved in research activities with undergraduates and the level of support that is provided to those who do. Relevant considerations include faculty compensation, teaching load, and promotion and tenure policies.

Compensation

Studies of faculty compensation for work with undergraduate students on research have revealed that such remuneration is apparently not a high priority at most institutions. In Blossey's (as cited by Hakim, 2000) survey of CUR members, only 40% indicated that they were compensated by their institutions for their work in summer undergraduate research programs. Of those who were compensated, 88% were paid in flat stipends, which averaged $2,500. The remainder were paid "an appropriate percentage of the academic salary" (p. 65). In a more recent survey of CUR members, representing 50 institutions, Visick (2006) found that only 14 (28%) institutions offered direct compensation to summer undergraduate research mentors in the form of grants or stipends. Of these 14 institutions, nine (64%) offered compensation on a competitive basis. The amount of the grants and stipends ranged from $500 to $5,000. Availability of grants or stipends was more common at private institutions (34%) than at public institutions (13%). Additionally, none of the doctoral institutions included in the study was found to offer compensation of any kind.

In a survey of chief academic officers at CUR member institutions, Chapdelaine (2012) queried participants on the degree to which undergraduate research was a factor in merit pay decisions on their campuses. Of the 35 who responded, 6% indicated that their institutions placed strong emphasis on such activity, 23% moderate emphasis, 46% slight emphasis, and 25% no emphasis. Given that all of the institutions included in the study held membership in CUR, it seems unlikely that the level of support conveyed in these findings would be lower than that found within American higher education generally.

Teaching Load

As an alternative to direct compensation, some institutions have recognized undergraduate research mentorship as part of the faculty teaching load. However, such recognition appears to be the exception to the rule, and is often heavily dependent on the form that such mentorship takes and the context in which it occurs.

In Visick's (2006) survey of 50 institutions, it was found that only one offered teaching credit for faculty involvement in its summer undergraduate research program. Such credit was based on a conversion factor of 0.3 semester hours per student. Another institution was found to offer accelerated sabbatical eligibility as an incentive for faculty to mentor summer undergraduate research students. Together, these institutions comprised only 4% of the total sample.

In an earlier study, Wenzel (2001b) queried CUR members on institutional policies concerning faculty compensation for both laboratory course instruction and other forms of undergraduate research mentorship. Of 199 respondents, 77 (39%) indicated that their institutions treated course-related laboratory supervision as equivalent to classroom instruction, for the purpose of calculating teaching loads. An additional 38 (19%) indicated that laboratory hours were deemed equivalent to two-thirds to three-quarters of classroom hours. A conversion factor of one-half was reported by 66 (33%) respondents and a factor of one-third was reported by eight (4%). Only one institution (less than 1%) was reported to offer no credit for laboratory supervision in determining teaching loads. The author provided no further details on the prevalence of other arrangements pertaining to course-related laboratory supervision. With regard to other forms of undergraduate research mentorship, 49 (24%) respondents indicated that their institutions offered teaching credit for such activity and 157 (76%) indicated that their institutions did not.

There is some limited evidence to suggest that policies may vary across academic departments within institutions and that even uniform policies may differentially affect certain disciplines. In commenting on his own findings, concerning teaching credit for course-related laboratory supervision, Wenzel (2001b) noted that:

> unless faculty members in other disciplines teach discussion sections or other scheduled activities that are not counted equivalent to classroom hours, most science faculty members who teach courses with labs have more scheduled contact hours than colleagues who teach courses without labs.
>
> *(p. 105)*

Because of the issues of equity that are implicit in such a discrepancy, the question of how best to credit laboratory supervision clearly warrants further investigation at the level of the individual institution.

Promotion and Tenure

It would seem that any discussion of faculty motivation must take into account institutional policies on tenure and promotion. As Paul (2011) aptly observed in an issue of the *Council on Undergraduate Research Quarterly* devoted to the topic, "tenure and promotion policies are the primary vehicle through which faculty roles are defined, recognized, and rewarded" (p. 2). In surveying the institutional climate for undergraduate research at American colleges and universities, attention must be given to the relative weight assigned to teaching and research in tenure and promotion policies, as well as the degree to which undergraduate research is recognized as incorporating both functions.

Citing data from a previous survey by Schrum, Hakim (2000) offered evidence of CUR member institutions' affirmation of undergraduate research within their systems of tenure and promotion. Of 65 baccalaureate and comprehensive institutions, 63% gave equal weight to independent faculty research and that done with undergraduate students, 26% gave greater weight to research with undergraduates, and 11% gave greater weight to independent research. Because the sample was limited to CUR member institutions, further generalization would not be appropriate. However, the congruity of criteria for promotion and tenure with these particular institutions' public support for undergraduate research offers encouragement to those seeking to create cultures of undergraduate research on those campuses.

Despite such promising findings, more recent research suggests that such informally observed patterns of priority may not fully align with official institutional stances. In her survey of chief academic officers at CUR member institutions, Chapdelaine (2012) probed more deeply into levels of support for undergraduate research, as reflected in written policy statements on tenure and promotion. When asked about the content of such statements, fewer than half of the respondents indicated that consideration of undergraduate research in faculty review was explicitly codified in relevant documents. Further, where references were made to such activity, it was generally in relation to evaluation of scholarship produced in collaboration with undergraduate students, as opposed to the inherent value of the mentoring process itself.

These findings were largely corroborated in a separate review of published criteria for tenure and promotion at 32 PUIs. Analysis of these documents revealed that 63% of the institutional policy statements included no specific mention of undergraduate research (Chapdelaine, 2012). Commenting on "the lack of well-defined valuation of faculty mentoring of undergraduate researchers" (p. 38), as reported by faculty on two campuses, Jones and Davis (2014) noted that "the vagueness regarding how mentoring [undergraduate researchers] would be counted toward tenure and promotion was a deterrent to faculty participation" (p. 39).

Administration of Undergraduate Research Programs

While administrators have been recognized as playing a key role in the creation of institutional conditions that are supportive of undergraduate research (Hakim, 2000; Wettack, 2007), there is no universal model for administrative oversight of institutional programs. Such programs are sometimes housed in offices of chief academic administrators or in offices of institutional research. In other cases, they are linked to honors programs or serve as the basis for separate offices of undergraduate research (Kinkead, 2003). The diversity of administrative models was evident in a collection of essays, profiling undergraduate research offices and programs at collegiate institutions of varying size, control, and location (Kinkead & Blockus, 2012).

Proponents of undergraduate research offices have cited their potential to increase visibility of undergraduate research on campus, to coordinate the efforts of multiple departments in the area of undergraduate research, to promote inter-disciplinary dialogue and broad understanding of multiple forms of scholarship, to provide students with information on undergraduate research opportunities, to ensure that adequate resources are available to support the intellectual and creative endeavors of undergraduate students and their faculty mentors, and to provide faculty development opportunities that are focused on the cultivation of mentoring skills (Brush et al., 2010; Crowe, 2007; Crowe & Sienerth, 2006; Pukkila, Taylor, & Gray-Little, 2001; Stocks, Ramey, & Lazarus, 2004). Institutional research by Vaughan (2011) revealed a 22.56% increase in self-reported under-graduate research among graduating seniors, following the establishment of an undergraduate research office on one state university campus.

In making the case for appointment of undergraduate research directors, Hakim (2000) cited the need for individual accountability and a level of focused attention that committees can rarely provide. To enhance the credibility of the position, he argued that it should be held by an individual with faculty rank. One indication of the growing prevalence of undergraduate research directorships is the establishment of the Undergraduate Research Program Directors Division of CUR (Hensel, 2006a). The Division includes both full-time administrators and faculty members who hold part-time administrative appointments (Stocks, 2006). A major initiative of the Division has been the creation of an institute for those interested in establishing undergraduate research offices on their campuses. The Division has also held its own conference in conjunction with the association's annual business meeting (Hensel, 2011c).

In categorizing administrative models, Malachowski (2003) has drawn a dis-tinction between centrally coordinated undergraduate research programs and those that arise through the initiative of individual departments or faculty mem-bers. Gavin (2000), on the other hand, has characterized the most successful pro-grams as those in which "both a bottom-up and a top-down support system" (p. 14) exist, meaning that faculty initiative serves as the driving force for under-graduate research, while administrative support provides the resources with which to realize program goals.

A recognized limitation of the traditional academic department, as an admin-istrative home for undergraduate research, is its singular disciplinary focus. Contemporary researchers frequently tackle complex questions that demand the expertise of scholars across multiple disciplines. The *institute* or *center* has emerged as an increasingly popular organizational structure for interdisciplinary undergrad-uate research (Husic, 2006; Scordilis & Litwin, 2005). These loosely configured units draw upon the motivation and creativity of faculty members, but because their lines of reporting exist outside the traditional departmental structure, they are well suited to promoting cooperation across disciplines.

In surveying the administrative structures of undergraduate research programs at the nation's research universities, the Boyer Commission (2001) found that 20.9% had strong centralized oversight of undergraduate research; 38.5% had loose coordination at the institutional level, coupled with primarily departmental control; 33% had exclusively departmental control, with no centralized coordination or oversight; and 6.6% had no administrative structures in place for undergraduate research. No relevant information was available on the remaining 1.1% of institutions surveyed.

Crowe and Sienerth's (2006) study of centralized undergraduate research offices revealed a variety of staffing patterns. Programmatic oversight was sometimes provided by faculty committees, without designation of a director, or by academic administrators whose duties were divided across multiple functional areas. Only about one-third of institutions had full-time directors of undergraduate research. Further analysis of the data revealed an overall mean time commitment of 63% for program directors. While full-time directors were often classified as "non-faculty administrative staff" (p. 55), part-time directors typically held faculty appointments and received course releases for their administrative duties. Of those undergraduate research offices on which data were available, over 80% were staffed in part with secretarial or administrative assistants, 70% with undergraduate assistants, and 50% with assistant or associate directors.

Conclusion

Building upon findings presented in the previous chapter, surveys of institutional provisions for undergraduate research shed further light on the discrepancy between existing opportunities for undergraduate research and actual rates of participation. Research courses, independent studies, and senior theses are commonly offered, but rarely required, which may account in part for what are often less than optimal rates of participation. Fellowship stipends seem to carry sufficient motivational value to promote student participation, but most fellowship programs are offered on a relatively small scale. Limited incentives for faculty participation appear to pose yet another obstacle to expansion of student participation in undergraduate research generally. While a number of models for administration of undergraduate research programs shows promise for maximizing student and faculty participation, there is a need for further research on their relative effectiveness in achieving this outcome.

PART IV
The Issues

8

EQUITY AND ACCESS IN UNDERGRADUATE RESEARCH

Over the past several decades, cultural and demographic changes in our nation have reshaped the composition of the academic community, and have placed new demands on colleges and universities. In this context, issues of equity in and access to learning opportunities have become a matter of paramount concern to our nation's higher education system (Altbach, 2011) and are inextricably linked to its efforts to promote the success of all students (Kuh et al., 2005; Newman, Couturier, & Scurry, 2004). Of further note, the challenge of creating inclusive learning environments in STEM disciplines has received special attention within the pedagogical literature (Boyd & Wesemann, 2009; Packard, 2016). In educating today's diverse student population, it would appear that undergraduate research has an important role to play.

Concerns of Specific Student Populations

Both the educational value of student diversity and the duty to support diverse student populations have been widely recognized within American higher education, as reflected in major reports issued by various professional associations (AAC&U, 2002; Chickering & Gamson, 1987; Kellogg Commission, 2001; Wingspread Group, 1993). Diversity has often been broadly conceived to include variation in religion (Nash, 2001), national origin (Glass, Wongtrirat, & Buus, 2015), sexual orientation (Wall & Evans, 2000), and socioeconomic status (Barratt, 2011), among other student characteristics. In the literature on undergraduate research, discussion of human diversity has most often centered on the unique concerns of three student populations: women, minorities, and students with disabilities.

Women: Shaping the Future of Science

Although great strides have been made in the education of women, with females now accounting for over half of all bachelor's, master's, and doctoral degrees conferred in the U.S. (National Center for Education Statistics, 2013), there remain concerns about an ongoing underrepresentation of women in scientific and technological fields. With the exception of the biological sciences and health-related fields, women have continued to show less affinity toward scientifically oriented academic majors than have men, based on both the expressed interests of incoming first-year students (Eagan et al., 2016) and the degrees conferred upon graduating seniors (National Center for Education Statistics, 2013). Further, at each transition point within the educational system, attrition of females from the study of science and engineering has been substantial (National Academy of Sciences et al., 2007b).

Even within those STEM-related professions where representation of women has increased, discrepancies in status remain. In higher education, for example, women now constitute over 30% of STEM faculty at four-year institutions generally. However, the percentage is much lower when limited to the most prestigious and research-intensive universities (Rosser, 2012). Within both laboratory science and medicine, women tend to be similarly concentrated in areas of specialization that hold relatively low status. Alluding to an undercurrent of sexism in this pattern, Hall (2007) observed that primary care physicians, of whom many are female, have come to be seen as the "housewives" (p. 206) of the medical profession. The persistence of barriers to women's advancement has prompted some scholars to speculate that science may be "the 'final frontier' for occupational gender equality" (Xie & Shauman, 2003, p. 1).

Why Gender Equity Matters

The underrepresentation of women in science at all levels is problematic for a number of reasons, first among which is our societal need for talented scientists and engineers. Our nation currently relies heavily on scientific and engineering talent drawn from overseas to fill the gap between supply and demand within the American workforce, a practice that has become progressively less tenable amidst the heightening of national security since September 11, 2001 and the expansion of competing economic opportunities abroad (*Enhancing Research*, 2003; Rosser, 2012). Under such circumstances, increased recruitment of women into scientific and technological fields is one means by which to ensure sufficient quantity and quality in our national labor pool (Xie & Shauman, 2003).

It has also been argued that the scientific disciplines themselves would benefit from the broadened perspectives that a more diverse corps of investigators would bring to their work, since the problems and hypotheses that serve as the foundation for research are often informed by the life experiences and values of individual scientists (*Enhancing Research*, 2003). On this basis, it would seem that greater gender balance among scientists could potentially eradicate what Rosser (2012) has referred to as an *androcentric bias* that pervades all aspects of clinical research, including not only the questions and hypotheses that are explored, but also the gender composition of participant samples, the methods of data collection and analysis that are employed, and the conclusions that are drawn from empirical findings.

Analyzing the Causes

In discussion of this issue, a frequent point of contention has been the relative influence of environmental conditions versus women's independent choices on their underrepresentation in science (Rosser, 2012). Hill, Corbett, and St. Rose (2010) have cited variation in the proportion of female scientists across nations and over time as evidence that American women's continued underrepresentation in STEM fields is largely a product of cultural forces. In a nuanced analysis of the issue, Xie and Shauman (2003) maintained that "gender inequalities in [science and engineering] careers are produced by the interaction of structural allocation and self-selection processes" (p. 13), meaning that women exercise autonomy in making life decisions, but do so under external conditions that often constrict the range of viable options before them. Findings from a recent qualitative study of distinguished female scientists lend credence to this contention, as the participants repeatedly spoke of opportunities that they had freely chosen, but only at some cost (Wolverton, Nagaoka, & Wolverton, 2015).

Researchers have identified a number of conditions that tend to discourage women's pursuit of scientific and technological careers, many of which have been directly linked to social aspects of the scientific enterprise (Etzkowitz, Kemelgor, & Uzzi, 2000). Based on several studies, focusing specifically on the engineering field, Mattis (2007) identified four conditions that act as obstacles to women's persistence and advancement within their organizations: (1) the absence of a "critical mass" (p. 350) of women to provide support and advocacy; (2) field locations that do not lend themselves to the creation of inclusive work environments; (3) limited opportunities for women to gain necessary managerial experience without substantial risk; and (4) significant disparities between the salaries of women versus those of men.

In studying female scientists in academe, Rosser (2012) found that they too experienced unique challenges in their professional lives that appeared to be linked to gender. Academic women often struggled to balance their work and family lives, and frequently faced discrimination and harassment in the workplace. Additionally, female faculty members typically found themselves called upon to engage in various service activities where a woman's perspective was needed. Despite the good intentions that might prompt their enlistment into such activities, a predictable consequence was for them to be placed at a disadvantage relative to men in meeting the more pressing demand for research productivity.

The 'Leaky Pipeline'

Much of the literature on women in science has focused on the early stages of career development, because it is here that potential problems can theoretically be averted. The analogy of a leaky pipeline is commonly used to illustrate the loss of talent that occurs as young women, for various reasons, abandon their pursuit of scientific and technological careers (Hill et al., 2010; Packard, 2016; Wolverton et al., 2015). Some authors have criticized this analogy as inadequately conveying the level of discouragement that young women typically face as they embark on their educational journeys (Etzkowitz et al., 2000). Cobb (1995) maintained that the obstacles confronting young women are more akin to a series of filters that actively hold them back, rather than leaks that simply allow them to fall away. In particular, she cited early patterns of socialization that reward females for docility and educational practices that discourage them from excelling in science and mathematics.

In an analysis of several national data sets, Xie and Shauman (2003) found proportionately fewer female high school seniors planning to pursue undergraduate science and engineering degrees, in comparison to their male peers. In examining students' paths to completion of the bachelor's degree in science or engineering, the authors found that males were more likely to have followed a continuous path of choosing a field of study within this cluster and persisting through to completion of the degree, whereas females were more likely to have entered science or engineering curricula after having initially chosen other fields. For many females, the decision to pursue a science or engineering degree coincided with the transition from high school to college.

Theoretical Perspectives on Women's Learning

As colleges and universities attempt to create more supportive academic environments for women, scholarship pertaining to gender differences in students' ways of thinking and learning offers a foundation for practice. Consistent with earlier theoretical works, which emphasized the significance of interpersonal relationships in women's identity development (Chodorow, 1978) and moral reasoning (Gilligan, 1982), influential theories of the past three decades have highlighted women's preferences for more connected approaches to learning in the college classroom.

Baxter Magolda (1992) put forth one such theory in which both male and female college students were characterized as passing through a common sequence of four increasingly complex stages of intellectual development, designated as *absolute knowing, transitional knowing, independent knowing,* and *contextual knowing.* Despite this uniform sequence, variations across the sexes were found to exist within individual stages. Most notably, as students progressed into the stage of transitional knowing, women tended to develop a preference for an *interpersonal* approach to learning, in which dialogue was favored, whereas men tended to prefer an *impersonal* approach, in which the rules of logic and debate prevailed. Similarly, at the stage of independent knowing, women tended to favor an *interindividual* approach, focused on understanding both their own thoughts and those of others, while men tended to favor an *individual* approach that was more singularly focused on their own thinking.

In research dealing specifically with women's views of knowledge and the learning process, Belenky et al. (1986) identified five commonly emerging patterns, which they termed *perspectives*. Although the authors stopped short of referring to the perspectives as stages, the emergence of each tended to follow a uniform sequence. The first perspective, *silence*, is characterized by a sense of powerlessness within the learning situation. Those who hold the second perspective, *received knowledge*, see themselves as having the power to take and reproduce knowledge imparted by authority figures, but do not feel empowered to produce original knowledge themselves. In contrast, *subjective knowledge* is seen as originating within the individual and as largely the product of personal intuition. Under the *procedural knowledge* perspective, the origin of knowledge is also seen as resting within the individual, but the process through which one gains new insight is believed to be guided by objective principles, which can be learned and applied. From the fifth perspective, *constructed knowledge*, women believe that all knowledge is contextual. As learners, they feel empowered to generate new knowledge, using both objective and subjective approaches.

In a subsequent analysis of Belenky et al.'s (1986) theory, Flannery (2000) observed that two of the five aforementioned perspectives could be linked to the concept of *connection*. In particular, she viewed subjective knowledge as "knowing in relation to oneself" (p. 114) and the subset of procedural knowledge called *connected knowing* as "knowing in relation to others" (p. 114). In a concurrent analysis by Hayes (2000), the concept of *voice* emerged as a central theme of Belenky et al.'s (1986) work. In a literal sense, voice is clearly linked to the interactive nature of women's learning. Speaking more figuratively, the concept of voice represents the female learner's identity and sense of empowerment, both of which crystallize as products of her maturation as a learner (Hayes, 2000).

Based on this view of women's development as learners, it would seem that an important aspect of college teaching is helping young women to find their voices. Despite evidence of stronger academic achievement and engagement among female students than among male students, findings from a national study by Sax (2008) revealed that the former tended to score lower on measures of academic self-confidence. Further analysis revealed that women's ratings of their own mathematical ability tended to decline as a result of dismissive reactions to their observations and opinions on the part of faculty members. Such reactions were also associated with declines in women's graduate degree aspirations. In contrast, Shapiro and Sax (2011) identified four conditions that were key predictors of women's decisions to major in STEM disciplines: (1) "self-confidence," (2) "sense of belonging in the STEM culture," (3) "family influences and expectations," and (4) "peers and social/cocurricular connections" (p. 11).

The Significance of Undergraduate Research

With its foundations in constructivist (and more specifically collaborative) learning theory, undergraduate research would appear to be a method of instruction well suited to the active and connected learning orientations that many women adopt as they become more mature learners. Indeed, the process of research itself might become a vehicle for advancing women's empowerment as learners if purposefully conducted as such. The National Research Council (2006) cited both undergraduate research and mentoring as important elements of a comprehensive strategy to recruit, retain, and advance female students, faculty members, and institutional leaders within the fields of science and engineering.

Studies directly addressing the influence of undergraduate research on women's development as scholars have yielded encouraging findings. In a qualitative study involving seven alumnae of a campus-based undergraduate research program, Campbell and Skoog (2004) found that the women credited their mentors with positively influencing their career development. The respondents also indicated that the undergraduate research experience had increased their self-confidence and prepared them for the demands of graduate school. In a survey of participants in an undergraduate research internship program at one university, Kardash et al. (2008) found that women more frequently cited collaborative relationships or increased self-efficacy as the principal benefit of the program than did men. In comparison to men, women also more often reported that their internships had increased their awareness of career options.

Recognizing the significance of the pre-college experience in women's development as scientists, the National Research Council (2006) has urged collegiate institutions to engage in outreach to the K-12 educational system in order to encourage school-age girls to consider careers in science and engineering and to prepare them for college-level work within these fields. Alexander and Herrera (2002) offered evidence of the potential for educational enrichment programs to promote early interest in science among female students, especially those from minority backgrounds. Shields et al. (2010) illustrated, further, how targeted recruitment of young women into a pre-college summer research program could be used to advance an agenda of inclusion, even without limiting enrollment by gender.

Minorities: Promoting Student Success

Just as postsecondary educators have become more sensitive to the educational needs of women, attention to minority student learning has become more pervasive as well. It appears that one factor in this growing concern is the expansion of the minority population itself. During the period from 2000 to 2010, the nation's Latino and Asian populations both increased by approximately 43%, while the White non-Hispanic population grew by only about 1%. Today, California, Hawaii, New Mexico, Texas, and the District of Columbia all have minority populations that collectively form over 50% of their total populations (Humes, Jones, & Ramirez, 2011). By 2060, it is anticipated that minorities will together constitute 57% of the population nationally (NSF, 2015a).

Despite their growing representation within the general population, racial and ethnic minorities, with the exception of Asian-Americans, have remained underrepresented in science and engineering. While African-Americans and Latinos together comprised approximately 29% of the nation's 18- to 64-year-old population in 2012, they accounted for only about 7% of doctoral degrees conferred in science and engineering (NSF, 2015a).

The Attainment Gap

The current situation with regard to minority representation in science and engineering is arguably more problematic than the underrepresentation of women, in that it mirrors a more general gap in educational attainment across ethnic groups. Using demographic data to project proportionality of racial and ethnic representation among graduates at each degree level in 2030, Longtine and Jones (2011) noted a cumulative trend that would predictably leave Hispanic students, in particular, woefully underrepresented at each level of educational attainment.

Thus far, non-Asian minority students have also typically been less prepared for college-level coursework in science and engineering than have White and Asian-American students, based on both the number of related courses taken in high school (Pryor et al., 2008) and scores on the mathematics and science scales of the *National Assessment of Educational Progress* (Snyder, de Brey, & Dillow, 2016). Additionally, Black and Native American students are less likely to have taken advanced placement (AP) courses in high school or even to have attended schools where such courses were offered (Pryor, Hurtado, DeAngelo, Palucki Blake, & Tran, 2009). Focusing specifically on the pre-college experiences of African-American males, Wood and Palmer (2015) identified five factors that tend to undermine such students' efforts to succeed in college: (1) poorly funded schools, (2) tracked curricula, (3) exclusion from gifted and AP courses, (4) underprepared teachers, and (5) low teacher expectations and high rates of suspension and expulsion.

Looking beyond academic preparedness, minority students have frequently expressed feelings of alienation from the student cultures within STEM disciplines on their campuses (Strayhorn, 2012). Such feelings of marginalization are pertinent to issues of minority student retention in STEM majors, as both academic and social integration have previously been identified as factors in persistence to degree completion (Tinto, 1993).

The Significance of Pre-College Outreach

As in the case of women, minority students' attitudes toward careers in mathematics and science are widely believed to be shaped by their pre-college experiences. Accordingly, multiple authors have emphasized the important role of colleges and universities in creating interventions that target pre-college students, in addition to undergraduate and graduate students. NSF has, likewise, been supportive of such initiatives and has offered funding for their creation through grant competitions (Wubah et al., 2000). Hill, Banks, and Floyd (2009) offered an illustrative example of how research opportunities for high school students could be used to create a "feeder program" (p. 157) within an historically Black college or university (HBCU) setting. St. Cloud State University has offered three summer research programs for pre-college students from populations underrepresented in STEM fields. The programs have targeted students at different levels of schooling, ranging from elementary and middle school through the 10th and 11th grades (Johnson, 2011).

It should be noted that the role of higher education in preparing minority students for college need not be focused exclusively on students themselves. Pearson et al. (2009) described how educational outreach for minority youth could be effectively combined with preparation of aspiring K-12 teachers for work with diverse student populations. Similarly, Morris, McConnaughay, and Wolffe (2009), Edgcomb et al. (2010), and Martins and Roth (2011) highlighted summer research programs that brought together both high school students and K-12 educators. Chicago State University, located in a predominantly African-American urban neighborhood, has offered instructional support to science educators in local schools, in addition to conducting a summer research program for local high school students (Abraha & Kanis, 2009).

Bridge programs have been cited as a particularly important means of promoting minority students' interest in science in advance of their entry into college (Wubah et al., 2000) and of smoothing their transition into a collegiate environment (Watford, 2007). Traditionally, bridge programs have been conducted during the summer immediately prior to enrollment in college, and have targeted specific segments of the incoming student population, such as minority, international, or first-generation students. A common goal of such programs is to increase retention, by promoting skills for student success. Summer bridge programs that are focused specifically on mathematics and science typically introduce students to laboratory research and problem-based learning. Such programs have been found to be common among institutions that graduate large numbers of minority scientists and engineers, and there is some evidence to suggest that summer bridge programs in general aid in students' social and academic adjustment to college (Kezar, 2000).

The Role of Mentors

A common element of many programs designed to support minority students in science is the provision of structured mentoring relationships. A review of the current literature reveals that mentoring opportunities are often incorporated into comprehensive minority support programs that include tutoring, orientation to the campus, and various other provisions. One such program for first-year students at Northern Kentucky University has been cited as promoting achievement, retention, and continued involvement in research beyond the duration of the program (Haik & Bullen, 2011). In addition to these benefits, a comparable program at Kansas State University has been lauded for its promise of increasing cultural diversity within the state by enhancing recruitment of minority students from other areas of the country (Webb & Cortez, 2009). The Miramontes Arts and Sciences Program for Excellence in Academics and Community, at the University of Colorado at Boulder, is noteworthy for its structured support of minority undergraduate students at three stages of their development as researchers. The program begins with a summer "boot camp" that introduces program participants to research in a group setting. Following this common experience, each student completes a series of paid research activities, under faculty supervision, and ultimately produces an honors thesis or other culminating work of independent scholarship (Keasley & Johnson, 2009).

Mentoring has played an important role in programs conducted on campuses throughout the nation, focused on preparing minority students for careers in research. The Louis Stokes Alliances for Minority Participation (LSAMP) program was developed by NSF specifically to encourage collaboration across institutional boundaries in the provision of support for minorities in science (Chubin & Ward, 2009; NSF, 2015b). Evanseck et al. (2009) described one LSAMP initiative that incorporated four fundamental strategies: *recruitment*, *support*, *mentorship*, and *partnerships*. In describing another such effort, Pukkila, Parikh, and Woodard (2009) stressed the importance of cooperation across administrative units in carrying out the multifaceted mission of the program.

Encouraging the use of mentoring to recruit and retain both minorities and women in STEM disciplines, Packard (2016) favored an approach in which specific underrepresented populations are targeted at key transition points in their preparation for STEM careers. With a goal of cultivating students' interest, capacity for success, and sense of belonging in STEM research environments, she urged faculty to analyze and devise plans for addressing shortcomings in three facets of their learning environments and disciplinary cultures: (1) the diversity of their faculty, staff, and students; (2) the public images of their departments; and (3) the resources available to support their departmental activities.

One of the challenges facing coordinators of minority undergraduate mentoring programs stems from the current demographics of the scientific community. Because protégées often feel a stronger connection to mentors whose backgrounds are similar to their own, the underrepresentation of minorities in science has long resulted in a suboptimal ratio of seasoned minority professionals to young people desiring mentorship in their fields (Boyce, 1997). Further, while minority faculty are often eager to serve as mentors to students following in their footsteps, such involvement is too often viewed primarily as service, holding the potential to divert faculty attention away from the more highly valued activities of teaching and research (Jackson & Guerrant, 2012). Possible solutions to this problem include the creation of mentoring relationships between graduate and undergraduate minority students (Boyce, 1997) and the recruitment of upper division students to serve as peer mentors to newly enrolled undergraduates (Blockus, 2009; Keasley & Johnson, 2009; Watford, 2007).

Patterns of Participation in Undergraduate Research

While undergraduate research clearly holds the potential to advance minority representation in STEM fields, rates of participation have remained uneven across racial and ethnic groups. In an analysis of 2012 *NSSE* data, Kuh (2013) found that only 18% of Black and Hispanic graduating seniors reported having worked with faculty on research, compared with 20% of Whites and 24% of Asians. Rates of participation in capstone experiences were reported at 25% for Hispanics, 29% for Blacks, 32% for Asians and other students, 34% for multiracial students, and 35% for Whites. In further analysis of the same data, disaggregated by race, Kuh and O'Donnell (2013) found that the educational benefits associated with both capstone experiences and collaborative research with faculty manifested themselves across all racial and ethnic groups.

There is some evidence to suggest that the interplay of race and gender results in unique barriers to minority women's participation in undergraduate research, even above and beyond the effects of an overall gender difference in rates of participation that slightly favors males (Kuh, 2013). In examining rates of voluntary engagement in undergraduate research prior to senior year, among students majoring in biology, Vieyra et al. (2011) found significantly higher rates for majority women and for men of all races than for minority women. In a related study, Vieyra, Carlson, Leaver, and Timmerman (2013) found that minority women majoring in biology at an institution where research was required were far more likely than other biology majors to indicate that they would not have participated in research in the absence of this requirement. Additionally, minority women were more likely than others to indicate that lack of time would have been a factor in the decision not to participate. In a multi-site study of NSF's REU program, which explicitly aims to increase diversity within the field of STEM research, Beninson et al. (2011) found proportionate representation of racial and ethnic minority groups and majority representation of women, ranging from 62% to 64% over a four-year period. These findings offer hope that parity can be attained through persistent and concerted efforts in support of underrepresented students.

Undergraduate Research as Inclusive Pedagogy

Beyond its potential for increasing representation of racial and ethnic minorities in science, undergraduate research exemplifies culturally inclusive teaching practices that apply to all disciplines. Building upon the work of Klump and Nelson, Tanner and Allen (2007) identified six such practices that have been supported in the educational research literature: (1) "employing active learning and hands-on teaching," (2) "developing a learning community among students," (3) "building knowledge of students and differentiating instruction," (4) "maintaining high expectations of all students," (5) "viewing culture as an asset to academic learning," and (6) "being explicit about cultural competence" (p. 252). Undergraduate research lends itself well to all of these practices, some of which are foundational to its very nature. Lee-Keller (2009) advocated the use of undergraduate research as a means of empowering both racial minorities and economically disadvantaged students and enabling them to view themselves as scholars.

Undergraduate research has also been advanced as a means of promoting faculty interaction with minority students outside of class and in turn creating more inclusive campus environments (Hurtado et al., 1999). Ishiyama (2007) found that African-American students who had participated in undergraduate research tended to value highly the personal support that was provided by their research mentors, suggesting that undergraduate research can be a powerful means of promoting minority students' satisfaction and engagement with their institutions. Dowling and Hannigan (2009) offered an example of how this effect could be further enhanced through the direct cultivation of a supportive peer culture.

Bayliss, Peterfreund, and Rath (2009) advocated the incorporation of undergraduate research into a multifaceted model of institutional transformation focused on the enhancement of educational opportunities for underrepresented minorities. This approach encompasses four broad components: (1) "developing a research environment," (2) "increasing research opportunities for students," (3) "instituting academic support programs," and (4) "developing a culture dedicated to the success of underrepresented minorities" (p. 284). Analyzing the successes of one urban state university, the authors cited numerous institutional initiatives that might be undertaken to achieve each of the four stated goals.

Based on a study of the National Center for Atmospheric Research's Significant Opportunities in Atmospheric Research and Science (SOARS) program, Laursen et al. (2010) identified four conditions particular to the effectiveness of programs focused on the advancement of minorities in the natural sciences: (1) early and sustained engagement over the course of the undergraduate experience, (2) direct cultivation of skills in written and oral communication, (3) access to multiple mentors, and (4) a supportive peer culture. These conditions were cited as having a powerful impact above and beyond that associated with more basic characteristics of effective undergraduate research programs.

Students with Disabilities: Moving Beyond Compliance

Another group that has drawn greater attention in higher education over the past four decades is students with disabilities. Although concern for accommodation of such students is likely fueled in part by a broader embrace of human diversity within today's academy, the influence of federal legislation protecting Americans with disabilities is undeniably an impetus as well. Among the key pieces of legislation that have been credited with advancing the rights of Americans with disabilities in higher education is Section 504 of the Rehabilitation Act of 1973, which ensured "otherwise qualified" individuals equal access to all programs and services supported by the federal government, regardless of their disabilities. In 1990, under the Americans with Disabilities Act (ADA), these protections were extended to include participation in programs and services not supported by the federal government as well. Pursuant to these laws, all institutions of higher learning are now required to attend to the educational needs of students with disabilities (Myers, Lindburg, & Nied, 2013). In fact, subsequent passage of the ADA Amendments Act of 2008 (ADAAA), together with the issuance of related administrative regulations by the Department of Justice in 2010, has resulted in a more liberal standard of eligibility for the protections offered under the original law and further clarification of the duties placed on colleges and universities to uphold them (Grossman, 2014).

Legal Requirements

Americans with disabilities are defined under ADA as those who have or are regarded as having ongoing physical or mental conditions that significantly impair their functioning in at least one area of *major life activity* (Myers et al., 2013). Access to higher education has been understood to include both *physical access* and *program access*. In other words, in addition to removing barriers to students' use of campus facilities, colleges and universities must make reasonable accommodations necessary to students' full participation in institutional programs and services (Simon, 2000). Elaborating on this point, Dietrich (2014) discussed the concept of *technology access*, meaning the availability of technology that enables students to participate in programs and services that would not be fully accessible to them otherwise.

Structural Provisions for Accommodation and Support

In carrying out their mandate to serve the needs of students with disabilities, colleges and universities have created a variety of administrative structures. One common approach is the establishment of centralized disability services offices, staffed by specialists who perform a wide range of duties (Cory, 2011; Oslund, 2015). Schuck and Kroeger (1993) identified 11 essential functions of a comprehensive disability services program: (1) *outreach*, (2) *verification and certification of disability*, (3) *assessment*, (4) *information and referral*, (5) *case management*, (6) *accommodations*, (7) *individual and group support*, (8) *advocacy*, (9) *training*, (10) *consultation*, and (11) *reporting and evaluation*. It should be noted, as well, that certain functions can also be carried out in a decentralized fashion, through cooperation of staff across multiple organizational units (Korbel, Lucia, Wenzel, & Anderson, 2011; Myers et al., 2013; Oslund, 2015).

Underlying Values

Moving beyond the focus on legal requirements, Hall and Belch (2000) recommended that university personnel turn to the traditional values of *community*, *equality*, and respect for *human dignity*, to guide them in their work with students who have disabilities. Adopting a holistic perspective, Brown and Broido (2015) called for the eradication of obstacles to both *academic* and *co-curricular* engagement in the life of the campus, with attention to a full range of *physical, institutional, attitudinal*, and *definitional* impediments to participation by those with disabilities. Similarly, Strange (2000) identified three progressively more supportive levels of learning environments for students with disabilities: (1) *safe and inclusive environments*, (2) *involving environments*, and (3) *communal environments*. This emphasis on the proactive design of inclusive campus environments is also evident in the growing endorsement of *universal design* (UD) as a guiding philosophy for facilities planning and *universal instructional design* (UID), also known as *universal design of instruction* (UDI) or *universal design for learning* (UDL), as a basic approach to serving the educational needs of all students. Under this model, inclusive pedagogy becomes the norm, even in work with nondisabled students, such that the need for special accommodations for students with disabilities is greatly reduced (Cory, 2011; Myers et al., 2013; Oslund, 2015).

Issues in Science and Engineering

Turning to the specific concerns of students with disabilities who are studying science and engineering, the situation differs from that of women and minorities, in that there does not appear to be a comparable pattern of underrepresentation. As of 2012, the proportion of undergraduate students with disabilities majoring in science or engineering was approximately one in four, a figure comparable to that of non-disabled students (NSF, 2015a). Accordingly, the literature on accommodation of students with disabilities in science has focused more on the quality of their learning experiences than on their recruitment into scientific fields.

Implications for Undergraduate Research

In the literature pertaining to undergraduate research, a number of issues that face students with disabilities and their teachers have been raised. While some of these issues are general, others are unique to specific disabilities. Among the conditions addressed in the literature are mobility limitations (McDaniel, 2011; Pence, Workman, & Riecke, 2003; Smyser, 2003), hearing impairments (Cebe, 2009;

MacDonald, 2009; Pagano, 2009; Seal, Wynne, & MacDonald, 2002), blindness or partial sightedness (Asher, 2001; Puglia, 2001), and learning disabilities (Muller, 2006), defined as a broad category of "neurological condition[s] manifested by significant difficulties in the acquisition and use of listening, speaking, reading, writing, reasoning, or mathematical skills" (Johnson & Clohessy, 2014, p. 11). The percentage of undergraduate students who have been diagnosed with learning disabilities has increased dramatically in recent years, rising from 0.5% of those entering college in 1983 to 3.3% of those entering in 2008 (Eagan et al., 2016), perhaps reflecting a heightened awareness of both the diagnosis itself and the accommodations to which students who are so classified have a right under the law.

One obvious area in which access issues are important is in the design of laboratory facilities that are safe and functional, particularly for students with sensory or mobility impairments (Manske, 2001; Pence et al., 2003; Smyser, 2003). In some instances, equipment must be modified as well, to accommodate the needs of students with disabilities (Asher, 2001; Puglia, 2001). Transcription and interpretation services, as well as alternative communication technology, also serve to broaden access to instruction for students who might otherwise be unable to benefit fully from a university education (Asher, 2001; MacDonald, 2009; Manske, 2001; Pagano, 2009; Puglia, 2001; Seal et al., 2002; Simon, 2000). In particular, it has been recommended that laboratory protocols and instrument manuals be prepared in multiple formats (Manske, 2001). Additionally, many of the needs of students with visual and hearing impairments can now be addressed through computer support (Simon, 2000). Use of group projects, rather than individual assignments, can also be beneficial insofar as it provides students who have disabilities with an opportunity to draw support and assistance from their peers (Cebe, 2009). Finally, adjustments in curricula, course assignments, and testing conditions can sometimes be made on an individual basis (Asher, 2001; Manske, 2001; Simon, 2000).

The Significance of Mentoring

Beyond these tangible accommodations, supportive relationships with faculty members and laboratory assistants have been recognized as important in facilitating adjustment to the research environment of the university among students with disabilities (Muller, 2006; Pence et al., 2003). However, the cultivation of such relationships can pose a challenge, in that many faculty members are skeptical of disabling conditions that do not manifest themselves physically and are resistant to accommodations that might appear to compromise the rigor of their courses or the undergraduate curricula of their institutions (Manske, 2001). Daughtry, Gibson, and Abels (2009) offered a detailed set of recommendations to mentors of individuals with disabilities, emphasizing the need for sensitivity to the protégé's specific condition and adoption of respectful patterns of communication within the mentoring relationship.

While the majority of accommodations made for undergraduate researchers with disabilities have been carried out informally, on a case-by-case basis, there is some evidence to suggest that more structured initiatives can also be highly effective. For example, the Eastern Alliance in Science, Technology, Engineering, and Mathematics (EAST) is one of ten NSF-funded regional organizations dedicated to the recruitment and support of students with disabilities in STEM-related fields. Using data on 42 students participating in an undergraduate research fellowship program sponsored by EAST, over a four-year period, Langley-Turnbaugh, Whitney, Lovewell, and Moeller (2014) documented academic, professional, personal, and relational benefits associated with participation.

Although much of the literature on accommodation of students with disabilities has emphasized supportive measures taken by their institutions, several authors have emphasized the need to foster independence within such students as well. Butler (2002) specifically advocated the teaching of skills in *self-regulated learning* to students with learning disabilities. Such skills enable learners to analyze academic problems, devise strategies for their solution, implement these strategies, and evaluate the results. In recounting the experiences of an undergraduate researcher with a degenerative fine motor condition, McDaniel (2011) cited ways in which the challenges of the research project itself prompted the student to independently adapt her behavior in ways that enabled her to function more effectively. In making the case for recognition of students with disabilities as an at-risk population that is worthy of special consideration for participation in undergraduate research, the author spoke further of both the challenges that such students face in their daily lives and the resiliency with which they can respond to these challenges when provided with appropriate support.

An Agenda for Inclusion

The goal of increasing diversity within American higher education has been strongly advanced by AAC&U, through its Making Excellence Inclusive initiative. This ongoing project emphasizes the fundamental coherence of institutional efforts to elevate standards of academic achievement while broadening access to higher learning. The overall intent of the initiative is:

> To help campuses: (a) integrate their diversity and quality efforts, (b) situate this work at the core of institutional functioning, and (c) realize the educational benefits available to students and to the institution when this integration is done well and is sustained over time.
>
> *(Clayton-Pedersen & Musil, 2005, p. iii)*

One of the first components of the initiative consisted of an extensive review of the prior research pertaining to the educational benefits of campus diversity and the conditions that maximize these benefits. Based on this review, Milem et al. (2005)

formulated a conceptual model of campus climate that takes into account social, psychological, historical, political, organizational, demographic, and behavioral factors, both internal and external to the academic institution.

In articulating the duties and functions of collegiate institutions, as they relate to AAC&U's goal of inclusive excellence, Bauman et al. (2005) drew a distinction between diversity and equity, calling upon colleges and universities to close the gap in achievement between majority students and their traditionally underrepresented peers, in addition to broadening the demographic profiles of their campus populations. The authors argued, further, that traditionally underrepresented students' success should not be defined solely in terms of their persistence to degree completion, but should instead be measured in terms of their academic performance over the course of their enrollment. Building upon the work of a research team at the Center for Urban Education, the authors presented the *Equity Scorecard* as an instrument for establishing institutional accountability for achievement outcomes.

Recognizing the depth of change implicit in AAC&U's vision of quality and inclusion, Williams et al. (2005) crafted a model of transformation grounded in contemporary understandings of organizational behavior, institutional culture, and outcomes assessment. The authors' framework situates the institution in an external environment that is shaped by social, economic, legal, political, and demographic conditions, which ultimately bear upon the internal climate of the organization as well. The authors also set forth multiple lenses through which the dynamics of the institution can be analyzed, each reflecting a distinct set of priorities, values, and assumptions. Echoing Bauman et al.'s (2005) call for tangible indicators of inclusive excellence, Williams et al. (2005) advocated the collection of evidence pertaining to four broad categories of outcome: (1) *access and equity*, (2) *diversity in the formal and informal curriculum*, (3) *campus climate*, and (4) *student learning and development*.

O'Neill (2009) advanced the Making Excellence Inclusive initiative as a foundation for institutional efforts to promote undergraduate research opportunities for diverse student populations. Consistent with the approach taken by the various authors associated with the initiative (Bauman et al., 2005; Milem et al., 2005; Williams et al., 2005), she urged proponents of undergraduate research to survey their institutional landscapes and to gauge the potential impact of historic and contemporary environmental factors on equitable and rigorous undergraduate research opportunities, to draw upon institutional strengths and resources to build such opportunities into an overall program of inclusive excellence, and to proactively eradicate institutional conditions that act as barriers to the creation of such opportunities.

In recognition of the unique challenges to diversity that exist in scientific disciplines, Building Engineering and Science Talent (BEST) was established in 2001, as "a public-private partnership dedicated to building a stronger, more diverse U.S. workforce in science, engineering and technology by increasing the participation of underrepresented groups." Using objective criteria to rate the effectiveness of diversity initiatives within the K-12, higher education, and employment sectors, a team of expert reviewers set out to identify exemplary programs and in turn to determine the specific factors that accounted for the success of these efforts. The project resulted in the articulation of eight elements of effective program design: (1) *institutional leadership*, (2) *targeted recruitment*, (3) *engaged faculty*, (4) *personal attention*, (5) *peer support*, (6) *enriched educational experience*, (7) *bridging to the next level*, and (8) *continuous evaluation* (BEST, 2004). The BEST design principles have served as a foundation for numerous undergraduate research initiatives at the local and regional levels, 33 of which were profiled in an influential CUR publication (Boyd & Wesemann, 2009). As more institutions adopt these principles in practice and share new insights with colleagues nationally, a more focused agenda for equity and access in undergraduate research is likely to emerge.

Conclusion

In light of the growing diversity of the undergraduate student population, as well as that of our nation as a whole, any discussion of undergraduate research programs must ultimately turn to matters of inclusion. In this chapter, issues of equity in and access to learning opportunities were discussed in relation to the unique concerns of women, minorities, and students with disabilities. While gains in women's educational attainment were acknowledged, their underrepresentation in scientific disciplines was raised as a matter of concern. Underrepresentation of racial and ethnic minorities in science was cited as only one aspect of a broader discrepancy in educational attainment that has continued to favor the majority population. While barriers to female and minority students' advancement in science have been primarily attributed to social, political, psychological, and organizational factors, students with disabilities often must also contend with physical obstacles to their full engagement in academic life, which can be even more daunting. A comprehensive strategy for promoting equity and access must address both the general conditions that inhibit advancement of all non-dominant populations and the unique concerns that are particular to women, minorities, and students with disabilities. Principles set forth by AAC&U and BEST provide a foundation for diversity initiatives in undergraduate research that combine the pursuit of both inclusion and achievement.

9

EXTENDING THE DISCIPLINARY FRONTIERS OF UNDERGRADUATE RESEARCH

Despite the potential benefits of scholarly collaboration between students and faculty members in nearly any field, the review of the literature presented in chapter 6 of this book provides striking evidence of discrepancies among the disciplines in rates of participation and levels of support for undergraduate research. The current climate, at both the national and the institutional levels, appears to be far more conducive to participation in undergraduate research by students in the natural sciences and engineering than by those in the humanities and social sciences.

Evidence of this pattern has been reported in several national studies over an extended period of time. For example, in the Boyer Commission's (2001) survey of American research universities, the percentage of institutions reporting majority participation in undergraduate research among science majors was over twice that reporting majority participation among social science and humanities majors. Likewise, in their analysis of *NSSE* data, Hu, Scheuch, et al. (2008) found that the percentage of biological and physical science majors who reported having participated in undergraduate research was over twice the percentage of arts, business, education, and other professional studies majors who reported such participation. Even in drawing comparisons among scientifically oriented majors, Russell (2008) pointed out large gaps in self-reported undergraduate research activity. Likewise, institutional data have revealed wide variation in levels of participation across departments, even at colleges and universities with strong undergraduate research programs (Cunningham & Murray, 2002; Goodman, 2006; Grabowski et al., 2008; Wilson et al., 2004).

Nationally, several conditions may factor into this participation gap. For one, funding opportunities for undergraduate research appear to strongly favor scientific disciplines (DeVries, 2001). Perhaps more important, development of a national network of faculty scholars committed to the advancement of opportunities for undergraduate research in the social sciences and, even more so, the humanities has been slow to materialize. Focusing exclusively on chemistry when it was founded in 1980, CUR moved quickly to expand into the remaining natural science disciplines within its first six years and added mathematics and computer science within its first nine years. The 1990s brought expansion into psychology and engineering, but it was not until 2001 and 2008 respectively that a comprehensive social science division and an arts and humanities division were established (CUR, 2009; Osborn, 2008). The applied social sciences have been even slower to achieve recognition as independent interest areas. It was not until 2015 that a designated education division was established (CUR, 2015, September), and as of this writing, a division for management faculty has yet to achieve even this milestone. Fortunately, prevailing sentiments within the organization have begun to favor broader participation in undergraduate research across the disciplines, as reflected in both conference programs and strategic planning documents (Ambos, 2012). However, successful expansion of opportunities for undergraduate students on American college and university campuses will require an understanding of existing barriers to full participation and an active effort to bring about a more supportive academic climate.

While the national and institutional conditions outlined in previous chapters of this book undoubtedly limit research opportunities for students in the social sciences and humanities, relative to those in the natural sciences, they do not fully account for the discrepant patterns of participation that have been observed in the literature. Even in institutional programs that are open to all academic majors, rates of participation have not always been uniform across disciplines (Wilson et al., 2004). In reflecting on his own experience as an undergraduate research program director, DeVries (2001), himself a humanist, observed that hardly any of the proposals that he had reviewed over the course of his tenure were from students in the humanities. Further, among those that were submitted, there was sometimes a straddling of the line between the humanities and social sciences, for example, in research designs that applied archeological methods to the study of historical cultures.

In this chapter, the root causes of discrepancies in undergraduate research participation across the disciplines will be further analyzed. In particular, differences in both the nature of the disciplines and the cultural norms that govern the conduct of research within them will be explored. Drawing upon successful disciplinary and interdisciplinary models, strategies for broadening participation in undergraduate research will then be discussed.

The Nature of the Disciplines

Disparities in both opportunities and rates of participation in undergraduate research among students in various fields can perhaps be explained by differences in the fundamental characteristics of the disciplines themselves. While academics, as a group, hold many values in common, not the least of which is an uncompromising commitment to the pursuit of truth, individual scholars' notions of truth and the methods by which they come to know it can differ dramatically according to their fields of study. Given these discordant world views, it should perhaps come as no surprise that undergraduate research—or any other form of pedagogy for that matter—would not be uniformly embraced across all disciplines.

Shulman (2005) coined the term *signature pedagogies* in reference to the predominant methods of instruction that are employed within specific fields of study. Although originally introduced in the context of professional education, the term has since come to be used more broadly in discussion of other academic disciplines as well (Gurung, Chick, & Haynie, 2009). In discussing the significance of these instructional practices, Shulman (2005) noted that they implicitly communicate how knowledge itself is defined within the respective disciplines.

Just as the signature pedagogies of the disciplines vary, so too do their characteristic forms of research. The reconceptualization of faculty scholarship that Boyer's (1990) work inspired, over 20 years ago, subsequently led to further reflection on how legitimate inquiry should be defined within specific disciplines, resulting in separate statements issued by learned societies across a wide range of academic subjects (Diamond & Adam, 1995, 2000). The variation among the models of scholarship put forth in these documents led Diamond and Adam (2000) to conclude that "there is no single definition or conceptualization of 'scholarship' that works easily across disciplines" (p. 5).

Taking into account variation in forms of both teaching and scholarship, Riordan and Roth (2005), together with their colleagues at Alverno College, characterized disciplines as *frameworks for student learning*. Viewing one's field of study in this way draws attention to the essential competencies and habits of mind that students must master, the developmental sequence through which these skills and patterns of thought become habituated, the methods by which instructors can most effectively facilitate and assess student learning, the manner in which faculty should conduct their own explorations of the discipline, and the types of institutional support that are necessary to promote student learning within the field (Riordan, 2005).

With a similar focus on student learning, Kreber (2009) portrayed disciplines as *lenses* through which students can examine and come to know various aspects of the world. Such imagery implies that understanding and differentiating among the disciplines can enable students to become more versatile learners and thus to better cope with the complexity and uncertainty that they will inevitably encounter in their adult lives. Insofar as aspects of both research and pedagogy have been found to vary across disciplines, it should perhaps come as no surprise that Boyer's (1990) scholarship of teaching has also taken unique forms within specific disciplines (Huber & Morreale, 2002).

In one of the most influential analyses of disciplinary perspectives to date, Biglan (1973) classified academic fields according to three criteria: (1) "existence of a paradigm," (2) "concern with application," and (3) "concern with life systems" (p. 195). Application of each criterion produces two dichotomous categories (hard vs. soft, pure vs. applied, life vs. non-life), resulting in eight disciplinary categories in total. Despite the passage of more than 40 years since its promulgation, and the emergence of numerous fledgling disciplines in the interim, Biglan's scheme remains a workable configuration for drawing comparisons across diverse fields of study.

Although Biglan's (1973) work has been particularly influential in shaping current understanding of disciplinary perspectives, a number of other taxonomies have also been advanced over the past 50 years. In another early analysis of differences across the disciplines, Thompson, Hawkes, and Avery (1969) drew comparisons based on the types of reasoning employed (codified vs. uncodified) and levels of reliance on experience (high vs. low). Dressel and Marcus (1982) classified academic fields based on both the problems that they address and the methods that they employ, with a focus on five distinct components of disciplinary structure. Becher (Becher & Trowler, 2001) offered a disciplinary typology that was unique in its use of both social and epistemological factors to differentiate among various fields of study.

Drawing upon these earlier works and others, Donald (2002) offered a comprehensive analysis of disciplinary perspectives that is applicable to the full range of specialties represented on American university campuses today. She observed that disciplines can be differentiated based on the degrees of abstraction in the subject matter on which they focus, the levels of openness in their systems of organization, the specific procedures and standards of validation upon which they rely, and the means of investigation that they employ. She also identified three systems of representation (*enactive, iconic,* and *symbolic*) and five predominant modes of inquiry (*hermeneutics, critical thinking, problem solving, scientific method,* and *expertise*) that are used to varying degrees across the disciplines.

Differences in Faculty Attitudes and Values

Studies of faculty members' views of teaching and scholarship suggest that the differences that various authors have cited among the disciplines are not simply a matter of theoretical abstraction. For example, in one study of faculty members' endorsement of course goals focused on knowledge acquisition, application, and integration, Smart and Ethington (1995) found that application was valued more highly in hard disciplines than in soft disciplines, and that acquisition and integration were valued more highly in soft non-life disciplines than in hard non-life disciplines. Further, the authors found that faculty members in pure disciplines placed more emphasis on acquisition than did those in applied disciplines, while the latter placed more emphasis on application and integration. Similarly, in comparing lessons in physics against those in engineering, Hativa (1995) found a greater emphasis on verification of principles in the former and a greater emphasis on application in the latter.

Citing multiple studies comparing faculty members' views of teaching across the disciplines, Braxton (1995) noted a number of contrasts between hard and soft disciplines that would seem to hold implications for undergraduate research. Most notably, faculty members in hard disciplines appeared to place more emphasis on student research than did their colleagues in soft disciplines. Conversely, the latter were more inclined to see a complementary relationship between their own research and teaching. They also tended to be more holistic in their educational goals, focusing on matters such as character development in addition to cognitive outcomes, and were more receptive to the adoption of pedagogical methods consistent with institutional efforts to improve teaching.

In analyzing disciplinary task force reports issued at the close of the second millennium, Lattuca and Stark (1995) found a greater emphasis on undergraduate research in the natural sciences than in either the social sciences or the humanities. More recently, Chapdelaine (2012) reported on a survey of chief academic officers, in which 39% of respondents indicated that undergraduate research was strongly emphasized in the natural sciences on their campuses, compared with 19% for the social and behavioral sciences and 6% for the humanities. In contrast, none of the chief academic officers indicated that emphasis on undergraduate research in the natural sciences on their campuses was slight, whereas fully 17% characterized the campus climate for undergraduate research in the humanities in this way. The results of the survey offered some evidence of progress in the advancement of undergraduate research in the social and behavioral sciences, as only 2% of the respondents reported slight emphasis on undergraduate research within these disciplines.

In commenting on their own experiences and those of their colleagues, a number of faculty in the humanities have cited common barriers to collaboration with undergraduate students in research. Among these barriers are the solitary nature of humanities scholarship (Armstrong, 2009; Klos, 2011; Young, 2011), declines in both enrollments in humanities programs and the perceived stature of these programs within their institutions (Baldus, 2009), the lack of appropriate models for undergraduate research in the humanities, the lack of recognition given to undergraduate research in evaluation of humanities faculty, and the relatively high levels of sophistication demanded of students in humanities research projects (Klos, 2011; Langford, 2011; LeMahieu, 2009; McDorman, 2004; Rogers, 2003; Uffelman, 1995; Young, 2011). LeMahieu (2009) cited, as well, an overall sense of resistance to applied research in the humanities, which might otherwise lend itself well to student participation. Dean and Kaiser (2010) pointed toward a more tangible barrier in the absence of laboratories in the humanities, noting that much of the collaboration that exists within the natural sciences occurs as a natural outgrowth of these shared spaces.

Placing responsibility more squarely on the shoulders of faculty, Grobman and Kinkead (2010a) shared their suspicion that undergraduate research has been slow to materialize in English studies in part because faculty "have not articulated to [their] students the methodology of inquiry in [their] fields except as injunctions in [their] classes to 'write a paper'" (p. x). The authors noted that methods of inquiry in the humanities differ from the scientific method in their ambiguity and lack of transparency, leaving research in the humanities as an activity that is seen by many as inaccessible to undergraduate students. Thus, the authors challenged faculty to make the methods of humanistic inquiry more explicit to students and to cultivate the perception that undergraduate students can make scholarly contributions to their fields.

Social scientists apparently face their own set of challenges in attempting to involve undergraduate students in collaborative research projects. Writing from the perspective of a sociologist, Howery (2001) cited the lack of exposure to her discipline in American high schools and the tendency for students to declare majors in the field relatively late in their college careers. She noted, as well, that sociology curricula tend not to follow a uniform sequence, that courses in the field often enroll large numbers of non-majors, and that research methods courses are often taken toward the end of students' degree programs. Such conditions make it difficult for faculty to identify promising student researchers and cultivate collaborative relationships with them over an extended period of time.

Despite the perceived kinship of their disciplines to the natural sciences, faculty scholars in mathematics and computer science have generally been less receptive to collaboration with undergraduate students in their research than have natural scientists. At the core of mathematicians' resistance is a widely held belief that the research itself is too complex to lend itself to participation by undergraduates and a belief that students themselves would benefit more fully from devoting their time to mastering basic mathematical principles. Like humanities scholarship, mathematical research has traditionally been a solitary pursuit (Greever & Gallian, 1995). Therefore, it would seem that expansion of undergraduate research opportunities within the discipline would demand a fundamental change in the disciplinary culture. It has been noted, as well, that evaluation of undergraduate research is more difficult in mathematics and computer science than in the natural sciences, because mathematics and computer science research tends to be guided by questions, rather than by hypotheses, and is less focused on adherence to prescribed protocols (Krone, 1997).

Strategies for Broadening Participation

In calling for an expansion of undergraduate research opportunities across the disciplines, Malachowski (1999, 2001) urged CUR to assume a leadership role in creating a more inclusive national academic culture. At the institutional level, he recommended the use of in-service programs to sell faculty members on the educational potential of undergraduate research, incorporation of goals for undergraduate research into strategic planning documents, implementation of rewards for research mentoring within the faculty review process, recognition of mentoring in calculation of faculty workloads, and more generous funding of research involving undergraduate students (Malachowski, 1999).

Other authors have shown how such practices can be successfully carried out on individual campuses. Werner and Sorum (2003), for example, described a comprehensive initiative at Union College, which incorporated virtually all of the strategies recommended by Malachowski (1999) and served as an excellent example of how institutions can work to promote undergraduate research across a broad range of academic fields. After the program was introduced, Union students' participation in NCUR by academic discipline became proportional to their distribution within the college. Other institutions have also adopted elements of Malachowski's agenda, with similarly favorable results (Etaugh & Liberty, 2001; Levesque & Wise, 2001; O'Hare, 2007; Ronco & Engstrom, 2003; Schilt & Gilbert, 2008; Vaughan, 2011). Faculty development, in particular, appears to hold promise of not only broadening student participation in research, but also increasing mutual respect among colleagues in different disciplines (Carr et al., 2013).

In addition to large-scale institutional initiatives, a variety of more narrowly defined strategies have shown promise of promoting undergraduate research within specific disciplines and groups of disciplines. Citing examples from such widely varied fields as English literature, philosophy, and social work, Ronnenberg and Sadowski (2011) illustrated how Boyer's (1990) alternative model of faculty scholarship could be used to guide the structuring of undergraduate research experiences across multiple academic fields. As the ranks of undergraduate research advocates have grown to include scholars across multiple disciplines, models for collaborative scholarship with undergraduates have grown to be more inclusive as well.

A Focus on Interdisciplinary Studies

In his call for reform, Malachowski (1999, 2003) advocated a *research-across-the-curriculum* movement, comparable to the *writing-across-the-curriculum* movement that has already taken hold on many campuses. Whereas a common characteristic of the latter is a blurring of the boundaries between the disciplines, it should perhaps come as no surprise that a number of authors have explicitly endorsed interdisciplinary studies as a means of promoting broader participation in undergraduate research. This approach has specifically been advanced as a strategy for creating research opportunities in the humanities (DeVries, 2001; Gesink, 2010; Pukkila et al., 2007; Young, 2008) and in community colleges (Owens & Murkowski, 2009). In commenting on the need for interdisciplinary perspectives in both teaching and research, several authors have noted the complexity of modern social problems, which rarely lend themselves to solutions drawn from single disciplines (Husic, 2006; Temple et al., 2010).

Elaborating on the concept of interdisciplinarity, Lattuca (2001) differentiated among four distinct types of relationship between disciplines in the context of teaching or research: (1) *informed disciplinarity*, (2) *synthetic interdisciplinarity*, (3) *transdisciplinarity*, and (4) *conceptual interdisciplinarity*. Under informed disciplinarity, theoretical perspectives or methods of inquiry are borrowed from one discipline to advance understanding of a topic that falls squarely within another discipline. In contrast, synthetic interdisciplinarity involves an actual bridging of the disciplinary divide in the topic itself. Transdisciplinarity takes this integration one step further through the use of tools of inquiry that are not identified with a single discipline. Finally, conceptual interdisciplinarity involves exploration of topics that are not firmly grounded in traditional disciplines at all and in some instances challenge traditional disciplinary perspectives. Hluchy (2002) drew a further distinction between *interdisciplinarity* and *multidisciplinarity,* noting that the former implies a more tightly woven integration of the disciplines than does the latter. Looking beyond the nature of interdisciplinarity itself, Klein (2010) examined the organizational contexts in which it occurs, resulting in five categories of interdisciplinary activities, each occurring at a different level within the organizational structure.

The literature on undergraduate research offers examples of interdisciplinary investigations on such widely varied topics as sexual assault (McKillip, 2009), human trafficking and migrant smuggling (Curley & Schloenhardt, 2014), fear and terror (Kitchens et al., 2010), and infectious disease (Shors & McFadden, 2009). In a uniquely innovative pilot course at The College of New Jersey, multiple student-faculty teams engaged in interdisciplinary research projects, organized around an overarching theme of freedom and tyranny (Friedman & Leigey, 2014).

The trend toward interdisciplinarity has given rise to entire academic fields that are inherently conducive to the integration of disciplinary perspectives in undergraduate research. Environmental studies, in particular, has been cited as a subject area replete with opportunities for interdisciplinary collaboration (Hluchy, 2002; Reggio, 2000). Environmental research projects have sometimes been conducted abroad (Best et al., 2007; Davis & Eves, 2005), which can increase natural science majors' participation in international education (Van Galen, 1995). Other such projects have been carried out on the university campus itself, focusing on various aspects of sustainable design (Pawlow & Retzlaff, 2012; Stocks, 2014). Synthetic biology has emerged as another field that is well suited to interdisciplinary undergraduate research, as it integrates elements of mathematics, engineering, and computer science with biological sciences (Eckdahl, Poet, Campbell, & Heyer, 2009). The relatively young field of neuroscience, with its roots in biology and psychology, also offers fertile ground for interdisciplinary undergraduate research (Temple et al., 2010).

With advances in technology, new methods and media are available to support undergraduate research, many of which lend themselves well to use in interdisciplinary studies. Geographic Information System (GIS) technology has emerged as a particularly popular tool for interdisciplinary undergraduate research, because of its broad applicability to multiple subject areas (A. B. Johnson, 2007), including environmental studies (Nyhus, Cole, Firmage, & Lehmann, 2002; Spieles & Cunfer, 2002). More recently, mobile devices and social media applications have shown similar capabilities (LaPlant, 2013b). Relying on more traditional technology, McKillip (2009) recounted how production of a television documentary brought together 12 Ball State University undergraduates, representing seven academic majors and three colleges, in a fully cooperative endeavor.

Although faculty sometimes feel misgivings toward interdisciplinary research (Husic, 2006), students tend to enthusiastically embrace its complexity and the learning opportunities that it provides (Stocks & Gregerman, 2009). As faculty mentors witness both the growing enthusiasm that their protégées feel toward their disciplines and the openness with which they cross disciplinary boundaries, faculty members' own interest in interdisciplinary research is likely to grow, leading to more widespread adoption of this promising approach to undergraduate research.

Undergraduate Research within Disciplines

Beyond interdisciplinary initiatives, creative approaches to undergraduate research within the disciplines have begun to bear fruit in providing broadened educational opportunities for students. Such efforts may require faculty to think in new ways about their scholarship, but a growing number of academics appear to be rising to the challenge, often with highly favorable results.

Humanities

The establishment of CUR's arts and humanities division (Osborn, 2008) has already begun to elevate the profile of undergraduate research within the associated disciplines. For example, in partnership with the social sciences division, arts and humanities affiliates have offered a workshop for faculty in both divisions, focused on ways of involving undergraduate students in original scholarship within their respective fields. Efforts have also been made to more prominently feature arts- and humanities-based scholarship in CUR's *Posters on the Hill* event (Hensel, 2011c). These initiatives are among several hopeful signs of a budding undergraduate research trend within the creative and literary-based disciplines. The dedication of a special issue of the *Council on Undergraduate Research Quarterly* to the theme, "Undergraduate Research in the Arts and Humanities" (Heinemann, 2008), coupled with the publication of four book-length compendia of best practices in undergraduate humanities scholarship (Behling, 2009a; Crawford, Orel, & Shanahan, 2014; Grobman & Kinkead, 2010b; Klos, Shanahan, & Young, 2011), attests to the growing receptivity to such activity among humanities faculty and offers a foundation for further expansion of this emerging trend.

According to Temple et al. (2010), much of the undergraduate research that has occurred in the humanities has been course-based. This pattern may be due in part to a sense, expressed by some humanities faculty, that incorporation of undergraduate research into their teaching is more beneficial than its incorporation into their scholarship (Armstrong, 2009). Shanahan (2011) offered course-based research as a cost-efficient means of engaging large numbers of undergraduate students in original scholarship and cultivating their investigative skills over an extended period of time. Her favored approach consists of a structured sequence of activities through which various aspects of research are *introduced, developed,* and *mastered.* Whereas certain skills have been identified as central to the production of original scholarship in the humanities, Temple et al. (2010) advocated the design of undergraduate research projects that are structured to promote specific forms of skill acquisition. McNely (2010) viewed writing courses, in particular, as a vehicle for promoting *rhetorical thinking,* which is informed by an understanding of "the role of language in knowledge-making and ontology" (p. 235). Lee-Keller (2009) presented a model for course-based research in the humanities that followed a three-stage sequence, with each stage organized around a specific group of skills in inquiry: (1) "investigation and discovery," (2) "interpretation and analysis," and (3) "analysis and synthesis" (p. 19).

Adoption of an inquiry-based curriculum in the humanities demands a shift in orientation away from a focus on coverage of content and toward engagement in dialogue (Hicok, 2009), yet it is important not to lose sight of students' need for domain-specific knowledge if they are to effectively apply general cognitive skills to the advancement of a given field of study (Tangney, 2009). In discussing the goals of a literary studies curriculum, Hedley and Schneider (2009) shared their desire to prepare students as scholars who are familiar with ongoing conversations in the field and are able to learn from the ideas of others, but not at the expense of their own capacity for original thought. Recounting her experiences in teaching an English course with "tripartite emphases on theory, research, and writing," Brown (2009, p. 101) described how she used research activity as a means of bringing literary theory to bear on the practice of writing. Grobman and Kinkead (2010a) saw a place for undergraduate research in courses on both literary criticism and writing and rhetoric.

In a course that emphasized critical ethnography, Rogers (2010) combined instruction in qualitative research methods with hands-on experience in design, data collection, analysis, and reporting. Though housed in a rhetoric department, the course integrated elements of the humanities and social sciences in ways that advanced the goals of interdisciplinarity that have been embraced by many of today's collegiate institutions. Similarly, Gabbert (2010) recounted how anthropological research methods were successfully incorporated into a course in folklore studies, through students' engagement in field-based research within the local community.

Addressing the issue of cultural resistance to collaboration, McDorman (2004) explained how peer review could be used to add a cooperative dimension to the more solitary forms of scholarship traditionally associated with the humanities.

The model that he presented could be used with either faculty-directed or student-directed projects. In faculty-directed projects, members of student groups would be assigned individual responsibility for drafting essays on discrete subtopics within a single area of investigation, which would then be reviewed by the other members of the group before being incorporated into a single work under the editorial oversight of the faculty mentor. In student-directed research, provisions would be made for direct feedback from the faculty mentor in one-on-one meetings throughout the research project.

In a variation on this approach, Fritzman and Gibson (2008) recounted how feedback from an undergraduate student was used to refine work that was initially drafted by a faculty member. Other authors have discussed the role that undergraduate research can play in reopening lines of faculty scholarship that have been abandoned or left dormant for extended periods of time (Armstrong, 2009; Dean & Kaiser, 2010; Young, 2011). Behling (2009b) described her one-on-one collaboration with undergraduate students on library and archival research, which involved composition of individual drafts, which were then integrated into joint works. Whitt and Henningsen (2010), a faculty mentor and an undergraduate researcher respectively, recounted their experiences in collaboratively editing an anthology of existing short stories on the topic of AIDS.

McDorman (2004) described, further, how writers' workshops could be used to introduce a communal dimension into undergraduate students' experiences of independent writing. He recommended that faculty mentors participate as actual members of such groups, so that students might learn from their examples, a process that he referred to as "faculty modeling" (p. 40). Collaboratively edited collections of individual essays can also serve as a medium for fostering cooperation and teamwork among groups of budding humanities scholars. LeMahieu (2009) offered examples of several such projects that he and his colleagues at Clemson University led, under the sponsorship of their institution's Creative Inquiry program.

The pedagogical models introduced here lend themselves well to use in the teaching of foreign languages. Rogers (2003), for example, described his use of an approach similar to that advocated by McDorman (2004), within a foreign language curriculum, and his overall satisfaction with the results. Boucquey (2009) recounted how six undergraduate students enrolled in a foreign language teaching practicum collaborated with their instructor to produce a collection of classroom activities, which was ultimately published in the form of a book. Embracing interdisciplinarity, Dellinger (2009) and Langford (2011) have advocated the use of foreign language in research on topics within other subject areas, a practice that can be especially powerful when conducted abroad (Dellinger, 2009; Edwards & Hogarth, 2008). Conliffe (2014) recounted how Willamette University's acquisition of a collection of Soviet-era political art became a vehicle for undergraduate research, involving not only translation from Russian to English, but cultural and historical analysis as well.

Though clearly a discipline that is driven by the creative vision of the individual, theatre is ultimately an interactive art, and is therefore uniquely suited to student-faculty collaboration. Reflecting on the complex nature of the discipline, Bell (2004) observed that stories created in solitude by the playwright can only be brought to life through cooperation with actors, directors, and audiences. As a faculty member, Bell has engaged his students in informal readings of his work and has benefited from their feedback. In one instance, he invited a group of students from another institution to join his students in performing separate acts of a single play, so that all could benefit from discussion of the various interpretations of the characters. Blackmer (2008), also a playwright, has taken student-faculty collaboration to an even higher level, by engaging 15 students in the creation of an original play, beginning with the writing of a script and culminating with the staging of a full theatrical production.

The fine and performing arts, in general, hold enormous potential for original work by individual students in integrative projects that apply multiple disciplinary perspectives to the examination of various art forms. Crawford, Huston-Findley, Mowrey, and Zurko (2011) explained how preliminary research during the junior year could be used to lay the foundation for creative senior projects in music, theatre, dance, art, and art history. According to the authors, this approach enables students to develop "a keen awareness of the historical, theoretical, and analytical components necessary for artists to move from investigation to application" (p. 24). Following a similar approach, students in the Department of Dance and Theatre at Manhattanville College complete a two-semester senior capstone experience. Under this model, each student writes a major research paper in the fall, which in turn informs a performance project in the spring (Posnick, 2014). One challenge in the oversight of undergraduate research in the fine arts is ensuring that the creative process itself is educational, an aspect of the project that cannot always be ascertained by examination of the finished work product alone (Temple et al., 2010).

Archival research has been cited as an activity ripe for undergraduate student participation across a variety of disciplines within the humanities (Gesink, 2010; Murray, 2014; Rogers, 2003; Wittner, 2007), and there is some precedent for involvement of undergraduate students in the conduct of interviews for historical research as well (Levesque & Wise, 2001; Murray et al., 2014; Shrum, 2011; Vaught, 2009). Archaeological remnants have also been used by undergraduate researchers as a basis for historical analysis (Langford, 2011), as have classical texts (Glew, 2007; Peeler, 2013) and historical news reports (Zeidel & Kramschuster, 2013). Students participating in a study abroad program, offered by Stetson University, have even scanned the British landscape for clues as to the nation's historical development (Reiter, 2014). Just as methods vary, work products of undergraduate research in history and related disciplines can take a variety of forms as well, ranging from curated museum exhibits to outlines of biographical narratives (Carr et al., 2013).

While there is no shortage of research designs that can be used in undergraduate scholarship of this nature, it is widely recognized that formal instruction in research methods is necessary for students to engage productively in any such activities. Whereas research courses have traditionally been taken relatively late in students' undergraduate experiences, leaving little time for application of newly acquired skills, Rogers (2003) proposed a reconfiguration of the undergraduate curriculum to provide earlier exposure to research methods. Wittner (2007) recounted how one history department resolved this dilemma by creating a mini-course in research methods, which was taken in advance of a two-course capstone experience that incorporated original research activity. Drawing upon the educational potential of undergraduate research itself, Schantz (2008) proposed a research apprenticeship model, in which students would serve as research assistants to faculty mentors, performing tasks that enable them to gain skills in research and engaging in a structured process of reflection that enables them to draw meaning from these experiences. Under this model, the primary focus would be on skill development, rather than on the production of significant works by the student.

While much of the literature on undergraduate research in the humanities has centered on the creation of opportunities for collaboration, where few have existed historically, Grobman (2007) argued in support of the tradition of the independent scholar and sought to identify ways in which undergraduate students' skills in independent research might be more effectively cultivated. Drawing upon her experience as a co-founder and editor of the undergraduate research journal, *Young Scholars in Writing: Undergraduate Research in Writing and Rhetoric,* she discussed the use of the review process as a means of providing undergraduate student writers with constructive feedback on their work, in addition to whatever guidance and support they might receive from faculty mentors on their own campuses. Another undergraduate research journal for students specializing in English, *The Oswald Review,* incorporates opportunities for them to also gain editorial experience by serving as staff interns (Mack, 2011).

Rejecting a forced choice between independent and collaborative approaches to undergraduate research in the humanities, Hicok (2009) favored a combination of the two approaches and challenged faculty to become facile in the application of both across a variety of circumstances. Baldus (2009) also advocated such a model, expressing her conviction that "humanities undergraduates can encounter research as an activity that is at once both solitary and communal, which underscores how the individual production of research constantly negotiates the communal discovery of academic knowledge" (p. 82). According to Downs and Wardle (2010), "even in the humanities, which value 'lone-genius' research, researchers form communities that share and develop their members' work" (p. 185).

A number of authors have discussed the significance of space to the cultivation of a supportive climate for undergraduate research and have sought to identify those places on campus where scholarship in the humanities can flourish. One such location is the writing center (Johnson, Hanson, & Kunka, 2011), characterized by DelliCarpini and Crimmins (2010) as a "new disciplinary space" (p. 192), where research projects can grow out of students' daily activities. Seeking to broaden common notions of disciplinary space, Dean and Kaiser (2010) noted that "humanists do not operate in the laboratory, but they do have their own *authentic contexts* or places where learning occurs, including increasingly on Internet sites" (p. 44). As undergraduate research in the humanities continues to come into its own, the spaces where it occurs will undoubtedly assume a more prominent place on the higher education landscape as well.

Social Sciences

The professional literature offers models of successful undergraduate research across a variety of social science disciplines, including psychology (Friedenberg, 1995), sociology (Howery, 2001), economics (Steele, 2008), political science (Chamely-Wiik et al., 2014), criminal justice (Robison, 2014), and geography (Cheong & Willis, 2015). There is support in the literature for course-based research in the social sciences, and a number of authors have recommended that research opportunities be woven through the entire undergraduate curriculum in certain majors (Chamely-Wiik et al., 2014; Friedenberg, 1995; Howery, 2001).

Research institutes have also proven to be popular within the social sciences, because they enable students and faculty to examine issues of broad public concern. Klinkner (2001), for example, described a comprehensive public policy institute at Hamilton College, which provided opportunities for students to participate in a wide variety of research projects pertaining to issues at all levels of government.

Undergraduate research in the social sciences can include either bibliographic research or collection and analysis of original data, and both faculty-directed and student-directed approaches can be appropriate (Joyce, 2004). With advances in technology, web-based surveys have emerged as a means of quickly and efficiently conducting social research within the financial and time constraints that are typically imposed on undergraduate research projects (Steele, 2008). Lancy (2003) described how ethnographic undergraduate research could be incorporated into both classroom instruction and the operations of an on-campus museum.

Community-based undergraduate research has proven to be especially popular within the social sciences. Projects of this nature have been incorporated into research methods courses in both psychology (Chapdelaine & Chapman, 1999) and sociology (Strand, 2000). In making the case for this approach, Strand (2000) cited the dual purpose of research methods courses, which have both *methodological* and *epistemological* aims. While the former are focused on students' practical understanding of the methods of social research, the latter relate to their understanding of the social significance of knowledge construction and who controls the process. Consistent with Stoecker's (2003) analysis of philosophical perspectives on community-based research, as discussed in chapter 2 of this book, Strand (2000) viewed the practice as a means of social empowerment. Exemplifying principles of feminist action research, Robison (2014) recounted her collaboration with several undergraduate students on a project that involved both teaching and research at a women's prison. In a variation on prevailing models of community-based undergraduate research, Girvan (1996) and Durso (1997) described programs that served local businesses, in addition to government and non-profit agencies. In yet another departure from the agency-based model, Walter (2013) described how first-year students at Denison University gained insight on renewable energy and sustainability by conducting energy audits on the homes of volunteers in the community, who in turn benefited from recommendations on how to increase energy efficiency.

In alignment with Hutchings and Clarke's (2004) recommendation that faculty involve students as collaborators in the scholarship of teaching and learning, Muir and van der Linden (2008) described an undergraduate psychology class in which students designed and conducted an assessment of their own service-learning project. Louis (2008) recounted how he and an undergraduate student used methods of ethnographic research to assess the impact of a community-based arts initiative, in a project that combined elements of both the humanities and the social sciences.

In addition to community-based research, institutional research can provide opportunities for students to cultivate their investigative skills, using the methods of the social sciences. In particular, Murray, Naimoli, Kagan, Kirnan, and Snider (2004) recommended that undergraduate research be used to assess educational outcomes of student affairs programs. Other authors have subsequently recounted instances in which undergraduate researchers have assessed outcomes of both curricular and co-curricular learning opportunities, including undergraduate research itself, emphasizing the potential for such projects to bring about institutional change (Anderson, Filer, & Lyon, 2012; Karkowski & Fournier, 2012; Sandover, Partridge, Dunne, & Burkill, 2012).

Moving beyond the local environment, several authors have advocated the incorporation of ethnographic research experiences into international education. Glass-Coffin and Balagna (2005), for example, described a study abroad program, sponsored by Utah State University, in which students spent five weeks during the summer immersed in the life of a small fishing village in Peru. Using a variety of anthropological research methods, students examined the social, cultural, and economic conditions of the region, and reported their findings both orally and in writing. According to the authors, this experience not only provided students with opportunities to cultivate their research skills, but often proved to be highly transformative on a personal level as well. Similar benefits were reported by Orr (2011), in her account of an international education program in which students from Linfield College traveled to Sweden and Norway to study the two nations' school systems, drawing upon both educational and sociological theory.

While most of the literature on undergraduate research in the social sciences has centered on pure disciplines, several innovative models for undergraduate research in applied fields have emerged as well. DeCosmo (2015) recently observed that undergraduate research is now:

> a critical component of the student experience in the professional disciplines, in some cases serving as a bridge for students to make connections between theory and practice and in other cases preparing undergraduates for lifelong careers that will require them to integrate research into their professional work.
>
> *(p. 4)*

Both course-based research (Khelifa, Sonleitner, Wooldridge, & Mayers, 2004) and senior theses (Morris & Labhard, 2005) have been incorporated into undergraduate curricula in family and consumer sciences. Curricular and co-curricular undergraduate research opportunities have been similarly offered in social work and communication-related fields (Hay, Snowball, Varallo, Hilton-Morrow, & Klien, 2014; Matich-Maroney & Moore, 2016; Shanahan et al., 2015).

Models of undergraduate research in business have typically emphasized collaboration among faculty, students, and corporate leaders (Bartkus, 2007; O'Clock & Rooney, 1996). However, Szymanski, Hadlock, and Zlotkowski (2012) cited ways in which research in the public sector could be used to cultivate appropriate skills for business majors as well. At Bridgewater State University, authentic research experiences have replaced textbook case studies in much of the undergraduate business curriculum (Shanahan et al., 2015). Sims et al. (2012) reported on the use of a credit-bearing independent study course to engage undergraduate students in research on various aspects of marketing and business communication. Hirsch et al. (2013) recounted how focus group research had been incorporated into a senior capstone course in conflict analysis and resolution. At Bentley University, where over 95% of students major in business-related fields, the Center for Integration of Science and Industry engages undergraduate students in research on application of scientific and technological advances to the design and delivery of consumer goods and services (Boulden, Hall, Oches, Szymanski, & Ledley, 2015). With similar goals in mind, Innovation to Enterprise Central (ITEC), an undergraduate research fellowship program at Indiana University–Purdue University Indianapolis (IUPUI), brings together students from multiple academic majors to engage in collaborative research, requiring both technical and entrepreneurial skills (White et al., 2013).

Within the field of education, certain obstacles to the creation of opportunities for undergraduate research are common, owing to both external constraints on teacher certification curricula and the role of research in the practice of teaching. In recognition of these challenges, Slobodzian and Pancsofar (2014) introduced what they have termed the *pragmatic model* of undergraduate research in teacher education. Grounded in the prior literature on classroom-based action research, this model emphasizes the use of evidence-based reflection on problems encountered in authentic educational settings, for purposes of improving the practice of teaching. In further elaboration on this model, Slobodzian, Pancsofar, Hall, and Peel (2016) offered illustrative examples of its application specifically to undergraduate research on literacy.

Other authors have offered examples of undergraduate research on a wide range of educational topics and in a variety of settings. Field-based research in teacher education has incorporated techniques of instructional evaluation and applied behavioral analysis (Hoppe, 2010; Luyben, 2005). Research has also been infused into foundational courses in education, as a form of constructivist pedagogy (Manak & Young, 2014). Shanahan et al. (2015) offered numerous examples of both course-based and co-curricular educational research involving undergraduates. Groth, Bergner, Burgess, Austin, and Holdai (2016) described a summer program in which undergraduate students were introduced to the collection and analysis of original data to inform their teaching of mathematics. Undergraduate education majors have also conducted surveys of professional opinions on controversial issues in the field (Jacobs, 2000). It should be noted, as well, that the institutional research model presented by Murray et al. (2004) proved applicable to both higher education and human resource development, reflecting the methodological grounding of both fields in the social sciences.

Mathematics and Computer Science

Undergraduate research in mathematics and computer science generally involves application of mathematical principles or computer programming skills to the solution of some practical problem in the real world. Such applications may relate directly to the career aspirations of the participating students, though not in all instances.

Advances in mathematical software have created new opportunities for mathematics students to engage in undergraduate research, often working with authentic data sets (Cerrito, 2008). Bendel (2008) explained how projects of this nature could be appropriately adapted to the skill levels of students with widely varied backgrounds in mathematics and computer science. The conviction that all undergraduate students can benefit from exposure to mathematical research has inspired its broad infusion into the mathematics curriculum at Ithaca College, resulting in a vibrant departmental research culture (Brown & Yurekli, 2007). According to Temple et al. (2010), undergraduate research in mathematically related fields typically consists of individual projects that are separate from the faculty mentor's primary line of research. However, in exploring theoretically oriented topics in mathematics, Beke (2010) has found that full collaboration with undergraduate students is possible through a process of dialogue that closely mirrors that which occurs among faculty colleagues.

Undergraduate research in computer science has often made use of a team-based approach (Bernat, Teller, Gates, & Delgado, 2000; Dahlberg et al., 2008;

Guo, 2008; Knox, DePasquale, & Pulimood, 2006; Way, 2006). Through applied projects, students have gained practical skills in various aspects of both design and management (Clear et al., 2001; Newman et al., 2003; Schummer, Lukosch, & Haake, 2005). Webster and Mirielli (2007), in particular, recounted how course-based service-learning had been used effectively to provide students with experience in developing an information system for a local non-profit agency. Greening and Kay (2002) advocated undergraduate students' use of educational research methods to assess the effectiveness of various approaches to the teaching of computer science. In addition to course assignments (Clear et al., 2001; Newman et al., 2003; Schummer et al., 2005), internships, fellowships, and other research program models have proven to be effective in introducing undergraduate computer science students to the world of original scholarship (Dahlberg et al., 2008; Knox et al., 2006). Underscoring the influence of mobile technology on undergraduate research, the Wireless Sensor Data Mining Lab at Fordham University has created new opportunities for undergraduate students to conduct original research in the development of smartphone applications (Weiss, 2013). Awong-Taylor et al. (2016) have cited the expansion of undergraduate STEM research programs to include "creative experiences" (p. 12), such as the development of electronic games or applications, as an important step toward greater inclusion.

The professional literature includes examples of undergraduate research opportunities in mathematics and computer science during both the summer and the academic year. Caristi and Gillman (2002), for example, described a program conducted by the Department of Mathematics and Computer Science at Valparaiso University, in which students worked together on teams for the full duration of the academic year to solve applied problems. Students were invited to participate in the program in their first year, and many chose to continue even after their initial projects had been completed. The length of students' commitment to their projects appeared to be an important factor in the program's success.

Conclusion

While undergraduate research has found an important place in the instructional practices of contemporary collegiate institutions, it continues to fall far short of universality within today's undergraduate experience. With roots deeply embedded in the natural sciences, it is only within the past two decades that interest in undergraduate research has begun to take hold on an appreciable scale in the humanities, the social sciences, and most professional fields. Under the leadership of CUR, the undergraduate research community has grown in disciplinary inclusivity, yet long-standing barriers to full participation remain. Variation in traditional methods of both teaching and research creates a more natural home for undergraduate research in some fields of study than in others. However, as interest in undergraduate research across the disciplines has grown, an expanding body of relevant literature has come to include corresponding models of best practice.

10

THE CHANGING ECONOMICS OF HIGHER EDUCATION AND UNDERGRADUATE RESEARCH

In analyzing the likely future of undergraduate research, it is important to consider the impact of economic factors on the availability of opportunities for our nation's students. While funding for undergraduate research is a matter of concern in even the best of times, the sustained economic downturn of the past several years has created new challenges for faculty and undergraduate students seeking to undertake collaborative inquiry. In this new economic climate, acquisition of financial resources has become a major focus of attention within the world of undergraduate research, and there is reason to believe that it will remain so, well into the future. Higher education's relationships with the federal government, corporations, and foundations will play an important role in the extension of research opportunities to future generations of undergraduate students.

The Role of the Federal Government

Though not a matter of constitutional mandate, the role of the federal government in education has grown dramatically over the course of our nation's history. Today, the federal government's influence over higher education comes primarily through tax policy, student financial aid, and research support (Mumper, Gladieux, King, & Corrigan, 2011). As is clear from the review of sponsoring agencies presented in chapter 5 of this book, the nation's colleges and universities are heavily dependent on the federal government for undergraduate research funding. Consequently, research opportunities for undergraduate students are shaped in part by both the state of the economy and the political priorities of the nation at any given point in time.

Under our currently strained economic conditions, calls for reductions in government spending have grown louder, and the societal benefits of investment in education have become increasingly obscured (Paul, 2010b; Conrad & Dunek, 2012). Passage of the Budget Control Act of 2011, which requires across-the-board reductions in discretionary spending in the event of a legislative impasse, has further jeopardized much of the financial support for undergraduate research on which colleges and universities have long relied (Cronin & Busch, 2013). In light of the major role the federal government has played in supporting undergraduate research, the continued availability of current opportunities will depend in part on academics' ability to clearly articulate to public officials the national interest that is served by both the cultivation of inquiry skills in our young and the expansion of our collective knowledge base through academic research. Evidence that links both undergraduate education and academic research to economic development appears to be especially persuasive in winning the support of members of Congress from both parties (Hensel, 2006b). Personal anecdotes that illustrate the benefits of undergraduate research and the need for public funding thereof are often seen as particularly compelling (Cronin, 2009).

Over the course of its history, CUR has emerged as an influential organization in Washington, due in large measure to its success in raising the visibility of the good work that is being carried out on campuses across the nation. In addition to providing students with an opportunity to gain skills in presenting their work, CUR's annual *Posters on the Hill* event serves as a means of expressing gratitude toward funding agencies and demonstrating to Congress the importance of continued support for undergraduate research (Hoagland, 1999).

In recent years, CUR has become more purposeful in advancing undergraduate research through lobbying activities in Washington. In addition to establishing its own advocacy advisory committee, the organization has engaged the services of a private consulting firm, Washington Partners, LLC, to guide and support its efforts to promote undergraduate research in the nation's capital (CUR, 2016e). In the first few years of its relationship with the firm, CUR hosted multiple informational events, communicated directly with key members of Congress, and secured representation on several key advisory committees. An important factor in CUR's ability to engage in dialogue on undergraduate research with influential decision-makers in Washington has been the close monitoring of developments on the legislative and policy fronts that the consulting firm has provided (Hensel, 2011c). In addition to providing consultation to the leadership of CUR, the firm has worked to keep the membership of the organization directly apprised of legislation affecting undergraduate research through monthly reports (Cronin & Busch, 2012).

The leadership of CUR has also encouraged students and educators to communicate directly with their elected representatives in Washington, concerning the educational and social benefits of undergraduate research and the significance of government support to its continued expansion (Husic, 2009b). Such outreach is important, insofar as elected members of Congress are directly accountable to their constituents and are therefore highly responsive to their concerns, especially in districts where margins of victory tend to be narrow (Cronin & Busch, 2012). Additionally, the organization has encouraged its members to elevate the profile of undergraduate research on their own campuses through communication and outreach to elected officials and influential community members. Urging members to reach out to their elected representatives at both the federal and state levels, one CUR president offered the following recommendations: (1) seek out ways to support legislators' own work through undergraduate research, (2) take advantage of opportunities to meet with members of Congress at their local offices during the August recess, (3) attend constituent events organized by elected officials themselves, (4) connect with elected officials through social media, (5) attend lobbying events organized by CUR and other relevant advocacy groups, and (6) invite legislators to attend undergraduate research events on campus (Crowe, 2012).

Such advice appears to have been taken to heart by proponents of undergraduate research on a number of campuses. Siena College has even gone so far as to appoint a designated staff member to serve as a liaison to state and federal officials (Medina, 2012). The Benjamin Center for Public Policy Initiatives, formerly the Center for Research, Regional Education, and Outreach (CRREO), at the State University of New York at New Paltz (SUNY New Paltz, n.d.), which engages undergraduate students in public interest research throughout the Hudson Valley, provides a natural mechanism for conveying the value of undergraduate research to elected officials through regularly published reports of sponsored projects (Morrow & Tobin, 2012). Szymanski et al. (2012) recounted how business majors at Bentley University have worked directly with state and local officials on public policy research. On other campuses, reports of similar research have been shared with individual legislators who have shown interest in the topics addressed (Gilbert & Guerra, 2012; Kvale et al., 2012).

While advocacy is important, a simultaneous reduction of dependence on the federal government can potentially shelter undergraduate research against the impact of shifting priorities within both the legislative and executive branches. As early as two decades ago, multiple observers predicted a softening of federal support for academic research (Massey, 1996; Scott, 1996). To make matters worse, such support has long been concentrated in the hands of a relatively small number of research universities (Mumper et al., 2011), rather than the predominantly undergraduate teaching institutions where much of the existing undergraduate research has taken place. Recent history suggests that the prevailing sentiment within the federal government has often favored an integration of basic and applied research, so as to maximize the societal benefit of our nation's investment in expanding the collective knowledge base (Lane, 1994; Scott, 1996). Therefore, academics would be well advised to adopt such an integrative approach in any projects for which federal funding is sought, while simultaneously exploring other sources of funding, such as local, regional, or industrial entities (Mills, 2010).

While the most direct impact of the federal government on undergraduate research comes by way of its funding of academic research generally, its role in student financial aid is not irrelevant, particularly in view of the cumulative effect of changes in financial aid policies and practices that have occurred over time. While the typical student financial aid package has long consisted of a combination of grants, loans, and employment, the trend in federal aid over the past several decades has been toward greater reliance on loans and less generous funding of grants. This trend has coincided with a rapid escalation of average sticker price and a reduction of emphasis on need-based institutional aid at public and private institutions alike (Clawson & Page, 2011; Cohen & Kisker, 2010; Levine, 2005); this at a time when a college degree has increasingly come to be seen as a necessity for gainful employment (Wadsworth, 2005), but by no means a guarantee of such (Kamenetz, 2007; Roksa & Arum, 2012; Stone, Van Horn, & Zukin, 2012).

The net effect of these trends is that a greater share of family income is now devoted to college tuition, especially among less affluent Americans (Arum & Roksa, 2011; Levine, 2005), even as potentially crippling student loan debt erodes the economic advantages traditionally bestowed upon college graduates (Roksa & Arum, 2012; Stone et al., 2012). Use of student loans to cover tuition and fees appears to be only the tip of the iceberg, as today's undergraduates have also shown growing reliance on credit cards and other forms of private interest-based financing to cover various expenses while in college (Arum & Roksa, 2011; Kamenetz, 2007). Noting that "the millennial generation increasingly views its collegiate experience as more transactional in nature than transformational," Daugherty (2012, p. 41) has raised the further prospect that the traditional allegiance of college graduates to their alma maters might quickly fade, as they come face to face with the reality of underemployment and unmanageable debt. Thus, a concurrent erosion of alumni support is not implausible.

Issues of affordability also affect the undergraduate experience itself, mainly by increasing the necessity of student employment. From the late 20th Century through the present, overall trends have shown an increase in both the percentage of students who work and the average number of hours worked per week (Arum & Roksa, 2011; Baum, 2010). Recognizing that the time available to students in a given week is finite, each hour devoted to one activity is one less hour devoted to another, and not all activities are of equal value in promoting students' intellectual development. In comparing the "work for wages" that constitutes most student employment against the "intellectual work" in which students and faculty engage through various other activities, Pusser (2010) observed that "intellectual work offers far more autonomy, allows for considerably more criticality, and is more often oriented to the production of public goods than are conventional employment relations" (p. 138).

In attempting to envision a truly transformational student employment experience, one would be hard pressed to find a more perfect example than the typical undergraduate research fellowship. Insofar as job responsibilities compete for students' time and energy with other learning opportunities, including most other forms of undergraduate research, it becomes clear that fellowships are an important component of any comprehensive institutional undergraduate research program that is based on principles of equity and inclusion. The undergraduate research literature offers multiple examples of how work-study funding can be used to expand paid undergraduate research opportunities on campus in ways that ensure openness to students for whom part-time employment has thus far remained an economic necessity (Blockus, 2009; Grabowski et al., 2008; Gregerman, 2009; Jonte-Pace & Gilbert, 2010; Nazaire & Usher, 2015; Pyles & Levy, 2009).

The Influence of Industry

Increased collaboration with industry is clearly one means by which to reduce higher education's reliance on federal funding, while also aligning the use of appropriated funds with governmental priorities. It should come as no surprise, therefore, that such collaboration has been explicitly endorsed by many within the federal government itself (Lane, 1994; Scott, 1996). Partnerships with industry have also been cited as an important means of advancing Boyer's scholarship of application (Braxton, Luckey, & Helland, 2002).

Even within the context of federally funded research, collaboration with industry has become increasingly common. A key factor in this trend was passage of the Bayh-Dole Act of 1980, which enabled academic institutions to retain ownership of intellectual property developed under federal research grants, and which included provisions to encourage *technology transfer* (Miller & Le Boeuf, 2009; Zemsky, Wegner, & Massy, 2006), defined in the professional literature as "the movement of knowledge and discoveries from the university to the public" (Ku, 2009, p. 17). In addition to communication of results through traditional academic venues, such as publications and conference presentations, technology transfer can occur through licensure agreements that allow discoveries to be applied to the delivery of goods and services to consumers (Ku, 2009). Over the past three decades, a number of innovative models of technology transfer have emerged, as a consequence of collaborative partnerships between academic and industrial organizations, which have yielded benefits to all concerned (Miller, Le Boeuf, & Associates, 2009). A thematic issue of the *Council on Undergraduate Research Quarterly,* dealing with "undergraduate research as a pathway to innovation," featured reports on several undergraduate research initiatives in which partnerships with industry were instrumental in promoting technology transfer (Stocks, 2013).

The aforementioned benefits notwithstanding, the trend toward collaboration with industry has not been universally embraced within the academy. In analyzing sources of resistance, Miller and Le Boeuf (2009) cited differences between academic and industrial cultures with respect to organizational governance, and more importantly, prevailing attitudes toward research. Other authors have also discussed this cultural divide, with a focus on the distinction between basic and applied research, and the relative value attached to each within the academic and commercial worlds. Traditionally committed to the pursuit of truth for its own sake, some faculty scholars are understandably apprehensive of a research culture in which the principal sponsors of investigations gauge the value of discoveries by the profitability of their commercial applications (Lorig, 1996; Scott, 1996). Under such circumstances, one might reasonably anticipate a narrowing of our nation's academic research agenda, to the exclusion of lines of inquiry that are not of immediate practical interest but are of potential theoretical value (Gregorian, 2005).

A further by-product of the profit motive that dominates industry is a constriction of communication among researchers that is often antithetical to traditional academic values. While faculty scholars are expected to share their discoveries with the academic community through publication, industrial researchers often have a competitive interest in maintaining secrecy surrounding their findings, and in some instances, obtaining patents to protect their discoveries against usage beyond their own organizations (Miller, 2009; Miller & Le Boeuf, 2009; Scott, 1996). The notion of a proprietary interest in one's discoveries raises further questions as to ownership of both the knowledge derived from collaborative research and the actual data from which conclusions are drawn.

The possibility that academic researchers might themselves profit from commercial application of their discoveries raises further cause for concern, insofar as economic interests hold the potential to erode their objectivity as social critics. One of the principal functions of the intellectual class has traditionally been to monitor the workings of various social institutions, including commercial organizations. It has been argued that faculty researchers' involvement in commercial ventures compromises their ability to render independent judgments of what is in the best interest of society (Scott, 1996; Washburn, 2005).

Cautioning against excessive commercialization of higher education, Gilde (2007) raised yet another way in which corporate sponsorship of research might lead the competitive culture of the business world to seep into the academic realm. Noting that industrial backers are often selective in choosing the objects of their largesse, he predicted further stratification of opportunity among academic institutions, as a relatively small number of elite universities emerge as their preferred beneficiaries. This prospect is troubling to those who embrace the undergraduate research community's goal of broad student participation in scholarly activities across all academic institutions. The lure of corporate funding also holds the potential to lend a favored status to those faculty members who are most adept in securing major research contracts, as opposed to those who are most fully committed to engaging students in meaningful learning (Washburn, 2005). The potential for the educational benefit of undergraduate research to be lost amidst the competition for corporate funding will demand the continued vigilance of the undergraduate research community.

In the absence of a shared set of norms and values across the academic and corporate worlds, faculty researchers who enter into collaborative relationships with industrial colleagues would be well advised to discuss with their collaborators the full range of issues that partnerships of this nature entail. Such conversations should occur well in advance of undertaking any joint projects (Lorig, 1996). Consistent with the norms of the particular industry, academic partners should be prepared to establish clear timelines for their projects with specific work products delivered at identified points along the way (Holman, 2006). At the same time, industrial partners may need to be reminded that undergraduate researchers are novices and that expectations placed upon them should reflect this fact. Provisions should likewise be made for regular communication between student researchers and their commercial sponsors, even if this means choosing only local or regional partners (Clear et al., 2001). In the course of negotiation, it is also important to be mindful of various constraints on academic institutions, with respect to public disclosure and assumption of risk, which may not be applicable to their industrial partners (Miller, 2009).

In navigating the rocky terrain surrounding the communication of findings, there would appear to be some potential for reconciliation of competing interests in a distinction that has sometimes been drawn between *applicable* and *applied* research. Conceivably, academic researchers could be free to publish findings related to the underlying scientific principles that support industrial innovation, while still ensuring appropriate protection of corporations' methods of applying these principles (Scott, 1996). One common approach to dealing with this dilemma is to delay publication of findings until after patent applications have been filed (Lorig, 1996). Hodapp (1996) suggested also that if patent authorship itself were recognized as faculty scholarship, the competing interests of industrial and academic partners could perhaps be more easily reconciled. In instances where corporate partnerships intermingle with federal grant funded projects, it is also important to differentiate the purview under which specific discoveries are made in order to properly assign patent ownership (Yavelow, 2006). In smaller projects, where no other external funding is involved, universities have sometimes opted to relinquish intellectual property rights to their industrial partners in the interest of securing research opportunities for their students (Carney, 2006). Others have retained ownership, but have granted either restricted or unrestricted use to their commercial partners (Clear et al., 2001).

Holman (2006) recommended that faculty seeking to initiate an academic-industrial partnership first identify an area of shared research interest and then form a team comprised of individual investigators who together bring the necessary expertise to the project. He recommended, further, that long-term collaborations be approached incrementally, with funding sought through a series of modest proposals, rather than a single major proposal. This approach serves to minimize the risk assumed by the industrial partner and provides academic researchers with an opportunity to demonstrate their good faith and reliability over an extended period of time.

Emphasizing the need for mutuality of benefit, Giedd and Baker (2006) offered a model of academic-industrial partnership, based on several key principles. First, they stressed accommodation of industrial partners' organizational priorities through a "focus on core interests" (p. 12). Second, they cautioned against simultaneous engagement with partners whose interests are at odds with one another, focusing instead on research and product development for companies that share common interests but differ in their specific applications of research findings. Finally, they offered a strategy for protecting the intellectual property interests of industrial partners based on the use of royalty agreements in lieu of university patent ownership.

If we are to continue providing meaningful research opportunities to undergraduate students, collaboration with industry appears to be both desirable and inevitable. However, as academics look toward a deepening of their involvement in such endeavors, they should anticipate potential areas of conflict and concern. Resolution of such matters will undoubtedly demand a different mindset of both faculty researchers and their industrial colleagues. New understandings will only come about through a process of dialogue, which in itself holds the potential for mutual benefit.

Building Educational Capital

Given the costs associated with academic research, it should perhaps come as no surprise that fundraising has become an increasingly important aspect of the faculty role in undergraduate research. With the economic downturn that our nation has experienced over the past several years, endowments have fallen both for academic institutions (LaPlant, 2010) and for many of the foundations that support them (Husic, 2009c), leaving faculty mentors and their students to vie for a more limited pool of private resources available to support their creative and investigative activities. Moreover, this struggle presents itself at a time when reductions in state and federal funding for higher education have made private philanthropy even more critical to the continuation of such activities (LaPlant, 2011b). To successfully initiate programs of undergraduate research, faculty members must familiarize themselves with sources of financial support and develop the skills necessary to access those resources that are available to them. Equally important to the integrity of the undergraduate research enterprise is the advancement of a philosophy of research funding that reflects the generative nature of the activity itself.

On the occasion of the 100th anniversary of the Carnegie Foundation for the Advancement of Teaching, Bacchetti and Ehrlich (2007a) undertook a major investigation of the state of educational philanthropy. Based on interviews with leaders of both educational and philanthropic organizations, the researchers identified a number of problematic conditions and issued recommendations for addressing them. Although their work focused specifically on the relationship between educational institutions and the private foundations that support them, the resultant vision of financial support for education applies equally well to fundraising efforts involving a wide variety of public and private benefactors.

At the heart of Bacchetti and Ehrlich's (2007b) vision is the concept of *educational capital*, defined as "the progressive accumulation, in forms usable by educators, of validated experience and knowledge about successful educational ideas and strategies" (p. 23). Under this model, the function of grants is not simply to address the immediate needs of individual institutions, but rather to spur the development of effective practices that can be replicated elsewhere. Elaborating upon this model, Shulman (2007) spoke of a "scholarship of philanthropy" (p. xiii), based on the core principles of Boyer's (1990) scholarship of teaching, namely transparency, critical review, and generalization of lessons learned locally. In their own recommendations for generating educational capital, Bacchetti and Ehrlich (2007b) emphasized the importance of grounding educational initiatives in prior research, identifying those elements of innovative practices that are deemed essential, devising plans for sustaining innovation over time, incorporating assessment into all stages of implementation, and integrating new initiatives into the existing contexts of educational organizations.

Similarly, in all of its programs to support undergraduate research, NSF applies two criteria to the evaluation of grant proposals: (1) *intellectual merit* and (2) *broader impacts*. Intellectual merit is established based on the weight of the problem that the proposed project is intended to address, the degree to which the project builds upon prior research, the soundness of the pedagogical and assessment procedures incorporated into the plan, the grant-writer's qualifications to carry out the project, and the depth of support for the project at the institutional level (NSF, 2004), as well as the transformative nature of the proposed research (Karukstis & Hensel, 2010). Projects that satisfy this criterion often fall into niche areas in which individual investigators have developed specialized knowledge (Coyne, 2004). Broader impacts include the project's potential contributions to the advancement of teaching, inclusion of traditionally underrepresented populations in scientific inquiry, and enhancement of the educational and research infrastructure, as well as the likelihood of widespread dissemination of findings and significant benefits to society (NSF, 2004).

This emerging vision of research funding is significant to the future of undergraduate research, because of the premium that it places on innovation and individual contributions to the advancement of the broader enterprise. Consistent with this view, Grant and Haynes (2001) drew parallels between the demands of undergraduate research leadership and those of entrepreneurship, emphasizing the need for independence, determination, tolerance for risk, and a strong desire to achieve. For both educators involved in undergraduate research and entrepreneurs involved in business ventures, the ability to craft a vision fueled by passion is critical to the successful acquisition of financial support. Recognizing the power of personal initiative and commitment, Knight (1999) articulated a role for faculty in fundraising to support undergraduate research at the departmental level. The direct involvement of new faculty members in grant-writing can offer the further benefit of focusing their research agendas and elevating their profiles as scholars within their fields (Crawford, Garg, & Neuhoff, 2008).

Faculty entering the world of grant-writing for the first time will find ample support for their efforts to obtain funding for their undergraduate research activities. Both CUR and NSF (2004) regularly offer faculty workshops dealing with grant-writing. CUR's offerings, in particular, have won praise from past participants, who have appreciated the opportunity to focus their undivided attention on grant-writing and to receive constructive feedback on their work (Reggio, 2002; Reingold, 2000). In seeking out potential sources of funding, faculty will find an abundance of information online at sites such as grants.gov and foundationcenter. org, which highlight publicly and privately supported grant programs respectively (Bolek & Forsythe, 2008). Additionally, NSF (n.d.b) maintains an online guide to its grant programs, organized by subject area and target population.

Institutional offices of sponsored research have also assumed an important role in supporting faculty efforts to secure external funding for undergraduate research (Hakim, 2000; McConnaughay & Rueckert, 2004). The Center for Undergraduate Research and Education in Science, Technology, Engineering, and Mathematics (CURE-STEM) at the University of Central Oklahoma maintains a comprehensive system of support for faculty mentorship of undergraduate research, which includes training and assistance in grant-writing. Institutional data, collected over a three-year period, revealed that increases in external funding far offset the investment of resources in the program (Barthell et al., 2013).

In addition to seeking external funding, faculty would be well advised to explore options available to them in-house. Doing so will enable them to ascertain the need for external support and to pinpoint the precise purpose for which it will be used (Bolek & Forsythe, 2008). A number of PUIs have established institutional foundations to support undergraduate research on their campuses (Cook & McCauley, 2003; Noice, 1999; Thabet, 1994). Others offer start-up grants to support faculty in conducting pilot studies related to new lines of research (Bolek & Forsythe, 2008; Crawford et al., 2008). Though relatively small, the grants offered through these programs are often sufficient to cover the costs of undergraduate research projects, such as travel expenses, equipment costs, and staff support (Rohs, 2011). Furthermore, the experience of applying for these and similarly small externally funded start-up grants can enable faculty members to develop skills in preparing proposals and to begin building records of successful grant-writing (Crawford et al., 2008). Shields (2010) recounted how one institution required recipients of institutional funding to subsequently submit proposals for external funding, thereby reinforcing this natural progression. Institutional support can be an important part of this process insofar as many granting agencies require matching funds or cost-sharing as conditions of their awards (Bolek & Forsythe, 2008).

Like undergraduate research itself, the process of grant-writing is one that is often collaborative in nature. Therefore, coalition-building is an important preliminary step in the pursuit of external funding. Grant proposals typically require letters from all participating institutions, affirming the support of the organizational leadership. To maximize "buy-in" among key individuals and constituencies, broad representation in the planning process and decision-making by consensus are important (Cheatham, Friedli, Robertson, & Rowell, 2005, p. 24; NSF, 2004). The planning team should also be chosen to include individuals with a variety of skills and talents, as well as complementary perspectives. It should be noted, as well, that coalition-building need not be confined to the institutional partners themselves. Advisory boards, composed of external consultants, can serve as an important source of expertise and objectivity in the planning process and can greatly enhance the credibility of the grant proposals that are ultimately produced (NSF, 2004).

While the format of the proposal will vary according to the specifications of the individual funding agency, certain elements are common. Applicants will typically be asked to prepare a proposal that includes four components: (1) a general description of the project, including a statement of its purpose and significance, as well as the hypotheses or questions that will guide the investigation; (2) a review of the relevant literature; (3) a detailed description of the methodology to be employed, as well as an account of any preliminary or pilot studies that might have been conducted; and (4) a proposed budget for the project (Halpern & Blackburn, 2005). Depending on the nature of the research and the proposed funding source, the principal investigator may also be required to provide assurances of compliance with various regulations pertaining to lobbying, biosafety, and ethical treatment of animals and human subjects (Bolek & Forsythe, 2008). In discussing the rhetoric of proposal writing, Halpern and Blackburn (2005) emphasized three overall goals: (1) to clearly articulate factual information about the proposed project, (2) to convince reviewers of the project's merit, and (3) to establish one's own qualifications to effectively execute the plan.

Beyond these general recommendations, various authors have addressed unique aspects of proposals for specific programs and funding sources (Cheatham et al., 2005; Chin, 2004; Coyne, 2004; Marusak, 2002). For a detailed description of the application process for NSF grants, readers are referred to the Foundation's *Proposal and Award Policies and Procedures Guide* (NSF, 2016). A more brief NSF (2004) publication, entitled *A Guide for Proposal Writing*, furnishes practical advice to researchers, regarding four phases of the application process: (1) preparation, (2) composition, (3) submission, and (4) notification of results.

While fundraising for undergraduate research has most often been framed in terms of grant-writing, students and faculty who are seeking to undertake such activities can also benefit from the generosity of alumni and other individual donors on whose support American colleges and universities have long depended. In a popular monograph on the subject, Kinkead (2010) situated fundraising for undergraduate research within the broader context of advancement, a realm of activity that also encompasses marketing and communication. With advances in technology, crowdfunding has become an increasingly popular approach to the solicitation of support for undergraduate research, in part because of its speed and efficiency (Fitzgerald, 2015).

Regardless of the source, the process of seeking funding is one that requires faculty scholars to think proactively about their research and to articulate the social significance of the problems that they have chosen to investigate. In the context of undergraduate research, this process also introduces opportunities for faculty mentors to discuss with students the practical utility of research, the responsible use of resources, and the necessity of careful planning.

Conclusion

This chapter addressed contemporary challenges in funding of undergraduate research, with a focus on the changing roles of the federal government, industry, foundations, and higher education institutions themselves. Both political and economic threats to government funding of academic research raise legitimate concerns, as does the shift of federal funding from grant-based student aid to loan aid. In anticipation of future reductions in research support, proponents of undergraduate research would be well advised to become more active in communicating its benefits to government officials, while simultaneously working to reduce reliance on public funding. Partnerships with industry are one possible strategy for coping with reductions of government funding for undergraduate research, though risks associated with such an approach must be acknowledged. An expansion of the faculty role in fundraising also appears likely, preferably guided by a philosophy of educational philanthropy that is focused on the accumulation of generalizable knowledge over time. It is anticipated that greater resourcefulness will be demanded of the undergraduate research community, moving forward. Thus, both the educational and advocacy roles that CUR has assumed in building a solid economic future for undergraduate research are expected to become even more important in the years ahead.

11

IMPLICATIONS OF SOCIAL AND POLITICAL CHANGE FOR THE FUTURE OF UNDERGRADUATE RESEARCH

In examining the national and international context in which undergraduate research is carried out, it becomes clear that a number of social and political factors will likely bear on the availability of research opportunities for our nation's undergraduate students in the years ahead, as well as the forms that such opportunities might take. Current trends that are likely to affect the future of undergraduate research include a growing emphasis on accountability at all levels of the American educational system, ongoing advances in educational technology, and a growing recognition of the interdependence that exists among the nations of the world.

The Education Reform Movement

Over the past four decades, education reform has gradually become a major political issue at all levels of government. The birth of the contemporary education reform movement has been widely traced to the publication of The National Commission on Excellence in Education's (1983) landmark report, *A Nation at Risk*, almost 35 years ago. This harsh critique of the nation's schools raised public awareness of deficiencies in school curricula, student achievement, and teacher preparation, and launched a call for greater accountability in education that has continued to this day.

A second milestone in the education reform movement came in 1989, when President George H.W. Bush convened the nation's governors for the Charlottesville Education Summit, which ultimately led to publication of *The National Education Goals Report* (National Education Goals Panel, 1993). Co-authored by a panel of governors, legislators, and White House officials, this document echoed previous calls for accountability and articulated a set of goals toward which reform efforts should be directed. These goals addressed six general issues: (1) school readiness, (2) high school graduation rates, (3) academic rigor and citizenship education, (4) science and mathematics education, (5) literacy for civic responsibility, and (6) reduction of youth substance abuse and delinquency. Within a year, these six goals, together with two additional goals pertaining to faculty development and parental involvement, were incorporated into a bill that passed both chambers of Congress and was signed into law by President Clinton, as the Goals 2000: Educate America Act (1994). This legislation served the purpose of establishing a national agenda for education and authorized federal spending to support state and local initiatives to equalize educational opportunities for all children.

The next phase of the education reform movement came several years later, when Congress passed and President George W. Bush signed into law the No Child Left Behind Act of 2001 (2002). Notably more directive than prior legislation, this law required states to enact educational standards and implement programs of assessment designed to hold schools accountable for attainment of the established standards. Although this particular piece of legislation has faced a barrage of criticism from educational commentators (Meier & Wood, 2004; Noddings, 2007; Ravitch, 2009), the prescriptive nature of its directives has ensured that it cannot be easily ignored by educators and policymakers at either the state or the local level.

Although the impact of No Child Left Behind has been felt most directly by elementary and secondary schools, indirect effects on colleges and universities have been noted in the literature as well. In analyzing the "testing culture" (p. 5) that now characterizes the K-12 system, with a focus on implications for higher education, Trolian and Fouts (2011) predicted greater passivity and extrinsic motivation among incoming undergraduate students in the years ahead, as well as a diminished capacity for critical analysis and a greater propensity toward academic misconduct. The authors' contention was that such tendencies would be a likely consequence of an elementary and secondary school system in which direct instruction in basic content is emphasized and external pressure to perform is imposed on both students and teachers.

Even prior to the passage of No Child Left Behind, Malcom (1995) anticipated that the emerging standards movement within the K-12 system would bring greater significance to undergraduate research within the nation's colleges and universities. One obvious demand that education reform places on higher education is the call for newly certified teachers who are well versed in both the substantive principles of the natural universe and contemporary methods of scientific inquiry, a point noted by subsequent authors as well (Daves, 2002; Ramaley, 2002). As a pedagogy that is based on active learning, undergraduate research not only enables aspiring science teachers to develop a deep understanding of their disciplines, but also directly models for them a highly effective form of science education.

Another consequence of education reform has been an increased demand for university outreach activities targeted at serving the educational needs of the nation's children and the K-12 school system. Undergraduate research programs have already begun to serve as one means by which collegiate institutions have responded to the needs of children in their communities. The literature includes examples of research institutes that have brought local high school students and teachers to campus during the summer months to engage in collaborative studies (Hamilton & Ingram, 1996), sometimes with undergraduate students serving as research mentors (Edgcomb et al., 2010; Morris et al., 2009). Additionally, at least one institution has created opportunities for high school seniors to observe and assist faculty and students participating in its regular undergraduate summer STEM research program (Felix & Zovinka, 2008). Summer STEM programs on other campuses have been designed specifically for school children from disadvantaged or underrepresented populations (Bender, 2007; Johnson, 2011; Martins & Roth, 2011). Other institutions have operated summer programs for school children that have extended beyond the STEM disciplines (Caldwell, 2007). It should be noted, as well, that STEM programs themselves have not been confined entirely to the summer months. For example, the Lawrence Math and Science Partnership is an afterschool STEM education initiative that pairs middle school students in Lawrence, Massachusetts, with undergraduate mentors from Merrimack College, who in turn benefit from this service-learning opportunity (Foote & DiFilippo, 2009; Merrimack College, n.d.).

Instructional programs for children represent just one type of partnership that has been formed between collegiate institutions and the K-12 school system. For example, Yost and Soslau (2009) recounted how two university professors provided consultation to a local educator, who used action research to determine the effectiveness of service-learning as a pedagogy for use at the upper elementary level. Holmes, Nieuwkoop, and Miedema (2011) reported on a professional development initiative for high school algebra teachers that Hope College has offered in cooperation with the regional intermediate unit in its area. Gardella, Maciejewski, and Huber (2009) described an even more ambitious partnership between the University of Buffalo and the Buffalo Public Schools, which included an afterschool service-learning initiative, faculty development opportunities for local teachers, mentoring of local students and parents, and support for presentations and fieldtrips. Although teacher preparation programs offer the most obvious opportunities for educational outreach, Chiang (2016) recounted how a 15-year partnership between a psychology department and a local Head Start program created both research opportunities for undergraduate students and support for early intervention services in the community.

Beyond the ripple effects associated with calls for reform of the K-12 system, higher education itself has become a target of increased scrutiny. Calls for reform of postsecondary education reached an elevated pitch in 2006, with the publication of *A Test of Leadership: Charting the Future of U.S. Higher Education* (U.S. Department of Education, 2006). Often referred to as the "Spellings Report," after then Secretary of Education Margaret Spellings, who commissioned it, this white paper presented a critical analysis of the state of postsecondary education in the U.S., along with a series of recommendations for reform. Identified areas of concern and corresponding recommendations were organized around seven broad themes: (1) *the value of higher education*, (2) *access*, (3) *cost and affordability*, (4) *financial aid*, (5) *learning*, (6) *transparency and accountability*, and (7) *innovation*.

Although the Spellings Report commanded special attention, because it carried the imprimatur of the federal government, its authors were not alone in their critique of American higher education. In the spirit of their forerunners of the late 20th Century, whose slings and arrows were instrumental in launching the undergraduate research trend, numerous educational researchers and social critics of today have independently raised a host of concerns about the state of American higher education, in regard to such matters as cost, accessibility, use of resources, instructional staffing patterns, faculty priorities, student culture, curricular relevance, and educational impact (Arum & Roksa, 2011; Bok, 2006; Brandon, 2010; Hacker & Dreifus, 2010; Hersh & Merrow, 2005; Taylor, 2010). Even among the general public, academic institutions have come to be viewed with growing skepticism. Reflecting the defensive posture into which the academic community has been cast, Hensel (2011a) observed that "with 57% of Americans questioning the value of higher education and the cost of a college degree skyrocketing, colleges and universities are seeking ways to communicate the value of college-level studies" (p. 4).

Even prior to release of the Spellings Report, both state governments and regional accrediting associations had come to see assessment as a necessary tool for holding colleges and universities accountable for the educational outcomes that they claimed to promote (Zemsky et al., 2006). Such calls for accountability gave rise to a major assessment movement within the academic community (Burke & Associates, 2005; Miller, 2007), which gained further traction after the Secretary of Education took up the cause (Borden & Pike, 2007). The release of the Spellings Report itself prompted three major higher education associations to undertake a systematic investigation of models for assessment of student learning, under the sponsorship of the Fund for the Improvement of Postsecondary Education (Hensel, 2009).

Recognizing the centrality of assessment to current accountability and reform efforts, proponents of undergraduate research have begun to devote considerable attention to the topic in national conversations and within the professional literature (LaPlant, 2015). For example, in one strategic planning session in which the leadership of CUR discussed its goals for the immediate future, "assessment of undergraduate research" was identified as one of six primary areas of focus (Ambos, 2012, p. 4). The association's publication of its statement of standards for undergraduate research programs, commonly known as COEUR (Rowlett et al., 2012), marked a major step in solidifying uniform criteria for evaluation of program quality, while concurrent (Hensel, 2012) and subsequent essays have offered guidance on its application across a variety of institutional contexts (Webster & Karpinksy, 2015).

It is important to recognize, of course, that the mere provision of undergraduate research opportunities is not evidence of student learning (Childress, 2015). However, the numerous outcome studies discussed in chapter 4 of this book present a compelling response to those who would demand such proof. As Scott (1994) noted, the concrete work products that are typically associated with undergraduate research, by their nature, directly substantiate student learning in a manner consistent with authentic assessment models. Citing two separate reporting initiatives established by a regional accrediting association and a voluntary coalition of public colleges and universities, Osborn (2009) offered evidence of a growing trend toward affirmation of undergraduate research as a powerful means of both facilitating and documenting student learning.

Despite the growing body of national outcomes data, the ongoing need for institutional data cannot be overstated. As Rueckert (2009) observed in introducing a thematic issue of the *Council on Undergraduate Research Quarterly*, dealing with outcomes assessment, "in the current climate of accountability, those working in higher education are being asked to document the value not only of what students learn in class, but also in co-curricular activities such as student research" (p. 8). Toward this end, systems of assessment have been devised to measure cognitive, professional, and personal growth associated with participation in undergraduate research (Osborn, 2009). One such system is the *Undergraduate Research Student Self-Assessment*, an online instrument used to measure students' perceptions of their own learning associated with research activities in the natural sciences (Hunter, Weston, Laursen, & Thiry, 2009).

The expansion of undergraduate research beyond the STEM disciplines poses new challenges, with regard to outcomes assessment, insofar as research in the arts and humanities often does not lend itself well to the types of quantitative measures used in other disciplines (Johnson & Gould, 2009). The NSF-funded ePorfolio Project allows undergraduate researchers in all disciplines and their mentors to assess outcomes manifest in submitted artifacts, using a scoring instrument known as the *NSF Electronic Rubric* (Wilson et al., 2009). Institutionally based assessment systems have also made use of both quantitative and qualitative data to document outcomes of undergraduate research across all disciplines (Cetkovic-Cvrlje, Ramakrishnan, Dasgupta, Branam, & Subrahmanyan, 2013; Singer & Weiler, 2009).

In addition to measuring impact, proponents of undergraduate research have come to recognize the importance of accurately gauging rates of student participation in research activities (Blockus, 2012; Campbell, 2012; Schneider, Sullivan, & Collado, 2016). As discussed in the opening chapter of this book, the trend in undergraduate research has long been toward greater inclusion. Efforts to quantify progress toward full participation are likely a reflection of both the priorities of the undergraduate research community itself and those of entities external to the academy. Amidst a reform movement that is largely focused on raising proficiency at the lower end of the performance continuum, demands for broader participation in undergraduate research are likely to grow even stronger in the years ahead.

Use of Technology

The modern-day explosion in information technology has led numerous thought leaders to conclude that continued social and economic progress will depend on adaptation of our educational system to a knowledge-based economy, where productivity will become less labor-intensive and lower in material costs, but more dependent on the generation of original ideas and creative uses of material resources (Van Dusen, 2000). As various scholars have sought to envision such a future, the pervasiveness of the anticipated impact of technology on higher education has prompted widespread use of such terms as the *virtual campus* (Van Dusen, 1997), the *digital university* (Losh, 2014), and the *virtual university* (Bates, 2000; Robins & Webster, 2002; Ryan, Scott, Freeman, & Patel, 2000; Tiffin & Rajasingham, 2003). Although some authors have defined such terms as encompassing only those institutions that provide instruction exclusively through electronic media (Bates, 2000), others have advanced broad definitions that take into account the many ways in which technology is used to support the operations of traditional brick-and-mortar institutions (Ryan et al., 2000).

The transformative potential of educational technology is perhaps most evident in its application to *distance learning*. Popular definitions of this term have typically highlighted five key attributes of distance learning systems: (1) separation of the instructor and student for over half the course of instruction, (2) temporal and geographical separation of the instructor and student, (3) use of instructional media to deliver content and facilitate interaction between the teacher and learner, (4) opportunities for interactive communication between the learner and the provider of instruction, and (5) exercise of autonomy by the learner in determining the pace of educational activities (California Distance Learning Project, 2005).

Among the most recent trends in distance learning is the emergence of *massive open online courses* (MOOCs), which provide educational opportunities, free of charge, via the Internet, to thousands of enrollees worldwide (Klobas, Mackintosh, & Murphy, 2015). Such courses are made available largely through host platforms maintained by for-profit companies, including Coursera, Udacity, EdX, and FutureLearn (Porter, 2015). While some companies contract with select groups of universities to develop MOOCs, others work directly with individual faculty members (Young, 2012). In addition to universities, various other providers of education and training have begun to test the waters of the growing MOOC enterprise as well (Klobas et al., 2015).

Although there is some variation in format, MOOCs typically include videotaped lectures by well-respected faculty members, along with electronically scored quizzes and other online activities (Gose, 2012). While there is currently no mechanism for accreditation of independent MOOC providers under which traditional college credit might be directly conferred (Dennis, 2012), the home institutions of cooperating faculty often make the courses that they teach available for credit to students on their own campuses (The attack of the MOOCs, 2013).

Traditional colleges and universities are also not prevented from offering transfer credit for other courses conducted by independent providers, an option that Colorado State University has elected to exercise under an agreement with Udacity (Dennis, 2012).

As distance learning has come into its own, proponents of this pedagogy have increasingly come to question the implicit dichotomy between its methods and those associated with more traditional classroom instruction. The desire for a more integrative paradigm has given rise to a third approach, which has been termed *blended learning*. Graham (2006) has defined blended learning systems as educational structures that "combine face-to-face instruction with computer-mediated instruction" (p. 5). This blending can occur at the level of the activity, the course, the program, or the institution. One form of pedagogy that has been supported by a blended learning format is the *flipped classroom* or *inverted classroom*. Under this model, the didactic component of a course takes place outside of class time, often facilitated through online videos or other forms of instructional technology. This, in turn, frees up class time for collaborative projects and other forms of active learning (Saitta, Morrison, Waldrop, & Bowdon, 2016).

It would appear that adoption of a blended learning model is often driven by a desire to optimize the role of peer interaction in the learning process. The cultivation of learning communities in cyberspace has been widely recognized as a necessary component of digitally based instruction, but one that poses unique challenges (Conrad & Donaldson, 2011; Garrison, 2011; Palloff & Pratt, 2005, 2007). Garrison and Vaughan (2008) advanced an approach to blended learning that places education in the context of a *community of inquiry*, which "supports connection and collaboration among learners and creates a learning environment that integrates social, cognitive, and teaching elements in a way that will precipitate and sustain critical reflection and discourse" (p. 8). Introduction of such elements into the operations of brick-and-mortar institutions illustrates how a blended learning environment can be used to enhance peer interaction beyond those levels that are typically associated with either traditional or distance learning models in isolation.

In regard to the overall instructional function of the university, technology holds implications for both content and process, as the use of computers becomes both a skill to be taught and a medium by which to teach (Frackmann, 1994). According to Gillespie (1998), technology changes teaching in five distinct ways: (1) it introduces a demand for course content focused on how computers function, (2) it creates new methods of supporting instruction, (3) it increases efficiency in the work of individuals, (4) it serves as a means of data transmittal, and (5) it facilitates communication between the teacher and learner. Coinciding with the growth of the assessment movement, as discussed previously, advances in instructional technology have made especially noteworthy contributions to increased efficiency and effectiveness in gauging student learning (Garrison & Vaughan, 2008; Ryan et al., 2000).

According to Palloff and Pratt (2007), one of the distinctive properties of technologically based instruction is that it can be either *synchronous,* meaning that it is temporally bound, or *asynchronous,* meaning that teachers and learners need not confer at a single point in time. This level of flexibility has been notably absent from traditional instruction, which has typically been bound by both time and place. Taking into account both factors, technologically based instruction can take any of four basic forms, depending on where the teacher and learner are situated in relation to each other: (1) *same time—same place,* (2) *same time—different place,* (3) *different time—same place,* and (4) *different time—different place* (Fontaine, 2002).

Insofar as technology can facilitate a sharing of instructional materials, even issues of staffing need not pose the limitations that they once did (Langenberg & Spicer, 2001). More widespread adoption of technologically based pedagogies might predictably lead students to assume more responsibility for their own learning, as instructors shift toward a more supportive role in the educational process (Baldwin, 1998). Instruction can also become more collaborative and tailored more closely to the needs of the individual student (Langenberg & Spicer, 2001). Under this evolving paradigm, faculty members need expertise in technological and interpersonal skills, in addition to knowledge of their subject areas (Baldwin, 1998).

While much of the discussion of technology's impact on education has centered on the processes of teaching and learning, on a more fundamental level, technology has changed the way that we view knowledge itself and the legitimacy that we ascribe to specific knowledge claims. Whereas publication has historically conferred authority upon the printed word, readers have long been accustomed to accepting published information unquestioningly. With the broad access to information-sharing that the Internet has created, there has come a realization that readers must independently analyze the veracity of claims that are made in print (Taniguchi, 2003).

This broad access has also changed our conceptions of how and where knowledge is stored and who owns it (Lynch, 2008). Historically, libraries held a special place on college and university campuses, as repositories of fixed bodies of knowledge that were made completely manageable through uniform cataloging systems. Today, academic libraries have increasingly come to be seen as gateways to a vast universe of knowledge beyond the campus, the limits of which cannot be known either to students or to those staff members who are charged with ensuring their access to information (Hensley, 2003). Weigel (2002) used the term, "knowledge navigators" (p. 117), to encapsulate the role of librarians as information specialists, whose principal function is to educate students on how to access and make use of an increasingly unwieldy body of information.

Technology has affected research in other ways as well. Just as teaching is no longer limited by time and place, collaboration in research is no longer event-driven, but has instead become ongoing. Further, it is no longer necessary for individual researchers to go to their sources of information, which can now be accessed from nearly anywhere in the world (Langenberg & Spicer, 2001). Additionally, electronic support for data analysis has enabled researchers to undertake more complex investigations than would have previously been possible. Finally, the Internet has opened up new outlets for dissemination of research findings, in the form of electronic journals and other web-based publications (Baldwin, 1998; Hannum, 2002), a number of which are devoted specifically to undergraduate research (Walkington, Edwards-Jones, & Grestly, 2013).

By virtue of its impact on both teaching and scholarship, technology clearly holds implications for undergraduate research. Writing specifically on this topic, Falbo-Kenkel (1997) recommended that *virtual classrooms* be used in conjunction with *research-based learning* (RBL) to promote student collaboration, particularly on campuses that are not primarily residential. Under this model, creation of the virtual classroom, in itself, is a collaborative endeavor, with students building websites through which class activities can be coordinated and information exchanged. Matich-Maroney and Moore (2016) advocated the use of a flipped classroom format to facilitate collaborative course-based inquiry, when faced with student resistance to research activity.

Other authors have offered specific examples of how various types of undergraduate research have been reformatted for the digital age, and how technology has been used to increase access to the educational opportunities that they provide (LaPlant, 2013b). Bates, Rodriguez, and Drysdale (2007), for example, recounted how a psychological research methods course had been successfully adapted to a distance education format. In an application of technology to non-course-based undergraduate research, Holland et al. (2004) explained how videoconferencing had been used effectively to monitor one undergraduate student's research activity in an off-campus laboratory. Several years ago, the University of Texas—Austin introduced a searchable database that provided a centralized source of information on undergraduate research opportunities and allowed students to connect with faculty members who shared their research interests (Schilt & Gilbert, 2008). Two commercial enterprises, ScholarBridge (2015) and the Student Opportunity Center (S.O.C.) (2016), have since developed systems to facilitate this process at a multi-campus level and to support undergraduate research administrators in managing data particular to their institutions. The recent acquisition of ScholarBridge by S.O.C. (M. Rauch, personal communication, November 1, 2016) will likely accelerate the continued development of the products' combined capabilities.

Although few forms of online learning have captured the imagination of the educational world more than the MOOC phenomenon has, its practical impact on traditional higher education to date has remained minimal, in comparison to more established models. Murphy, Kalbaska, Horton-Tognazzini, and Cantoni (2015) have distinguished among four distinct forms of online learning: (1) *resources*, (2) *tutorials*, (3) *courses*, and (4) *MOOCs*. While the practice of undergraduate research has, thus far, been largely immune to the impact of MOOCs, other forms of online learning have begun to make their mark. Interestingly, some of the most dramatic innovation in this realm has arisen from a growing industry of technological firms committed to supporting the work of traditional colleges and universities, working in partnership with the academic community itself. One such company is Epigeum (n.d.), which develops online courses that are made available to collegiate institutions on a subscription basis. Its growing catalog of offerings addresses such topics as research skills and human subjects protections. Another firm, Labster (n.d.), offers highly sophisticated online laboratory simulation modules that can be used in traditional undergraduate courses to facilitate active learning in a safe and engaging format.

In discussing the long-term impact of technology on undergraduate research, amidst the surge of online activity that marked the close of the 20th Century, Massey (1996) predicted that both students and faculty would benefit from more independent access to information during the years ahead, with educational institutions no longer serving as the sole "guardians of information" (p. 95). In the years since then, the impact of technology has become evident in the growing number of online education providers, which have introduced a new breed of competition into the academic marketplace. The prospect of students one day fully satisfying general education requirements through participation in MOOCs raises the potential for traditional four-year colleges and universities to experience an erosion of their dominance in this arena, which parallels previous blows suffered at the hands of community colleges and proprietary universities. In entertaining such a scenario, LaPlant (2013c) saw opportunities for undergraduate research to take on added significance within those institutions where its roots run deepest. Through the incorporation of undergraduate research into the general education curriculum, traditional four-year institutions can continue to distinguish themselves from their competitors in ways that will likely yield an ongoing marketing advantage.

The Move toward Globalization

One of the principal effects of advances in communication technology is the creation of a more globally integrated society, the nature of which has affected nearly all areas of human activity, whether social, economic, or political (Urry, 2002). Indeed, the virtual university itself has been characterized as an institution that is global in nature (Delanty, 2002; Robins & Webster, 2002; Tiffin & Rajasingham, 2003). According to Massey (1996), one significant effect of globalization is the formation of scholarly groups that transcend national boundaries, while building upon shared academic interests. This fundamental change in prevailing notions of an intellectual community holds the potential to shape the future of undergraduate research in a number of ways.

Beyond the impact of technological advancement, globalization of scientific research has been fueled by a broad constellation of ecological concerns that threaten to adversely affect all regions of the world and that demand the collective attention of its populace. Environmental problems that must be resolved in the years ahead include climate change, ozone depletion, deforestation, overpopulation, and species endangerment. Coupled with world hunger, disease, terrorism, and other shared concerns, these conditions provide a common focus for the attention of both natural and social scientists worldwide (Scott, 1995). Under the leadership of the United Nations, diverse disciplinary perspectives have been brought to bear on international discussions of numerous global challenges (Husic, 2010).

The demand for international cooperation in research has been accompanied by a growing recognition of the need for educational institutions to prepare future generations of Americans to live as global citizens. Understanding of international perspectives and skills in cross-cultural communication and collaboration are among the competencies that today's educators most fervently seek to instill in our young people. Although the goals of equipping students with an understanding of the world beyond our nation's borders and preparing them for responsible citizenship are not new, the fusion of global understanding with preparation for citizenship that is now at the forefront of the academic community's consciousness is a relatively recent phenomenon (Plater, 2011). Among the conditions that have been cited in the literature as contributing to this new global education imperative are the spread of antagonism toward the U.S. internationally, the rise of economies in historically underdeveloped regions of the world, and a persistent sense of parochialism within American culture (Stearns, 2009).

Not long ago, under the sponsorship of AAC&U, a panel of leading scholars in the field of higher education issued a report entitled *College Learning for the New Global Century* (National Leadership Council for Liberal Education & America's Promise, 2007). In this report, the world of the 21st Century was characterized as one in which change is inevitable. In this dynamic context, advanced knowledge is necessary to adaptation, innovation is necessary to prosperity, civic engagement and social responsibility are necessary to the common good, and practical wisdom is necessary to problem-solving.

Colleges and universities in the U.S. have responded to the call for global education in a variety of ways, including the infusion of global perspectives into their formal curricula, expansion of opportunities for study abroad, recruitment and support of international students, opening of branch campuses overseas, and formation of partnerships with institutions in other parts of the world. Together, such efforts serve a twofold purpose of (1) equipping American students with the knowledge and skills necessary to function effectively in today's global environment and (2) capitalizing on the strength of American higher education to establish collaborative and mutually beneficial relationships that will enhance the nation's standing in the world (Stearns, 2009).

A common goal of global education initiatives is the promotion of *intercultural competence*, meaning an ability to successfully adapt to different cultural settings. According to Bennett (2008), there are cognitive, behavioral, and affective dimensions to this broadly defined capacity, which she has labeled the *mindset, skillset,* and *heartset,* respectively. In consultation with experts on global education, Deardorff (2008) has developed a model of intercultural competence that builds upon this basic framework of knowledge, skills, and attitudes to illustrate a process of personal transformation that yields both internal and outwardly visible changes in the individual.

Reflecting the trend toward globalization in higher education, study abroad programs have grown dramatically in recent years, and have taken on a variety of forms, including short-term experiences of a week to a semester in duration, in addition to the more traditional junior year abroad (Savicki, 2008; Spencer & Tuma, 2007). Consistent with the constructive developmentalist perspective discussed in chapter 2 of this book, study abroad programs have been characterized as transformative, because they combine academic learning with personal development. While traditional classroom instruction can serve as an effective means of familiarization with the structural variation that exists among the nations of the world, the cultural variation that lives in the perceptions of the world's people is often more deeply understood as a consequence of spending time among them (Selby, 2008). Drawing upon the work of Mezirow, Hunter (2008) differentiated between *normative* responses to cross-cultural immersion, meaning those that result in incorporation of new insights into existing cognitive or behavioral frameworks, and *transformative* responses, meaning those that result in fundamental changes in one's perceptions.

International service-learning is an increasingly popular approach to global education that combines the transformative potential of both service-learning and study abroad. The principle of reciprocity applies to international service-learning, just as it would apply to service-learning in any other context. However, in an international setting, this mutuality of benefit demands a higher level of intercultural competence on the part of students. Thus, in addition to the combination of academic work and experiential learning that characterizes all service-learning, international service-learning must also include intercultural learning (Pusch & Merrill, 2008). Bringle and Hatcher (2011) characterized international service-learning as occurring at the intersection of service-learning, study abroad, and international (i.e., global) education, and elaborated on how the three pedagogies complement one another.

Given the changes that globalization has inspired in both research and education, its impact specifically on undergraduate research would seem inevitable. While the natural sciences have long been at the forefront of undergraduate research, global education has more traditionally been viewed as falling within the province of the humanities and social sciences (Stearns, 2009). Thus, the trend toward globalization has coincided well with the expansion of undergraduate research into disciplines beyond the natural sciences. Nevertheless, it would be a mistake to assume that natural scientists or those in professional fields can remain on the sidelines of the global education trend. According to Stearns (2009), "engineers and managers have just as much need, as citizens, for a grasp of global education as do Latin American anthropologists; and their work may provide at least as many opportunities, if sometimes unexpected, for international competence or an appreciation of international impacts" (p. 5).

The trend toward globalization has begun to manifest itself in both the composition and priorities of the undergraduate research community itself. For example, among CUR's identified strategic planning foci is "internationalization of undergraduate research" (Ambos, 2012, p. 4). Additionally, the *Council on Undergraduate Research Quarterly* has introduced a feature entitled *From the International Desk*. Articles published under this banner have highlighted undergraduate research initiatives within the higher education systems of various countries, including Australia, Canada, Denmark, England, Germany, Ireland, Japan, the Netherlands, New Zealand, and Scotland. Even prior to the introduction of this feature, the journal occasionally featured contributions from international colleagues involved in undergraduate research. In a book-length report, sponsored by the U.K.-based Higher Education Academy, Healey and Jenkins (2009) reviewed undergraduate research initiatives in England, Ireland, Scotland, Australia, New Zealand, Canada, Denmark, and the Netherlands, in addition to the U.S., lending further credence to the notion that undergraduate research is no longer a uniquely American phenomenon.

The U.K., in particular, has assumed a leadership role in expanding undergraduate research opportunities globally. Modeled on NCUR, the British Conference of Undergraduate Research (BCUR) was founded in 2010, under the sponsorship of the Higher Education Funding Council for England (HEFCE) and the University of Central Lancashire, and held its first conference the following year (BCUR, 2010a). The organization has since introduced a British counterpart to CUR's *Posters on the Hill*, entitled *Posters in Parliament* (BCUR, 2010b). In 2016, BCUR partnered with CUR and Qatar University to conduct the first World Congress on Undergraduate Research (CUR, 2016f), a truly international event, which advanced a global educational agenda.

It should be noted, as well, that a number of collegiate institutions in the U.S. have begun to create opportunities for American undergraduate students to directly engage in research within an international context (Barkin, 2016; Bender, 2012; Best et al., 2007; DeCosmo, 2014; Dellinger, 2009; Edwards & Hogarth, 2008; Glass-Coffin & Balagna, 2005; Orr, 2011), sometimes working in cooperation with colleges and universities in other parts of the world (Jakubowski & Jianping, 2007; Scott, 1995). As the trend toward globalization continues, it would seem likely that initiatives of this type will emerge on numerous other campuses throughout the nation as well. Whereas such opportunities remain a relatively new phenomenon, few systematic studies of their unique educational impacts have been undertaken to date. Looking toward the future, articulation and verification of the educational benefits of such programs must remain high on the agenda of the undergraduate research community (Laursen et al., 2010).

Conclusion

This chapter presented an analysis of the current social and political climate for undergraduate research, with attention to how it might influence the advancement of inquiry-based learning in the years ahead. Three specific trends were explored: (1) the education reform movement, (2) advances in instructional technology, and (3) increasing global interdependence. The impact of education reform on undergraduate research was seen in community-based research initiatives undertaken in partnership with the K–12 system, as well as in the growing emphasis placed on assessment of educational outcomes associated with undergraduate research itself. The influence of technology on the future of undergraduate research was recognized as inescapable, given its significant impact on both teaching and research. The greater ease with which researchers can now engage in collaboration, collection and analysis of data, and communication of findings illustrates how advances in technology have supported the growth of undergraduate research. The trend toward globalization has shaped both the research agenda of the scientific community and the educational priorities of the academic community. With growing emphasis on the cultivation of students' intercultural competence, community-based undergraduate research is becoming an increasingly common element of international education initiatives.

PART V

The Outlook

12

REFLECTIONS AND RECOMMENDATIONS

Given the general purpose of this book and the diversity of its target audience, the scope of its content was necessarily broad, raising the potential for key points to be lost amidst the minutiae. In this final chapter, major themes will be highlighted, and implications for the practices of undergraduate research mentorship and program administration will be explored. Additionally, limitations in the existing body of literature will be examined and recommendations for further research presented.

Discussion of Findings

The preceding chapters addressed a number of subtopics pertaining to undergraduate research, which were grouped under four main topics: (1) the concept, (2) the rationale, (3) the conditions, and (4) the issues. Together, the information presented in these 11 chapters provides the foundation for discussion of the book's fifth major theme, the outlook, which serves as the focus of this final chapter.

The Concept

In chapter 1, undergraduate research was presented as an innovative pedagogical model that builds research competencies in students while simultaneously contributing to the shared body of knowledge within the relevant disciplines. Forms of undergraduate research can vary according to the respective roles of the student and the faculty mentor, as well as provisions for academic credit or financial compensation. Common forms of undergraduate research include course assignments, independent studies, theses, and fellowships.

Consistent with the dual functions of undergraduate research in supporting student learning and advancing the disciplines, dissemination of results is an
important component of the undergraduate research experience. Beyond the traditional publications and meetings of various learned societies, a growing number
of undergraduate research journals and conferences have been formed specifically
to serve as outlets for student work.

With the growth of interest in undergraduate research, proponents have set
their sights on institutionalization of the practice on individual campuses. Carried
to its ultimate end, the process of institutionalization leads to conditions under
which all students participate in some form of undergraduate research over the
course of their enrollment.

The Rationale

Chapters 2, 3, and 4 offered justification for undergraduate research, based on
contemporary educational theory, the history and cultural values of American
higher education, and a growing body of assessment data that attests to the impact
of undergraduate research on participating students. This integration of theoretical, historical, philosophical, and empirical perspectives mirrors the unitive nature
of undergraduate research itself and offers a persuasive argument in favor of its
adoption across a full range of academic disciplines.

The theoretical rationale for undergraduate research, as discussed in chapter 2,
is grounded in constructive developmentalism, an ascending school of thought
that draws upon the constructivist branch of learning theory, together with the
cognitive-structural and psychosocial branches of developmental theory. This
integration of theoretical perspectives results in an approach to teaching that is
focused on the promotion of identity formation, growth in cognitive complexity, and mastery of disciplinary content, through processes of active learning and
personal reflection.

The theme of integration is also central to much of the literature on the evolving culture of the academy. As discussed in chapter 3, concern for the competing
demands of teaching, research, and service has led to a reconceptualization of
faculty scholarship, resulting in a more complementary relationship among the
various facets of the faculty role. Integration of students into the campus community and a softening of the boundaries between their academic and non-academic
lives have also emerged as common institutional priorities. On a broader scale,
integration of future scholars into the global intellectual community has remained
a shared priority of the academic profession. Consistent with this goal of enculturation, the role of the professor as a mentor to undergraduate students has come
to be seen as increasingly important.

As indicated in chapter 4, the past 15 years have brought dramatic growth
in the body of empirical literature on educational outcomes of undergraduate
research. In alignment with the unitive nature of the pedagogy itself, the studies to

date have attested to its benefits for participating students within both the cognitive and the affective realms. Likewise, the mentoring relationship with the faculty advisor has been widely cited as a benefit of program participation.

The Conditions

Chapters 5, 6, and 7 surveyed current patterns of participation in undergraduate research, as well as conditions at the national and institutional levels that support or inhibit such participation. In addition to descriptive information on overall rates of participation, this review included comparisons across institutional and disciplinary categories.

As is evident from the information presented in chapter 5, the national climate is supportive of undergraduate research and continues to grow increasingly so. Both formal and informal networks within American higher education provide faculty mentors and other advocates of undergraduate research with mechanisms to promote interest in the chosen pedagogy and to increase opportunities for student participation. These groups have been supported in this endeavor by a variety of other public and private organizations that have generously funded undergraduate research and facilitated its dissemination.

At the institutional level, as discussed in chapter 6, it appears that opportunities for undergraduate research are common as a matter of policy, but less so as a matter of practice. Few institutions have reached a point where it is presumed that each undergraduate student will engage in original research prior to graduation. Moreover, institutions that have achieved this standard are limited almost entirely to the four-year sector of American higher education. Additionally, participation in undergraduate research has been found to be far more common in engineering and the natural sciences than in the humanities and social sciences.

As discussed in chapter 7, limited faculty incentives to mentor undergraduate researchers may be a factor in the aforementioned patterns of participation. For example, it appears that direct compensation for involvement in undergraduate research is rare and of little more than token value. Consideration of such activity in determination of individual teaching loads varies across different types of research activity, and is rarely proportionate to the demands placed on faculty who choose to participate. On an optimistic note, institutions that have made a public commitment to undergraduate research, by way of their membership in CUR, have widely honored this commitment in their weighting of undergraduate research mentorship in tenure and promotion decisions. However, many of these same institutions apparently have yet to codify such validation in written statements of policy.

The Issues

Chapters 8, 9, 10, and 11 addressed a number of contemporary issues, within American higher education and beyond, which bear upon the future of undergraduate research and have commanded the attention of its proponents. These issues include expansion of opportunities across diverse student populations and academic disciplines, funding of undergraduate research initiatives, and navigation of an ever changing social and political landscape.

In chapter 8, issues of equity in and access to learning opportunities were discussed in relation to the unique concerns of women, minorities, and students with disabilities. While gains in women's educational attainment were acknowledged, their underrepresentation in scientific disciplines was raised as a matter of concern. Underrepresentation of racial and ethnic minorities in science was cited as only one aspect of a broader discrepancy in educational attainment that has continued to favor the majority population. While barriers to female and minority students' advancement in science have been primarily attributed to social, political, psychological, and organizational factors, students with disabilities often must also contend with physical obstacles to their full engagement in academic life, which can be even more daunting.

While undergraduate research has found an important place in the instructional practices of contemporary collegiate institutions, its disciplinary breadth continues to fall far short of the ideal, as discussed in chapter 9. With roots deeply embedded in the natural sciences, it is only within the past two decades that interest in undergraduate research has begun to take hold on an appreciable scale in the humanities, the social sciences, and most professional fields. Under the leadership of CUR, the undergraduate research community has grown in disciplinary inclusivity, yet longstanding barriers to full participation remain.

Perhaps the most formidable challenge to expansion arises from the nature of the disciplines themselves. Longstanding variation in methods of both teaching and research across the disciplines creates a more natural home for undergraduate research in some fields of study than in others. In particular, the creative and solitary nature of faculty scholarship in the humanities has stood in sharp contrast to the shared conventions and traditions of collaboration that have long characterized academic research in the natural sciences.

Chapter 10 addressed contemporary challenges in funding of undergraduate research. Both political and economic threats to government funding of academic research were cited as cause for concern, as was the shift of federally funded student aid from a grant-based model to one that is primarily loan-based. Building partnerships with industry was cited as one possible strategy for coping with reductions of government funding. However, such an approach has remained controversial, due in part to differences in the cultures of the academy and the corporate world, as well as the functions of research within the two settings. Although private foundations have often more closely aligned with educational institutions in their organizational goals, so too have they aligned in the ebb and flow of their economic fortunes. Consequently, the financial lifeline that they offer has sometimes become frayed just when it has been needed most.

Chapter 11 presented an analysis of the current social and political climate for undergraduate research, with attention to how it might influence the advancement of inquiry-based learning in the years ahead. Three specific trends were explored: (1) the education reform movement, (2) advances in instructional technology, and (3) increasing global interdependence.

The chapter began with an historical overview of the contemporary education reform movement that gave birth to the No Child Left Behind Act of 2001. The demand for well-trained science teachers has inspired a new level of university outreach to the K-12 system, often in the form of community-based teaching and research initiatives. Although the education reform movement has focused primarily on the K-12 system, higher education has also faced new demands for accountability from state and federal governments, regional accrediting agencies, and independent critics and analysts. The consequence of this added scrutiny has been a growing emphasis on outcomes assessment, which has taken hold in both the undergraduate research community and higher education generally.

Over the past three decades, instructional practices in the nation's colleges and universities have also been shaped by the rapid pace of advances in technology. While the most dramatic changes that technology has brought to higher education have emerged in the area of distance learning, most recently with the advent of the massive open online course (MOOC), traditional instruction has also been affected. Blended learning is an increasingly popular approach to instructional delivery, which combines online and classroom-based pedagogies. As instructional technology continues to advance, it is anticipated that higher education will become more collaborative and less teacher-centered.

Closely related to the technological revolution is the trend toward globalization, which holds further implications for the future of undergraduate research. Advances in communication technology have helped to erode barriers to interaction across national boundaries in nearly all areas of human endeavor, including research. Additionally, the nations of the world hold a common interest in eradicating various threats to their shared well-being, which has created an incentive for global cooperation in research.

Recognition of the need for international cooperation has also shaped the educational agenda of American colleges and universities. Although there are numerous facets to globalization of undergraduate education, study abroad programs have been among the more prominent strategies employed, and such efforts have increasingly incorporated undergraduate research activities in the host countries. Concurrent with this trend, there has been an expansion of CUR's reach to colleagues overseas, who have become partners in the advancement of undergraduate research globally.

Implications for Practice

In reviewing the previous chapters of this book, it becomes evident that the body of literature pertaining to undergraduate research has matured considerably in the past 20 years, fueled in large measure by the growth of CUR and other professional associations. It has also coincided with a more general trend toward adoption of inquiry-based teaching methods across the disciplines. While this overall trend may be cause for celebration, the impact of undergraduate research on our nation's student population clearly has yet to reach its full potential. Therefore, any review of the relevant literature would be incomplete without a proper examination of implications for practice.

In chapter 2, the compatibility of undergraduate research with constructive developmentalism was explored in relation to four pedagogical models: (1) experiential learning, (2) discovery learning, (3) service-learning, and (4) collaborative learning. The alignment of undergraduate research with contemporary understandings of experiential learning was observed in both the direct immersion of students in the research process and the individualization of research activities based on student interests. The dual focus of undergraduate research on promotion of student learning and advancement of the disciplines was found to complement the goals of discovery learning. Both inquiry learning and problem-based learning were found to be suitable models for undergraduate research, based on current practices within the field. Community-based undergraduate research was introduced as a form of service-learning that holds promise of advancing the holistic educational goals inspired by constructive developmentalism. Finally, the inherently collaborative nature of undergraduate research was found to be consistent with the interactive approaches to teaching and learning that have grown out of this same school of thought.

As an inherently unitive form of pedagogy, undergraduate research also aligns closely with the shift toward a more integrative academic culture, as discussed in chapter 3. In addition to promoting a complementary relationship between faculty members' teaching and research activities, the close interaction that students experience with their mentors holds the potential to increase their own feelings of connection to the institution. Additionally, the co-curricular nature of many undergraduate research activities can contribute to a more harmonious relationship between students' in-class and out-of-class lives. Finally, both the relationship with the faculty mentor and the research activity itself can play an important role in facilitating students' entry into the world of scholarship and adoption of high standards of ethical conduct.

The alignment of undergraduate research with theoretical and philosophical perspectives that have been widely embraced within American higher education offers its advocates a strong basis on which to build institutional support for its expansion. Additionally, the general literature on active learning offers a ready foundation for the actual practice of undergraduate research. Where the path is not so well worn is in the adaptation of existing pedagogical models to accommodate challenges particular to undergraduate research. In chapters 8, 9, 10, and 11, a number of such challenges were discussed, including issues of equity and access, disciplinary breadth, funding, educational reform, technology, and globalism.

As becomes clear in chapter 8, any comprehensive strategy for promoting equity and access must address both the general conditions that inhibit advancement of all non-dominant populations and the unique concerns that are particular to women, minorities, and students with disabilities. Mentoring and early exposure to research have been cited as key factors in promoting interest in science among female and minority students. Safe and accessible facilities, coupled with appropriate academic support, play an important role in promoting the academic success of students with disabilities. In chapter 8, principles set forth by AAC&U and BEST were presented as a foundation for diversity initiatives in undergraduate research and numerous examples of successful institutional strategies based on these principles were introduced.

While the disciplinary disparities in undergraduate research opportunities that were noted in chapter 6 have remained stubbornly persistent, the situation has begun to improve over the past decade. Growing interest in undergraduate research across the disciplines has given rise to an expanding body of relevant literature, which served as the basis for chapter 9. As noted, interdisciplinary research has been offered as an approach to scholarly inquiry that is often more conducive to collaboration than is traditional disciplinary based scholarship. Additionally, new models for scholarship within traditional disciplines have created more fertile ground for the infusion of authentic research into the undergraduate curriculum. Strategies employed in literary-based disciplines include incorporation of peer review into processes of iterative writing, coupled with the creation of communal spaces in the real or virtual world. Community-based undergraduate research has proven to be highly compatible with the instructional goals of many courses in the social sciences. The infusion of community-based projects into study abroad programs has further expanded the relevance of this approach to social science disciplines in which international perspectives are emphasized. Finally, applied research has been shown to enhance learning opportunities in mathematics and computer science, and combines nicely with the pedagogy of service-learning.

In anticipation of future reductions in research support, proponents of undergraduate research were encouraged, in chapter 10, to become more proactive in communicating its benefits to government officials, while simultaneously working to reduce reliance on public funding. Although partnerships with industry may offer a viable alternative to government funding, sensitivity to potential tradeoffs in such arrangements is critical. Faculty members seeking to partner with industrial colleagues would be well advised to establish detailed agreements, concerning such matters as intellectual property and research timelines, prior to undertaking any joint ventures. As colleges and universities compete for the limited funds available through philanthropic foundations, it appears that grant-writing will also become an increasingly important aspect of undergraduate research mentorship during the years ahead. Therefore, it is incumbent upon faculty to cultivate their own skills in this area and equally important for institutions to offer relevant faculty development opportunities.

Changes in allocation of financial aid, together with the rising cost of college attendance, hold implications for undergraduate research participation, insofar as growing numbers of students are now working to fund their education and working longer hours as well. Unless fellowships remain a major component of comprehensive undergraduate research programs, there is a risk that opportunities for students to engage in original scholarship will become further stratified, based on socioeconomic status. Federal work study funding, which aligns with the currently prevalent self-help philosophy toward student aid, has been used successfully to support undergraduate research on a number of campuses and should not be overlooked as a viable source of revenue in the future.

Although the education reform movement has focused primarily on the K-12 school system, its impact on colleges and universities is inescapable, by virtue of their role in preparing future teachers. In this context, undergraduate research takes on added significance, as a means of introducing teacher certification candidates to the methods of inquiry-based teaching, as well as the use of research to evaluate and improve instructional practice. Consistent with the more general goal of expanding undergraduate research across the disciplines, the recent formation of CUR's Education Division will likely play a significant role in generating new models for undergraduate research in teacher preparation programs.

Emerging models of undergraduate research in teacher education have frequently incorporated field-based action research in K-12 settings. This approach nicely dovetails with an array of existing outreach activities conducted by collegiate institutions for children in their surrounding communities. While many of these initiatives are currently housed in traditional arts and sciences departments, partnerships with faculty colleagues in teacher preparation programs could potentially enhance their educational impact. Offerings such as afterschool and summer enrichment programs, as well as school-based service-learning activities, could provide ready opportunities for practitioner research by aspiring teachers, while continuing to improve learning outcomes for local children.

By virtue of its impact on both research and teaching, instructional technology is clearly significant to the future of undergraduate research. However, its adoption further complicates the institutionalization of undergraduate research by posing new logistical challenges, which will demand the attention of faculty and institutional leaders. The goal of universal participation in undergraduate research has remained elusive, in part due to the demand for mentoring that such broad opportunities would entail. The promise of emerging technologies for facilitating collaboration among large numbers of students offers hope for increased participation in undergraduate research. However, more efficient mentoring models will likely be necessary to fully harness this potential.

The trend toward globalization, which has been advanced largely by innovations in the technological realm, likewise holds implications for undergraduate research. As noted previously, study abroad has emerged as an educational practice uniquely conducive to the development of intercultural competencies that are critical to students' success as global citizens, and the infusion of community-based undergraduate research into study abroad programs has rapidly taken hold as a means of attaining this outcome. The expansion of such opportunities will depend on the cultivation of faculty partnerships that transcend national boundaries. With the ongoing expansion of the undergraduate research community beyond American shores, the time is right for CUR and other professional associations to assume a leadership role in facilitating such connections.

Recommendations for Research

With the growth of interest in undergraduate research over the past several years, the pedagogy itself has emerged as an increasingly frequent object of investigation. Based on a growing number of studies, much has been learned about both the prevalence and the educational impact of undergraduate research, as well as the conduciveness of current conditions to its expansion. However, due to the recency of even the most rudimentary investigations of the topic, there remains a need for further research. Proponents of undergraduate research have set an ambitious agenda for the future, one that will require a substantial investment of time and resources. Moving forward, a full body of evidence will be needed to bolster the case for such an investment, and ultimately to maximize its return.

On a very basic level, there is a need for more complete information on student and faculty participation in undergraduate research, as well as institutional support for the practice. While CUR has done an admirable job in collecting data on current practices among its member institutions, more general conclusions about the state of undergraduate research nationally would not be warranted, based solely on data pertaining to this select consortium. In particular, there is a need for further research on institutional policies pertaining to tenure and promotion, across the broader academic community, as well as on the impact of such policies on actual rates of faculty participation in undergraduate research mentorship.

Another aspect of the institutional climate for undergraduate research that bears further investigation is the range of organizational structures used to administer undergraduate research programs and their respective benefits. Anecdotal accounts of successes associated with various program models, as well as rationally based arguments in their favor, are readily available in the literature of the field. However, systematic comparisons of objectively measured outcomes associated with these models, based on comprehensive national data sets, have yet to materialize. While each of the various models has its proponents, there will need to be further research before any consensus is likely to emerge, with regard to best practices in this area.

Despite advances in current understanding of the educational outcomes of undergraduate research generally, there is a need for further studies in this area. Thus far, most of the research has centered on specific programs, some of which have included provisions for mentoring far beyond what is typically offered on

American college and university campuses. Generalizability has, therefore, been limited. Further, it has not always been clear which program provisions have accounted for changes in students' knowledge, attitudes, and behaviors. Relatively few studies have included control groups, and where such groups have been used, non-equivalency has sometimes been an issue. Consistent with the prevalence of undergraduate research across the disciplines, much of the recent outcomes assessment has occurred within the natural sciences. Consequently, relatively little is known about the outcomes of undergraduate research in other fields, most notably in the humanities. Further research could potentially fill these gaps in the existing literature, and is therefore strongly recommended.

Conclusion

Based on this chapter's analysis of the literature reviewed in the previous sections of the book, it is clear that interest in undergraduate research has increased dramatically over the past three decades. A sound philosophical and theoretical rationale for the practice has been articulated, and a wide range of beneficial outcomes associated with it have been documented, using empirical methods. Both national and local conditions have grown increasingly hospitable to undergraduate research, and its community of supporters has continued to expand in both its geographical and disciplinary reach. Nevertheless, there remains work to be done in building more inclusive practices. Additionally, ongoing changes in social, cultural, political, and economic conditions will continue to pose new challenges during the years ahead. Nevertheless, the record to date is one of resiliency and innovation, which clearly points toward a promising future for undergraduate research.

REFERENCES

Abraha, A. & Kanis, D. R. (2009). Growing a vibrant research program with non-traditional students: Strategic use of time and energy. In M. K. Boyd & J. L. Wesemann (Eds.), *Broadening participation in undergraduate research: Fostering excellence and enhancing the impact* (pp. 307–318). Washington, DC: Council on Undergraduate Research.

Ahern-Rindell, A. & Quackenbush, A. (2015). Applied ethics can foster the teacher-scholar model and impact undergraduate research campus-wide. *Council on Undergraduate Research Quarterly, 36 (1)*, 19–24.

Alexander, B. B. & Herrera, O. L. (2002). *Engaging ethnic minority girls in science: An evaluation of the Girls Are G.R.E.A.T. science enrichment program.* Madison, WI: LEAD Center, University of Wisconsin-Madison. Retrieved August 15, 2008, from Wisconsin Center for Educational Research, School of Education, University of Wisconsin-Madison website, https://www.wcer.wisc.edu/publications/LEADcenter/grgeval.pdf.

Altbach, P. G. (2011). Patterns of higher education development. In P. G. Altbach, P. J. Gumport, & R. O. Berdahl (Eds.), *American higher education in the twenty-first century: Social, political, and economic challenges* (3rd ed.) (pp. 15–36). Baltimore, MD: Johns Hopkins University Press.

Ambos, E. (2012). Undergraduate and faculty researchers change themselves, their educational institutions… and CUR. *Council on Undergraduate Research Quarterly, 33 (1)*, 4–5.

Ambos, E. (2016). From CUR's Executive Officer. *Council on Undergraduate Research Quarterly, 36 (4)*, 2.

Ambos, E. L. & Rivera, J. (2015). From CUR's Executive Officer and Past President. *Council on Undergraduate Research Quarterly, 36 (2)*, 2–3.

American Chemical Society (ACS) (2016). *About the ACS Petroleum Research Fund.* Retrieved December 18, 2016, from http://www.acs.org/content/acs/en/funding-and-awards/grants/prf/about.html.

Anderson, M., Lyons, K., & Weiner, N. (2014). *The honors thesis: A handbook for deans, directors, and faculty advisors.* Lincoln, NE: National Collegiate Honors Council.

Anderson, M. A., Filer, K., & Lyon, J. S. (2012). Undergraduate research on UR leads to college-wide change. *Council on Undergraduate Research Quarterly, 33 (1)*, 8–12.

Archambault, C. (2008). Programs to look for. In Meredith (Ed.), *America's best colleges* (2009 ed.) (pp. 36–37). Washington, DC: U.S. News & World Report.

Armstrong, P. (2009). Incorporating undergraduate research into a seventeenth-century French literature seminar. In L. L. Behling (Ed.), *Reading, writing, research: Undergraduate students as scholars in literary studies* (pp. 92–99). Washington, DC: Council on Undergraduate Research.

Arum, R. & Roksa, J. (2011). *Academically adrift: Limited learning on college campuses.* Chicago, IL: University of Chicago Press.

Ash, S. L. & Clayton, P. H. (2004). Service-learning: Integrating inquiry and engagement. In V. S. Lee (Ed.), *Teaching & learning through inquiry: A guidebook for institutions & instructors* (pp. 229–242). Sterling, VA: Stylus.

Asher, P. (2001). Teaching an introductory geology course to a student with visual impairment. *Journal of Geoscience Education, 49,* 166–169.

Association of American Colleges and Universities (AAC&U) (n.d.). *Project Kaleidoscope (PKAL).* Retrieved December 23, 2016, from http://aacu.org/pkal.

Association of American Colleges and Universities (AAC&U) (2002). *Greater expectations: A new vision for learning as a nation goes to college.* Washington, DC: Author.

Astin, A. W. (1984). Student involvement: A developmental theory for higher education. *Journal of College Student Personnel, 25,* 297–308.

Astin, A. W. (1993). *What matters in college? Four critical years revisited.* San Francisco, CA: Jossey-Bass.

Austin, A. E. & Wulff, D. H. (2004). The challenge to prepare the next generation of faculty. In A. E. Austin & D. H. Wulff (Eds.), *Paths to the professoriate: Strategies for enriching the preparation of future faculty* (pp. 3–16). San Francisco, CA: Jossey-Bass.

Austin, C. G. (1986). Orientation to honors education. In P. G. Friedman & R. C. Jenkins-Friedman (Eds.), *Fostering academic excellence through honors programs* (pp. 5–16). New Directions for Teaching and Learning, n. 25. San Francisco, CA: Jossey-Bass.

Awong-Taylor, J., D'Costa, A., Giles, G., Leader, T., Pursell, D., Runk, C., & Mundie, T. (2016). Undergraduate research for all: Addressing the elephant in the room. *Council on Undergraduate Research Quarterly, 37 (1),* 11–19.

Bacchetti, R. & Ehrlich, T. (2007a). Foundations and education: Introduction. In R. Bacchetti & T. Ehrlich (Eds.), *Reconnecting education & foundations: Turning good intentions into educational capital* (pp. 3–20). San Francisco, CA: Jossey-Bass.

Bacchetti, R. & Ehrlich, T. (2007b). Recommendations: Building educational capital. In R. Bacchetti & T. Ehrlich (Eds.), *Reconnecting education & foundations: Turning good intentions into educational capital* (pp. 21–45). San Francisco, CA: Jossey-Bass.

Baldus, K. (2009). Empowering undergraduate research in the humanities: Negotiating the dynamics of individual research within academic communities. In L. L. Behling (Ed.), *Reading, writing, research: Undergraduate students as scholars in literary studies* (pp. 78–91). Washington, DC: Council on Undergraduate Research.

Baldwin, R. G. (1998). Technology's impact on faculty life and work. In K. H. Gillespie (Ed.), *The impact of technology on faculty development, life, and work* (pp. 7–21). New Directions for Teaching and Learning, n. 76. San Francisco, CA: Jossey-Bass.

Banta, T. W. (Ed.) (2003). *Portfolio assessment: Uses, cases, scoring, and impact.* San Francisco, CA: Jossey-Bass.

Barkin, G. (2016). Undergraduate research on short-term, faculty-led study abroad. *Council on Undergraduate Research Quarterly, 36 (4),* 26–32.

Barkley, E. F., Cross, K. P., & Major, C. H. (2005). *Cooperative learning techniques: A handbook for college faculty.* San Francisco, CA: Jossey-Bass.

Barlow, A. E. L. & Villarejo, M. (2004). Making a difference for minorities: Evaluation of an educational enrichment program. *Journal of Research in Science Teaching, 41,* 861–881.

Barnett, B. (1992, June 3). Teaching and research are inescapably incompatible. *The Chronicle of Higher Education,* A40.

Barratt, W. (2011). *Social class on campus: Theories and manifestations.* Sterling, VA: Stylus.

Barthell, J. F., Chen, W. R., Endicott, B. K., Hughes, C. A., Radke, W. J., Simmons, C. K., & Wilson, G. M. (2013). Encouraging and sustaining a culture of student-centered research at a predominantly undergraduate institution. *Council on Undergraduate Research Quarterly, 34 (1),* 41–47.

Bartkus, K. R. (2007). Fostering student/faculty collaborations through the "research group" model: An application to colleges and schools of business. *Council on Undergraduate Research Quarterly, 28 (2),* 6–10.

Bates, A. W. (2000). *Managing technological change: Strategies for college and university leaders.* San Francisco, CA: Jossey-Bass.

Bates, S. C., Rodriguez, M. D., & Drysdale, M. J. (2007). Supporting and encouraging behavioral research among distance education students. *Council on Undergraduate Research Quarterly, 28 (1),* 18–22.

Battistoni, R. M. (1997). Service learning and democratic citizenship. *Theory into Practice, 36,* 150–156.

Bauer, K. W. & Bennett, J. S. (2003). Alumni perceptions used to assess undergraduate research experience. *The Journal of Higher Education, 74,* 210–230.

Bauer, K. W. & Bennett, J. S. (2008). Evaluation of the undergraduate research program at the University of Delaware: A multifaceted design. In R. Taraban & R. L. Blanton (Eds.), *Creating effective undergraduate research programs in science: The transformation from student to scientist* (pp. 81–111). New York, NY: Teachers College Press.

Baum, S. (2010). Student work and the financial aid system. In L. W. Perna (Ed.), *Understanding the working college student: New research and its implications for policy and practice* (pp. 3–20). Sterling, VA: Stylus.

Bauman, G. L., Bustillos, L. T., Bensimon, E. M., Brown, M. C., & Bartee, R. D. (2005). *Achieving equitable educational outcomes with all students: The institution's roles and responsibilities.* Washington, DC: Association of American Colleges and Universities.

Baxter, Magolda, M. B. (1992). *Knowing and reasoning in college: Gender-related patterns in students' intellectual development.* San Francisco, CA: Jossey-Bass.

Baxter, Magolda, M. B. (1999). *Creating contexts for learning and self-authorship: Constructive-developmental pedagogy.* Nashville, TN: Vanderbilt University Press.

Baxter, Magolda, M. B. (2000). Teaching to promote holistic learning and development. In M. M. B. Baxter (Ed.), *Teaching to promote intellectual and personal maturity: Incorporating students' worldviews into the learning process* (pp. 88–98). New Directions for Teaching and Learning, n. 82. San Francisco, CA: Jossey-Bass.

Baxter, Magolda, M. B. (2004a). Self-authorship as the goal of 21st Century education. In M. M. B. Baxter & P. M. King (Eds.), *Learning partnerships: Theory and models of practice to educate for self-authorship* (pp. 1–35). Sterling, VA: Stylus.

Baxter, Magolda, M. B. (2004b). *Making their own way: Narratives for transforming higher education to promote self-development.* Sterling, VA: Stylus.

Bayliss, F. T., Peterfreund, A. R., & Rath, K. A. (2009). Institutional transformation: Establishing a commitment to research and student success. In M. K. Boyd & J. L. Wesemann (Eds.), *Broadening participation in undergraduate research: Fostering excellence and enhancing the impact* (pp. 281–294). Washington, DC: Council on Undergraduate Research.

Baynham, P. J. (2016). Fostering students' identity as scientists as they search for new antimicrobial drugs. *Council on Undergraduate Research Quarterly, 37 (2)*, 19–23.

Bean, J. C. (2011). *Engaging ideas: The professor's guide to integrating writing, critical thinking, and active learning in the classroom* (2nd ed.). San Francisco, CA: Jossey-Bass.

Becher, T. & Trowler, P. R. (2001). *Academic tribes and territories: Intellectual enquiry and the culture of disciplines* (2nd ed.). Philadelphia, PA: Society for Research into Higher Education & Open University Press.

Becker, K. (2005). Cutting-edge research by undergraduates on a shoestring? *Journal of Computing Sciences in Colleges, 21*, 160–168.

Beckman, M. & Hensel, N. (2009). Making explicit the implicit: Defining undergraduate research. *Council on Undergraduate Research Quarterly, 29 (4)*, 40–44.

Beere, C. A., Votruba, J. C., & Wells, G. W. (2011). *Becoming an engaged campus: A practical guide for institutionalizing public engagement*. San Francisco, CA: Jossey-Bass.

Behling, L. L. (Ed.) (2009a). *Reading, writing, research: Undergraduate students as scholars in literary studies*. Washington, DC: Council on Undergraduate Research.

Behling, L. L. (2009b). What I did on my summer vacation: Faculty-student collaborative research in literary and cultural studies. In L. L. Behling (Ed.), *Reading, writing, research: Undergraduate students as scholars in literary studies* (pp. 128–142). Washington, DC: Council on Undergraduate Research.

Beke, T. (2010). Undergraduate research is possible in math. *Council on Undergraduate Research Quarterly, 31 (1)*, 31.

Belenky, M. F., Clinchy, B. M., Goldberger, N. R., & Tarule, J. M. (1986). *Women's ways of knowing: The development of self, voice, and mind*. New York, NY: Basic.

Belkhir, J. A., Jack, L., Adaboye, D., Kambhampati, M., Johnson, C. P., Omar, A., Taylor, W. P., Das, S., Heath, P., Omojola, J., & Carey, A. (2002). Second SUNO undergraduate research day: Students' contributions at the Southern University at New Orleans. *Council on Undergraduate Research Quarterly, 23*, 30–31.

Bell, J. (2004). Facilitating creative activity and student involvement. *Council on Undergraduate Research Quarterly, 24*, 168.

Bendel, C. P. (2008). Computational mathematics: An opportunity for undergraduate research. *Council on Undergraduate Research Quarterly, 29 (1)*, 48–51.

Bender, C. (2007). It all began with a simple question…. *Council on Undergraduate Research Quarterly, 28*, 11–15.

Bender, C. (2012). Undergraduate research abroad. In J. Kinkead & L. Blockus (Eds.), *Undergraduate research offices and programs: Models & practices* (pp. 162–164). Washington, DC: Council on Undergraduate Research.

Bender, G. (2010). Undergraduate research in a foundations of architecture course. *Council on Undergraduate Research Quarterly, 31 (2)*, 40.

Beninson, L. A., Koski, J., Villa, E., Faram, R., & O'Connor, S. E. (2011). Evaluation of the Research Experiences for Undergraduates (REU) sites program. *Council on Undergraduate Research Quarterly, 32 (1)*, 43–48.

Bennett, J. M. (2008). On becoming a global soul: A path to engagement during study abroad. In V. Savicki (Ed.), *Developing intercultural competence and transformation: Theory, research, and application in international education* (pp. 13–31). Sterling, VA: Stylus.

Bernat, A., Teller, P. J., Gates, A., & Delgado, N. (2000). Structuring the student research experience. *ACM SIGCSE Bulletin, 32 (3)*, 17–20.

Best, A. A., DeJongh, M., Barton, A. J., Brown, J. R., & Barney, C. C. (2007). Models of interdisciplinary research and service learning at Hope College. *Council on Undergraduate Research Quarterly, 28 (2)*, 18–23.

Bettison-Varga, L. (2006). Creative activity and undergraduate research across the disciplines. *Peer Review, 8 (1)*, 19–21.

Biglan, A. (1973). The characteristics of subject matter in different academic areas. *Journal of Applied Psychology, 57*, 195–203.

Birkhead, W. S. & Stanton, G. E. (2011). Columbus State University's approach to undergraduate research in biology. *Council on Undergraduate Research Quarterly, 32 (1)*, 20–22.

Blackmer, J. (2008). The gesture of thinking: Collaborative models for undergraduate research in the arts and humanities—plenary presentation at the 2008 CUR National Conference. *Council on Undergraduate Research Quarterly, 29 (2)*, 8–12.

Blauth, J. R. & Schrum, D. P. (2005). Service learning and field research at the University of Redlands: Desert restoration in Joshua Tree National Park. *Council on Undergraduate Research Quarterly, 26*, 63–65.

Blockus, L. (2003). The growth of undergraduate research opportunities at a research university. *Council on Undergraduate Research Quarterly, 23*, 126–129.

Blockus, L. (2009). Opening a gateway to research for freshman and sophomore students: Providing opportunities and mentoring. In M. K. Boyd & J. L. Wesemann (Eds.), *Broadening participation in undergraduate research: Fostering excellence and enhancing the impact* (pp. 341–344). Washington, DC: Council on Undergraduate Research.

Blockus, L. (2012). The challenge of "the count." *Council on Undergraduate Research Quarterly, 32 (3)*, 4–8.

Blockus, L. & Wilson, A. (2012). Undergraduate research in locations external to campus. In J. Kinkead & L. Blockus (Eds.), *Undergraduate research offices and programs: Models & practices* (pp. 197–210). Washington, DC: Council on Undergraduate Research.

Bloom, B. S., Hastings, J. T., & Madaus, G. F. (1971). *Handbook on formative and summative evaluation of student learning.* New York, NY: McGraw-Hill.

Bok, D. (2006). *Our underachieving colleges: A candid look at how much students learn and why they should be learning more.* Princeton, NJ: Princeton University Press.

Bolek, C. & Forsythe, R. (2008). Funding: What you need to know about grant writing. *Council on Undergraduate Research Quarterly, 29 (1)*, 9–13.

Boone, C. K. (2003). Entering the community of scholars: Summer research at Denison. *Council on Undergraduate Research Quarterly, 23*, 113–115.

Borden, V. M. H. & Pike, G. R. (Eds.) (2007). *Assessing and accounting for student learning: Beyond the Spellings Commission.* New Directions for Institutional Research Assessment Supplement. San Francisco, CA: Jossey-Bass.

Boucquey, T. (2009). Published book at Scripps College spurs school district to mull new program. *Council on Undergraduate Research Quarterly, 29 (4)*, 33.

Boulden, R. M., Hall, G. J., Oches, E. A., Szymanski, D. W., & Ledley, F. D. (2015). Connecting business and STEM education through undergraduate research. *Council on Undergraduate Research Quarterly, 35 (4)*, 17–23.

Bowen, H. R. & Schuster, J. H. (1986). *American professors: A national resource imperiled.* New York, NY: Oxford University Press.

Boyce, C. A. (1997). Increasing graduate studies interest and admissions among [sic] African-American undergraduates: A role for graduate students. In H. T. Frierson, Jr. (Ed.), *Mentoring and diversity in higher education* (pp. 93–102). Diversity in Higher Education, v. 1. Greenwich, CT: JAI.

Boyd, M. K. & Wesemann, J. L. (Eds.) (2009). *Broadening participation in undergraduate research: Fostering excellence and enhancing the impact.* Washington, DC: Council on Undergraduate Research.

Boyer, E. L. (1987). *College: The undergraduate experience in America*. New York, NY: Harper & Row.

Boyer, E. L. (1990). *Scholarship reconsidered: Priorities of the professoriate*. San Francisco, CA: Jossey-Bass.

Boyer Commission on Educating Undergraduates in the Research University (1998). *Reinventing undergraduate education: A blueprint for American research universities*. Retrieved December 27, 2003, from http://naples.cc.sunysb.edu/Pres/boyer.nsf/673918d46fbf65 3e852565ec0056ff3e/d955b61ffddd590a852565ec005717ae/$FILE/boyer.pdf.

Boyer Commission on Educating Undergraduates in the Research University (2001). *Reinventing undergraduate education: Three years after the Boyer report*. Retrieved October 30, 2003, from http://www.sunysb.edu/pres/0210066-Boyer%20Report%20Final.pdf.

Brakke, D. F., Crowe, M. L., & Karukstis, K. (2009). Perspective: Reasons deans and provosts (and presidents) should value, support, and encourage undergraduate research. *Council on Undergraduate Research Quarterly, 30 (1)*, 10–14.

Brandenberger, J. R. (2013). Teaching innovation through undergraduate research. *Council on Undergraduate Research Quarterly, 34 (1)*, 18–23.

Brandon, C. (2010). *The five-year party: How colleges have given up on educating your child and what you can do about it*. Dallas, TX: BenBella.

Brandt, L. S. E. & Hayes, J. L. (2012). Broader impacts of undergraduate research at a community college: Opening doors to new ideas. *Council on Undergraduate Research Quarterly, 33 (1)*, 17–21.

Braxton, J. M. (1995). Disciplines with an affinity for the improvement of undergraduate education. In N. Hativa & M. Marincovich (Eds.), *Disciplinary differences in teaching and learning: Implications for practice* (pp. 59–64). New Directions for Teaching and Learning, no, 64. San Francisco, CA: Jossey-Bass.

Braxton, J. M., Luckey, W., & Helland, P. (2002). *Institutionalizing a broader view of scholarship through Boyer's four domains*. ASHE-ERIC Higher Education Report v. 29, n. 2. San Francisco, CA: Jossey-Bass.

Brew, A. (2006). *Research and teaching: Beyond the divide*. New York, NY: Palgrave Macmillan.

Bringle, R. G. & Hatcher, J. A. (2011). International service learning. In R. G. Bringle, J. A. Hatcher, & S. G. Jones (Eds.), *International service learning: Conceptual frameworks and research* (pp. 3–28). Sterling, VA: Stylus.

British Conference of Undergraduate Research (BCUR)(2010a). *About BCUR*. Retrieved July 2, 2016, from http://www.bcur.org/about/.

British Conference of Undergraduate Research (BCUR) (2010b). *Posters in Parliament*. Retrieved July 2, 2016, from http://www.bcur.org/about/posters-in-parliment/.

Brothers, M. & Higgins, T. (2008). Research models that engage community college students. *Council on Undergraduate Research Quarterly, 29 (1)*, 12–17.

Brown, D. R., Higgins, T. B., & Coggins, P. (2007). The increasing presence of undergraduate research in two-year colleges. *Council on Undergraduate Research Quarterly, 28 (2)*, 24–28.

Brown, D. R. & Tyner, K. L. (2009). Leading the way: Creating an institutional culture of undergraduate research. In M. K. Boyd & J. L. Wesemann (Eds.), *Broadening participation in undergraduate research: Fostering excellence and enhancing the impact* (pp. 230–233). Washington, DC: Council on Undergraduate Research.

Brown, D. & Yurekli, O. (2007). Undergraduate research in mathematics as a curricular option. *International Journal of Mathematical Education, 38*, 571–580.

Brown, K. & Broido, E. M. (2015). Engaging students with disabilities. In S. J. Quaye & S. R. Harper (Eds.), *Student engagement in higher education: Theoretical perspectives and practical approaches for diverse populations* (2nd ed.) (pp. 187–207). New York, NY: Routledge.

Brown, M. (2009). Research and reflection: Teaching literary theory and writing to undergraduates. In L. L. Behling (Ed.), *Reading, writing, research: Undergraduate students as scholars in literary studies* (pp. 100–111). Washington, DC: Council on Undergraduate Research.

Brown, P. C. & Morrison, A. (2009). Redevelopment: A case study at Mercer University. *Council on Undergraduate Research Quarterly, 29 (4)*, 14–17.

Brownell, J. E. & Swaner, L. E. (2010). *Five high-impact practices: Research on learning outcomes, completion, and quality.* Washington, DC: Association of American Colleges and Universities.

Bruffee, K. A. (1995). Sharing our toys: Cooperative learning versus collaborative learning. *Change, 27 (1)*, 12–18.

Bruffee, K. A. (1999). *Collaborative learning: Higher education, interdependence, and the authority of knowledge* (2nd ed.). Baltimore, MD: Johns Hopkins University Press.

Bruner, J. S. (1960). *The process of education.* Cambridge, MA: Harvard University Press.

Bruner, J. S. (1973). The act of discovery. In J. S. Bruner, *Beyond the information given: Studies in the psychology of knowing.* New York, NY: Norton. (Original work published 1961)

Bruno, B. C., Thomas, S., James, L., & Frazier, M. (2011). Student perspectives on facilitating positive undergraduate research experiences. *Council on Undergraduate Research Quarterly, 32 (2)*, 37–40.

Brush, E., Cox, M., Harris, A., & Torda, L. (2010). Undergraduate research as faculty development. *Council on Undergraduate Research Quarterly, 31 (1)*, 11–16.

Building Engineering & Science Talent (BEST) (2004). *A bridge for all: Higher education design principles to broaden participation in science, technology, engineering, and mathematics.* San Diego, CA: Author. Retrieved July 3, 2009, from the Building Engineering & Science Talent website, http://bestworkforce.org/PDFdocs/BEST_BridgeforAll_High EdFINAL.pdf.

Burke, J. C. & Associates (2005). *Achieving accountability in higher education: Balancing public, academic, and market demands.* San Francisco, CA: Jossey-Bass.

Burke, J. D. (1996). What companies do in support of undergraduate research. *Council on Undergraduate Research Quarterly, 16*, 200–202.

Butler, D. L. (2002). Individualizing instruction in self-regulated learning. *Theory into Practice, 41*, 81–92.

Caldwell, B. D. (2007). An alternative research model of faculty, undergraduate, and high school student collaboration. *Council on Undergraduate Research Quarterly, 28 (2)*, 29–34.

California Distance Learning Project (2005). *What is distance learning?* Retrieved August 23, 2011, from http://www.cdlponline.org/index.cfm?fuseaction=whatis&pg=2.

Camille & Henry Dreyfus Foundation, Inc. (n.d.). *Overview.* Retrieved December 18, 2016 from http://www.dreyfus.org/awards/overview_and_programs.shtml.

Campbell, A. & Skoog, G. (2004). Preparing undergraduate women for science careers: Facilitating success in professional research. *Journal of College Science Teaching, 33 (5)*, 24–26.

Campbell, B. (2011). From the CUR President. *Council on Undergraduate Research Quarterly, 32 (1)*, 2–3.

Campbell, B. (2012). From the CUR President. *Council on Undergraduate Research Quarterly, 32 (3)*, 2–3.

Cantor, J. A. (1995). *Experiential learning in higher education: Linking classroom and community.* ASHE-ERIC Higher Education Report No. 7. Washington, DC: The George Washington University, Graduate School of Education and Human Development.

Caristi, J. & Gillman, R. A. (2002). Engaging first-year students in mathematical research. *Council on Undergraduate Research Quarterly, 23*, 95–98.

Carnegie Foundation for the Advancement of Teaching (2006a). *Institution lookup.* Retrieved July 27, 2006, and June 27, 2007, from http://www.carnegiefoundation. org/classifications/index.asp?key=782.

Carnegie Foundation for the Advancement of Teaching (2006b). *Basic classification description.* Retrieved July 27, 2006, and June 28, 2007, from http://www.carnegiefoundation. org/classifications/index.asp?key=791.

Carnegie Foundation for the Advancement of Teaching (2010a). *Institution lookup.* Retrieved August 1, 2013, from http://classifications.carnegiefoundation.org/lookup_ listings/institution.php.

Carnegie Foundation for the Advancement of Teaching (2010b). *Classification description.* Retrieved August 1, 2013, from http://classifications.carnegiefoundation.org/descriptions/basic.php.

Carney, M. J. (2006). Polymerization catalyst development: Collaborative research with Chevron Phillips Chemical Company. *Council on Undergraduate Research Quarterly, 27 (1)*, 22–26.

Carr, K. S., Davis, S. D., Erbes, S., Fulmer, C. M., Kats, L. B., & Teetzel, M. U. (2013). Developing first-year students as scholars. *Council on Undergraduate Research Quarterly, 33 (4)*, 8–15.

Carter, D., Fox, L., Priest, T., & McBride, F. (2002). Student involvement in community-based research. *Metropolitan Universities, 13*, 56–63.

Carter, O. (2011). Fueling a future beyond the coal mines. *Council on Undergraduate Research Quarterly, 31 (3)*, 23–28.

Castley, A. J. (2006). Professional development support to promote stronger teaching and research links. In C. Kreber (Ed.), *Exploring research-based teaching* (pp. 23–31). New Directions for Teaching and Learning, n. 107. San Francisco: Jossey-Bass.

Cebe, P. (2009). Taking a team approach in an internship program for deaf and hard-of-hearing undergraduate students. In M. K. Boyd & J. L. Wesemann (Eds.), *Broadening participation in undergraduate research: Fostering excellence and enhancing the impact* (pp. 215–218). Washington, DC: Council on Undergraduate Research.

Cejda, B. D. & Hensel, N. (2008). Undergraduate research in community colleges: A summary of the CUR/NCIA conversations. *Council on Undergraduate Research Quarterly, 29 (1)*, 7–11.

Cejda, B. D. & Hensel, N. (Eds.) (2009). *Undergraduate research at community colleges.* Washington, DC: Council on Undergraduate Research.

Center for Engaged Learning (2016, July 27). *George Kuh on ePortfolio as high-impact practice.* Retrieved December 30, 2016, from https://www.youtube.com/watch?v=5r9WuHB_ Yo0&feature=youtu.be.

Cerrito, P. B. (2008). Classroom research for undergraduate mathematics majors and general education students. *Council on Undergraduate Research Quarterly, 29 (1)*, 52–57.

Cetkovic-Cvrlje, M., Ramakrishnan, L., Dasgupta, S., Branam, K., & Subrahmanyan, L. (2013). A multi-disciplinary analysis of intensive undergraduate research. *Council on Undergraduate Research Quarterly, 33 (4)*, 16–22.

Chamely-Wiik, D., Dunn, K., Heydet-Kirsch, P., Holman, M., Meeroff, D., & Peluso, J. (2014). Scaffolding the development of students' research skills for capstone experiences: A multi-disciplinary approach. *Council on Undergraduate Research Quarterly, 34 (4)*, 18–25.

Chapdelaine, A. (2012). Including undergraduate research in faculty promotion and tenure policies. In N. H. Hensel & E. L. Paul (Eds.), *Faculty support and undergraduate research:*

Innovations in faculty role definition, workload, and reward (pp. 115–132). Washington, DC: Council on Undergraduate Research.

Chapdelaine, A. & Chapman, B. L. (1999). Using community-based research projects to teach research methods. *Teaching of Psychology, 26,* 101–105.

Chaplin, S. B., Manske, J. M., & Cruise, J. L. (1998). Introducing freshmen to investigative research—a course for biology majors at Minnesota's University of St. Thomas. *Journal of College Science, 27,* 347–350.

Cheatham, T., Friedli, A., Robertson, W., & Rowell, G. H. (2005). Planning, securing, and jumpstarting an NSF-STEP grant. *Council on Undergraduate Research Quarterly, 26 (1),* 22–26.

Cheong, S. & Willis, S. (2015). Integrating research and education: Undergraduate field work in geography. *Council on Undergraduate Research Quarterly, 36 (1),* 40–45.

Cherry, G. (2001). Research day for regional universities: Highlighting research in predominantly undergraduate institutions. *Council on Undergraduate Research Quarterly, 21,* 130–132.

Chiang, T. (2007). Utilizing a senior capstone research course to promote undergraduate research. In K. K. Karukstis & T. E. Elgren (Eds.), *Developing and sustaining a research-supportive curriculum: A compendium of successful practices* (pp. 240–241). Washington, DC: Council on Undergraduate Research.

Chiang, T. (2016). Undergraduate researchers partner with local Head Start programs. *Council on Undergraduate Research Quarterly, 36 (4),* 45.

Chickering, A. W. & Gamson, Z. F. (1987). Seven principles for good practice in undergraduate education. *AAHE Bulletin, 39 (7),* 3–7.

Chickering, A. W. & Reisser, L. (1993). *Education and identity* (2nd ed.). San Francisco, CA: Jossey-Bass.

Childress, H. (2015). The outcomes are the outcomes: Making sure we assess what we actually care about. *Council on Undergraduate Research Quarterly, 35 (3),* 6–8.

Chin, J. (2004). Most common questions about NIH-AREA grant applications. *Council on Undergraduate Research Quarterly, 24,* 111–119.

Chmielewski, J. G. (2007). Undergraduate research: Our institutional goal. In K. K. Karukstis & T. E. Elgren (Eds.), *Developing and sustaining a research-supportive curriculum: A compendium of successful practices* (pp. 587–589). Washington, DC: Council on Undergraduate Research.

Chodorow, N. (1978). *The reproduction of mothering: Psychoanalysis and the sociology of gender.* Berkeley, CA: University of California Press.

Chubin, D. E. & Ward, W. E. (2009). Building on the BEST principles and evidence: A framework for broadening participation. In M. K. Boyd & J. L. Wesemann (Eds.), *Broadening participation in undergraduate research: Fostering excellence and enhancing the impact* (pp. 21–30). Washington, DC: Council on Undergraduate Research.

Clawson, D. & Page, M. (2011). *The future of higher education.* New York, NY: Routledge.

Clayton-Pedersen, A. & Musil, C. M. (2005). Introduction to the series. In D. A. Williams, J. B. Berger, & S. A. McClendon (Eds.), *Toward a model of inclusive excellence and change in postsecondary institutions* (pp. iii–ix). Washington, DC: Association of American Colleges and Universities.

Clear, T., Goldweber, M., Young, F. H., Leidig, P. M., & Scott, K. (2001). Resources for instructors of capstone courses in computing. *ACM SIGCSE Bulletin, 33 (4),* 93–113.

Cobb, J. P. (1995). Looking ahead. *Council on Undergraduate Research Quarterly, 16,* 19–23.

Coggins, P. (2009). Linking research and learning: A journey of discovery and creativity. In M. K. Boyd & J. L. Wesemann (Eds.), *Broadening participation in undergraduate research:*

Fostering excellence and enhancing the impact (pp. 101–107). Washington, DC: Council on Undergraduate Research.

Cohen, A. M. & Kisker, C. B. (2010). *The shaping of American higher education: Emergence and growth of the contemporary system* (2nd ed.). San Francisco, CA: Jossey-Bass.

Colbeck, C. L. (2008). Professional identity development theory and doctoral education. In C. L. Colbeck, K. A. O'Meara, & A. E. Austin (Eds.), *Educating integrated professionals: Theory and practice on preparation for the professoriate* (pp. 9–16). New Directions for Teaching and Learning, n. 113. San Francisco, CA: Jossey-Bass.

Coleman, J. (2005). Undergraduate research participation as an essential component of a research university: A perspective of a chief research officer. *Council on Undergraduate Research Quarterly, 25,* 154–155.

College Student Experiences Questionnaire (CSEQ) Assessment Program (2007). *CSEQ and CSXQ survey operations closed in 2014.* Retrieved December 19, 2016, from http://cseq.indiana.edu/cseq_closeInfo.cfm.

Conliffe, M. (2014). Turning unexpected resources into undergraduate research in the humanities. *Council on Undergraduate Research Quarterly, 35 (1),* 43–47.

Conrad, C. & Dunek, L. (2012). *Cultivating inquiry-driven learners: A college education for the 21st century.* Baltimore, MD: Johns Hopkins University Press.

Conrad, R. & Donaldson, J. A. (2011). *Engaging the online learner: Activities and resources for creative instruction* (updated ed.). San Francisco, CA: Jossey-Bass.

Conway, P., Hanson, B., Wages, J., Gonnella, T., Super, H., Sens, D., Doze, V., Cisek, K., & Boeckel, J. (2012). Recruiting students into science: Evaluating the impact of the North Dakota IDeA Network of Biomedical Research Excellence. *Council on Undergraduate Research Quarterly, 32 (3),* 34–39.

Cook, J. A. & McCauley, A. M. (2003). Summer research at Albion College: The impact of the Foundation for Undergraduate Research, Scholarship, and Creative Activity. *Council on Undergraduate Research Quarterly, 23,* 121–125.

Cook, M. & Kelly, S. Q. (2013). Connecting the dots: Web 3.0 and interdisciplinary freshman research. *Council on Undergraduate Research Quarterly, 34 (2),* 8–16.

Cooke, D. & Thorme, T. (2011). *A practical handbook for supporting community-based research with undergraduate students.* Washington, DC: Council on Undergraduate Research.

Cook-Sather, A., Bovill, C., & Felten, P. (2014). *Engaging students as partners in learning and teaching: A guide for faculty.* San Francisco, CA: Jossey-Bass.

Cory, R. C. (2011). Disability services offices for students with disabilities: A campus resource. In W. S. Harbour & J. W. Madaus (Eds.), *Disability services and campus dynamics* (pp. 27–36). New Directions for Higher Education, n. 154. San Francisco, CA: Jossey-Bass.

Council for the Advancement of Standards in Higher Education (CAS) (2009). *CAS professional standards for higher education* (7th ed.). Washington, DC: Author.

Council for the Advancement of Standards in Higher Education (CAS) (2016a). *Thirty-five years of CAS.* Retrieved December 15, 2016, from http://www.cas.edu/history.

Council for the Advancement of Standards in Higher Education (CAS) (2016b). *Standards.* Retrieved July 22, 2015, from http://www.cas.edu/standards.

Council on Undergraduate Research (CUR) (n.d.). *Institutional members.* Retrieved July 27, 2006, from http://www.cur.org/instmem.asp.

Council on Undergraduate Research (CUR) (2009). *CUR Timeline.* Retrieved December 15, 2016, from http://www.cur.org/about_cur/history/timeline/.

Council on Undergraduate Research (CUR) (2009, August). Council on Undergraduate Research (CUR) and National Conferences on Undergraduate Research (NCUR).

CUR E-News. Retrieved August 5, 2009, from http://www.cur.org/newsletter/news-letter080309.html.

Council on Undergraduate Research (CUR) (2015, September 17). *CUR E-newsletter*. Retrieved September 7, 2016, from http://www.multibriefs.com/briefs/CUR/CUR 091715.php.

Council on Undergraduate Research (CUR) (2015, December 31). *Constitution & bylaws*. Retrieved December 15, 2016, from http://www.cur.org/about_cur/constitution_and_bylaws/.

Council on Undergraduate Research (CUR) (2016a). *About CUR*. Retrieved December 15, 2016, from http://www.cur.org/about_cur/.

Council on Undergraduate Research (CUR)(2016b). *What is NCUR?* Retrieved December 15, 2016, from http://www.cur.org/conferences_and_events/student_events/ncur/.

Council on Undergraduate Research (CUR) (2016c). *NCUR for faculty and administrators*. Retrieved December 15, 2016, from http://www.cur.org/conferences_and_events/student_events/ncur/faculty/.

Council on Undergraduate Research (CUR) (2016d). *Posters on the hill*. Retrieved December 15, 2016, from http://www.cur.org/conferences_and_events/student_events/posters_on_the_hill/.

Council on Undergraduate Research (CUR) (2016e). *Advocacy advisory committee*. Retrieved December 15, 2016, from http://www.cur.org/governance/committees/advocacy_advisory_committee/.

Council on Undergraduate Research (CUR) (2016f). *World Congress on Undergraduate Research*. Retrieved July 2, 2016, from http://www.cur.org/world_congress/.

Coyne, R. (2004). NSF's RUI program: Perspectives from the inside. *Council on Undergraduate Research Quarterly, 25*, 62–66.

Crampton, S. B. (2001). Questions from the past for the future. In *Academic excellence: The sourcebook: A study of the role of research in the natural sciences at undergraduate institutions* (pp. 59–63). Tucson, AZ: Research Corporation.

Craney, C. & Dea, P. (2003). Connecting to neighboring community colleges through NSF-REU site grants. *Council on Undergraduate Research Quarterly, 23*, 169–171.

Crawford, I., Garg, S., & Neuhoff, J. (2008). Undergraduate research as faculty development: The College of Wooster experience. *Council on Undergraduate Research Quarterly, 29 (1)*, 14–17.

Crawford, I., Huston-Findley, S., Mowrey, P., & Zurko, K. M. (2011). Undergraduate research in the fine arts at The College of Wooster. In N. Y. Klos, J. O. Shanahan, & G. Young (Eds.), *Creative inquiry in the arts & humanities: Models of undergraduate research* (pp. 23–32). Washington, DC: Council on Undergraduate Research.

Crawford, I., Orel, S. E., & Shanahan, J. O. (Eds.) (2014). *How to get started in arts and humanities research with undergraduates*. Washington, DC: Council on Undergraduate Research.

Creamer, E. G. (2005). Insight from multiple disciplinary angles: A case study of an interdisciplinary research team. In E. G. Creamer & L. R. Lattuca (Eds.), *Advancing faculty learning through interdisciplinary collaboration* (pp. 37–44). New Directions for Teaching and Learning, n. 102. San Francisco, CA: Jossey-Bass.

Cronin, D. B. (2009). The role of undergraduate research in federal public policy. *Council on Undergraduate Research Quarterly, 29 (4)*, 10–13.

Cronin, D. B. & Busch, A. (2012). The voice of undergraduate research on Capitol Hill. *Council on Undergraduate Research Quarterly, 33 (2)*, 7.

Cronin, D. B. & Busch, A. (2013). Special feature: How the flawed federal budgeting process damages the national undergraduate research agenda. *Council on Undergraduate Research Quarterly, 34 (2)*, 7.

Crowe, M. (2007). The role of campus-wide undergraduate research centers in supporting a research-rich curriculum. In K. K. Karukstis & T. E. Elgren (Eds.), *Developing & sustaining a research-supportive curriculum: A compendium of successful practices* (pp. 495–505). Washington, DC: Council on Undergraduate Research.

Crowe, M. (2012). From CUR's President. *Council on Undergraduate Research Quarterly, 33 (2)*, 2–3.

Crowe, M. & Sienerth, K. (2006). Budgeting for a centralized office of undergraduate research. *Council on Undergraduate Research Quarterly, 27*, 54–60.

Cuban, L. (1999). *How scholars trumped teachers: Change without reform in university curriculum, teaching, and research, 1890–1990.* New York, NY: Teachers College Press.

Cunningham, B., Gaffield, G., Halpern, A., & Rackoff, J. (2001). Starting an institutional review board at a PUI. *Council on Undergraduate Research Quarterly, 22*, 57–60.

Cunningham, B. A. & Murray, J. L. (2002, June). *Undergraduate research across the disciplines.* Presentation conducted at the Council on Undergraduate Research National Conference, New London, CT.

Curley, M. & Schloenhardt, A. (2014). Undergraduate research and human rights: An Australian case study on human trafficking and migrant smuggling. *Council on Undergraduate Research Quarterly, 34 (3)*, 24–29.

Dahlberg, T., Barnes, T., Rorrer, A., Powell, E., & Cairco, L. (2008). Improving retention and graduate recruitment through immersive research experiences for undergraduates. *ACM SIGCSE Bulletin, 40 (1)*, 466–470.

Daloz, L. A. (1999). *Mentor: Guiding the journey of adult learners.* San Francisco, CA: Jossey-Bass.

Daugherty, B. (2012). The debt threat. *Currents, 38 (7)*, 40–43.

Daughtry, D., Gibson, J., & Abels, A. (2009). Mentoring students and professionals with disabilities. *Professional Psychology: Research and Practice, 40 (2)*, 201–205.

Daves, G. D., Jr. (2002). The national context for reform. In J. L. Narum & K. Conover (Eds.), *Building robust learning environments in undergraduate science, technology, engineering, and mathematics* (pp. 9–14). New Directions for Higher Education, n. 119. San Francisco, CA: Jossey-Bass.

Davis, L. E. & Eves, R. L. (2005). The natural history of a modern carbonate ecosystem: Field studies that integrate undergraduate research. *Council on Undergraduate Research Quarterly, 25*, 175–179.

Dean, J. M. & Kaiser, M. L. (2010). Faculty-student collaborative research in the humanities. *Council on Undergraduate Research Quarterly, 30 (3)*, 43–47.

DeAngelo, L. & Hasson, T. (2009). Quantifying success: Using control groups to measure program effectiveness. *Council on Undergraduate Research Quarterly, 29 (3)*, 39–45.

Deardorff, D. K. (2008). Intercultural competence: A definition, model, and implications for education abroad. In V. Savicki (Ed.), *Developing intercultural competence and transformation: Theory, research, and application in international education* (pp. 32–52). Sterling, VA: Stylus.

DeCosmo, J. (Ed.) (2014). From the CURQ issue editor. *Council on Undergraduate Research Quarterly, 35 (2)*, 5.

DeCosmo, J. (2015). Undergraduate research and the professional schools. *Council on Undergraduate Research Quarterly, 35 (4)*, 4–5.

DeCosmo, J. (Ed.) (2016). From the CURQ issue editor. *Council on Undergraduate Research Quarterly, 37 (2)*, 3.

DeCosmo, J. & Gould, L. (Eds.) (2015). *Council on Undergraduate Research Quarterly, 36 (1)*.

Dehn, P. F. (2009). Community health-based internships as an entry into research. In M. K. Boyd & J. L. Wesemann (Eds.), *Broadening participation in undergraduate research: Fostering excellence and enhancing the impact* (pp. 334–336). Washington, DC: Council on Undergraduate Research.

Dehn, P. F. (2010). Responsible conduct of research: Administrative issues concerning research integrity and compliance. *Council on Undergraduate Research Quarterly, 30 (3)*, 27–34.

Deicke, W., Gess, C., & RueB, J. (2014). Increasing students' research interests through research-based learning at Humboldt University. *Council on Undergraduate Research Quarterly, 35 (1)*, 27–33.

Delanty, G. (2002). The university and modernity: A history of the present. In K. Robins & F. Webster (Eds.), *The virtual university? Knowledge, markets, and management* (pp. 31–48). New York, NY: Oxford University Press.

van Delden, S. (2012). A circular model for framing the undergraduate research experience. *Council on Undergraduate Research Quarterly, 33 (1)*, 40–47.

DelliCarpini, D. & Crimmins, C. (2010). The writing center as a space for undergraduate research. In L. Grobman & J. Kinkead (Eds.), *Undergraduate research in English studies* (pp. 191–211). Urbana, IL: National Council of Teachers of English.

Dellinger, M. A. (2009). Endless possibilities: Undergraduate research in a second language. *Council on Undergraduate Research Quarterly, 29 (4)*, 34–39.

Dellinger, M. A. & Walkington, H. (2012). The curriculum and beyond. In D. A. Hart (Ed.), *How to start an undergraduate research journal* (pp. 24–33). Washington, DC: Council on Undergraduate Research.

Dennis, M. (2012). The impact of MOOCs on higher education. *College & University, 88 (2)*, 24–30.

Detweiler-Bedell, J. & Detweiler-Bedell, B. (2007). Transforming undergraduates into skilled researchers using laddered teams. In K. K. Karukstis & T. E. Elgren (Eds.), *Developing and sustaining a research-supportive curriculum: A compendium of successful practices* (pp. 402–406). Washington, DC: Council on Undergraduate Research.

DeVries, D. N. (2001). Undergraduate research in the humanities: An oxymoron? *Council on Undergraduate Research Quarterly, 21*, 153–155.

Dewey, J. (1963). *Experience and education*. New York, NY: Collier. (Original work published 1938)

Diamond, R. M. & Adam, B. E. (Eds.) (1995). *The disciplines speak: Rewarding the scholarly, professional, and creative work of faculty*. Washington, DC: American Association for Higher Education.

Diamond, R. M. & Adam, B. E. (Eds.) (2000). *The disciplines speak II: More statements on rewarding the scholarly, professional, and creative work of faculty*. Washington, DC: American Association for Higher Education.

Dietrich, G. (2014). Technology access: An institutional responsibility. In M. L. Vance, N. E. Lipsitz, & K. Parks (Eds.), *Beyond the Americans with Disabilities Act: Inclusive policy and practice for higher education* (pp. 69–82). Washington, DC: NASPA.

Divine, R. A. (1993). *The Sputnik challenge*. New York, NY: Oxford University Press.

Dolan, T. (2011). One program, three pathways to success. *Council on Undergraduate Research Quarterly, 32 (1)*, 35.

Donald, J. G. (2002). *Learning to think: Disciplinary perspectives*. San Francisco. CA: Jossey-Bass.

Dowling, C. B. & Hannigan, R. E. (2009). Developing cohorts, fostering retention, and nurturing careers. In M. K. Boyd & J. L. Wesemann (Eds.), *Broadening participation in undergraduate research: Fostering excellence and enhancing the impact* (pp. 219–222). Washington, DC: Council on Undergraduate Research.

Downs, D. & Wardle, E. (2010). What can a novice contribute? Undergraduate researchers in first-year composition. In L. Grobman & J. Kinkead (Eds.), *Undergraduate research in English studies* (pp. 173–190). Urbana, IL: National Council of Teachers of English.

Dressel, P. D. & Marcus, D. (1982). *On teaching and learning in college: Reemphasizing the roles of learners and the disciplines.* San Francisco, CA: Jossey-Bass.

Dressel, P. L. & Thompson, M. M. (1973). *Independent study.* San Francisco, CA: Jossey-Bass.

D'Souza, M., Dwyer, P., Allison, B., Miller, J., & Drohan, J. (2011). Wesley College ignites potential with undergraduate research program. *Council on Undergraduate Research Quarterly, 32 (2),* 41–45.

Durso, F. T. (1997). Corporate-sponsored undergraduate research as a capstone experience. *Teaching of Psychology, 24 (1),* 54–56.

Eagan, M. K., Stolzenberg, E. B., Ramirez, J. J., Aragon, M. C., Suchard, M. R., & Rios-Aguilar, C. (2016). *The American freshman: Fifty-year trends, 1966–2015.* Los Angeles, CA: Higher Education Research Institute, UCLA.

Eckdahl, T. T., Poet, J. L., Campbell, A. M., & Heyer, L. J. (2009). Synthetic biology as a new opportunity for multidisciplinary undergraduate research. *Council on Undergraduate Research Quarterly, 30 (2),* 39–44.

Eddins, S. G. N., Williams, D. F., Bushek, D., Porter, D. & Kineke, G. (1997). Searching for a prominent role of research in undergraduate education: Project Interface. *Journal on Excellence in College Teaching, 8 (1),* 69–81.

Edgcomb, M. R., Crowe, H. A., Rice, J. D., Morris, S. J., Wolffe, R. J., & McConnaughay, K. D. (2010). Peer and near-peer mentoring: Enhancing learning in summer research programs. *Council on Undergraduate Research Quarterly, 31 (2),* 18–25.

Edwards, N. & Hogarth, C. (2008). Using short-term study abroad to further undergraduate research. *Council on Undergraduate Research Quarterly, 29 (2),* 14–17.

Egger, A. E. & Klemperer, S. L. (2011). Recruiting undergraduates into the earth sciences through research. *Council on Undergraduate Research Quarterly, 32 (2),* 22–31.

Einstein, G. (2003). *Undergraduate Research at Furman and Beyond.* Retrieved November 30, 2003, from http://www.furman.edu/engaged/research-einstein.html.

Elgren, T. E., Billiter, W. J., & Paris, D. C. (2007). Using institutional funds to promote undergraduate research across the college: A strategic initiative. In K. K. Karukstis & T. E. Elgren (Eds.), *Developing and sustaining a research-supportive curriculum: A compendium of successful practices* (pp. 591–594). Washington, DC: Council on Undergraduate Research.

Elgren, T. & Hensel, N. (2006). Undergraduate research experiences: Synergies between scholarship and teaching. *Peer Review, 8 (1),* 4–7.

Enhancing research in the chemical sciences at predominantly undergraduate institutions (2003, August). A report from the Undergraduate Research Summit, Lewiston, ME.

Epigeum (n.d.). *About Epigeum.* Retrieved September 18, 2016, from https://www.epigeum.com/epigeum/.

Erbes, S. (2008). Interdisciplinary efforts used to assess research experiences for undergraduates. *Council on Undergraduate Research Quarterly, 29 (2),* 34–42.

Erikson, E. K. (1968). Life cycle. In D. L. Sills (Ed.), *International encyclopedia of the social sciences* (pp. 286–292). New York, NY: Macmillan.

Etaugh, C. & Liberty, S. (2001). Building a foundation for institution-wide student-faculty collaboration in research and creative production: What role can accreditation play? *Council on Undergraduate Research Quarterly, 21,* 122–125.

Etzkowitz, H., Kemelgor, C., & Uzzi, B. (2000). *Athena unbound: The advancement of women in science and technology.* New York, NY: Cambridge University Press.

Evanseck, J. D., Gawalt, E. S., Huisso, A., Madura, J. D., Nunes, S. S., Oki, R. R., Seybert, D. W., & Venkatraman, R. (2009). Optimizing research productivity while maintaining educational excellence: A collaborative endeavor. In M. K. Boyd & J. L. Wesemann (Eds.), *Broadening participation in undergraduate research: Fostering excellence and enhancing the impact* (pp. 65–76). Washington, DC: Council on Undergraduate Research.

Fairweather, J. S. (1996). *Faculty work and public trust: Restoring the value of teaching and public service in American academic life.* Boston, MA: Allyn and Bacon.

Falbo-Kenkel, M. (1997). From conceptual physics to senior research: Building a research community using technology. *Council on Undergraduate Research Quarterly, 18,* 24–25, 47–48.

Feldman, K. A. & Newcomb, T. M. (1994). *The impact of college on students.* New Brunswick, NJ: Transaction. (Original work published 1969)

Felix, A. & Zovinka, E. P. (2008). One STEP: Enhancing student retention through early introduction of research for STEM majors. *Council on Undergraduate Research Quarterly, 29 (1),* 30–35.

Fink, L. D. (2003). *Creating significant learning experiences: An integrated approach to designing college courses.* San Francisco, CA: Jossey-Bass.

Firmage, D. H., Tietenberg, T. H., & Cole, F. R. (2005). Research-based learning in an introductory environmental studies course. *Council on Undergraduate Research Quarterly, 25,* 191–200.

Fitzgerald, N. (2015). Crowdfunding undergraduate research projects. *Council on Undergraduate Research Quarterly, 36 (2),* 18–21.

Flannery, D. D. (2000). Connection. In E. Hayes & D. D. Flannery (Eds.), *Women as learners: The significance of gender in adult learning* (pp. 111–137). San Francisco, CA: Jossey-Bass.

Flannery, J. L. (1994). Teacher as co-conspirator: Knowledge and authority in collaborative learning. In K. Bosworth & S. J. Hamilton (Eds.), *Collaborative learning: Underlying processes and effective techniques* (pp. 15–23). New Directions for Teaching and Learning, n. 59. San Francisco, CA: Jossey-Bass.

Flores, B. C., Darnell, A., & Renner, J. (2009). The emergence of undergraduate research in the course of institutional change. In M. K. Boyd & J. L. Wesemann (Eds.), *Broadening participation in undergraduate research: Fostering excellence and enhancing the impact* (pp. 295–306). Washington, DC: Council on Undergraduate Research.

Foertsch, J., Alexander, B. B., & Penberthy, D. (2000). Summer research opportunity programs (SROPS) for minority undergraduates: A longitudinal study of program outcomes, 1986–1996. *Council on Undergraduate Research Quarterly, 20,* 114–119.

Fontaine, G. (2002). Presence in "Teleland." In K. E. Rudestam & J. Schoenholtz-Read (Eds.), *Handbook of online learning: Innovations in higher education and corporate training* (pp. 29–52). Thousand Oaks, CA: Sage.

Foote, L. C. & DiFilippo, J. E. (2009). STEM literacy, civic responsibility, and future vision: Examining the effects of the Lawrence Math and Science Partnership. In T. Kelshaw, F. Lazarus, & J. Minier (Eds.), *Partnerships for service-learning: Impacts on communities and students* (pp. 165–205). San Francisco, CA: Jossey-Bass.

Fox, C. (2010). Advancing research in English through honors. In L. Grobman & J. Kinkead (Eds.), *Undergraduate research in English studies* (pp. 162–172). Urbana, IL: National Council of Teachers of English.

Frackmann, E. (1994). Introduction. In G. M. Bull, C. Dallinga-Hunter, Y. Epelboin, E. Frackmann, & D. Jennings (Eds.), *Information technology: Issues for higher education management* (pp. 1–11). Bristol, PA: Kingsley.

Freed, L. & Farnsworth, F. V. (2001). Dealing with federal compliance issues at a predominantly undergraduate institution. *Council on Undergraduate Research Quarterly, 22*, 61–63.

Friedenberg, L. (1995). If you build it, they will come: How academic departments can foster faculty involvement in undergraduate research. *Council on Undergraduate Research Quarterly, 15*, 133–135.

Friedman, E. G. & Leigey, M. E. (2014). Faculty-student collaborative "jazz" in a research seminar. *Council on Undergraduate Research Quarterly, 34 (3)*, 7–12.

Friedman, P. G. (1986). Independent study, fieldwork, and peer teaching. In P. G. Friedman & R. C. Jenkins-Friedman (Eds.), *Fostering academic excellence through honors programs* (pp. 87–98). New Directions for Teaching and Learning, n. 25. San Francisco, CA: Jossey-Bass.

Fritzman, J. M. & Gibson, M. (2008). Collaborative faculty/student research at Lewis & Clark College. *Council on Undergraduate Research Quarterly, 29 (2)*, 18–21.

Fukami, C. V. (1997). Struggling with balance. In R. Andre & P. J. Frost (Eds.), *Researchers hooked on teaching: Noted scholars discuss the synergies of teaching and research* (pp. 3–13). Thousand Oaks, CA: Sage.

Funke, L. A. (2000). Origin and programs of the Petroleum Research Fund. In M. P. Doyle (Ed.), *Academic excellence: The role of research in the physical sciences at undergraduate institutions* (pp. 173–179). Tucson, AZ: Research Corporation.

Gabbert, L. (2010). Exploring local communities: Conducting undergraduate research in folklore studies. *Council on Undergraduate Research Quarterly, 30 (4)*, 37–42.

Gafney, L. (2005). The role of the research mentor/teacher: Student and faculty views. *Journal of College Science Teaching, 34 (4)*, 52–56.

Gaglione, O. G. (2005). Underground existence of research in chemistry in two-year college programs. *Journal of Chemical Education, 82*, 1613–1614.

Gappa, J. M., Austin, A. E., & Trice, A. G. (2007). *Rethinking faculty work: Higher education's strategic imperative.* San Francisco, CA: Jossey-Bass.

Gardella, J. A., Maciejewski, H. M., & Huber, M. B. (2009). Service-learning in an urban public school district: The Buffalo experience. In D. P. Redlawsk & T. Rice (Eds.), *Civic service: Service-learning with state and local government partners* (pp. 189–212). San Francisco, CA: Jossey-Bass.

Garrison, D. R. (2011). *E-learning in the 21st Century: A framework for research and practice* (2nd ed.). New York, NY: Routledge.

Garrison, D. R. & Vaughan, N. D. (2008). *Blended learning in higher education: Framework, principles, and guidelines.* San Francisco, CA: Jossey-Bass.

Gary, T., de la Rubia, L. A., Brinkley, M., & Thompson, M. (2010). "The Scholar in U Experience" at Tennessee State University. *Council on Undergraduate Research Quarterly, 31 (1)*, 6–10.

Gasparich, G. E. (2009). Facilitating seamless transitions from two-year to four-year institutions. In M. K. Boyd & J. L. Wesemann (Eds.), *Broadening participation in undergraduate research: Fostering excellence and enhancing the impact* (pp. 331–333). Washington, DC: Council on Undergraduate Research.

Gavin, R. (2000). The role of research at undergraduate institutions: Why is it necessary to defend it? In M. P. Doyle (Ed.), *Academic excellence: The role of research in the physical sciences at undergraduate institutions* (pp. 9–17). Tucson, AZ: Research Corporation.

Gazdik, M. A. & Powell, J. D. (2012). The impact of student-directed research at an undergraduate liberal arts institution. *Council on Undergraduate Research Quarterly, 33 (1)*, 22–27.

Gerlach, J. M. (1994). Is this collaboration? In K. Bosworth & S. J. Hamilton (Eds.), *Collaborative learning: Underlying processes and effective techniques* (pp. 5–14). New Directions for Teaching and Learning, n. 59. San Francisco, CA: Jossey-Bass.

Gesink, I. F. (2010). Speaking stones: The cemetery as a laboratory for undergraduate research in the humanities. *Council on Undergraduate Research Quarterly, 30 (4)*, 9–13.

Giedd, R. E. & Baker, J. P. (2006). Innovative models for corporate and academic relationships: Missouri State's Jordan Valley Innovation Center. *Council on Undergraduate Research Quarterly, 27 (1)*, 11–17.

Gilbert, B. & Guerra, F. (2012). From the classroom to the assembly floor: Making students' research count. *Council on Undergraduate Research Quarterly, 33 (2)*, 27.

Gilde, C. (2007). The overcommercialization of higher education. In C. Gilde (Ed.), *Higher education: Open for business* (pp. 21–39). Lanham, MD: Lexington.

Gillespie, F. (1998). Instructional design for the new technologies. In K. H. Gillespie (Ed.), *The impact of technology on faculty development, life, and work* (pp. 39–52). New Directions for Teaching and Learning, n. 76. San Francisco, CA: Jossey-Bass.

Gilligan, C. (1982). *In a different voice: Psychological theory and women's development.* Cambridge, MA: Harvard University Press.

Girvan, R. B. (1996). Undergraduate research and service for external agencies through the Center for the Study of Local Issues at Clarion. *Council on Undergraduate Research Quarterly, 16*, 215–217.

Glass, C. R., Wongtrirat, R., & Buus, S. (2015). *International student engagement: Strategies for creating inclusive, connected, and purposeful campus environments.* Sterling, VA: Stylus.

Glass-Coffin, B. & Balagna, C. (2005). The ethnographic field school as a venue for undergraduate research. *Council on Undergraduate Research Quarterly, 25*, 169–174.

Glassick, C. E., Huber, M. T., & Maeroff, G. I. (1997). *Scholarship assessed: Evaluation of the professoriate.* San Francisco, CA: Jossey-Bass.

Glew, D. G. (2007). Designing a research-driven history program. In K. K. Karukstis & T. E. Elgren (Eds.), *Developing and sustaining a research-supportive curriculum: A compendium of successful practices* (pp. 388–389). Washington, DC: Council on Undergraduate Research.

Goals 2000: Educate America Act (1994). Retrieved July 9, 2004, from http://www.ed.gov/legislation/GOALS2000/TheAct/intro.html.

Golde, C. M. (2006). Preparing stewards of the discipline. In C. M. Golde & G. E. Walker (Eds.), *Envisioning the future of doctoral education: Preparing stewards of the discipline* (pp. 3–20). San Francisco, CA: Jossey-Bass.

Golde, C. M. & Walker, G. E. (Eds.) (2006). *Envisioning the future of doctoral education: Preparing stewards of the discipline.* San Francisco, CA: Jossey-Bass.

Golphin, V. F. A. & Smith, D. T. (2007). Livin' for the city: An interdisciplinary course. In K. K. Karukstis & T. E. Elgren (Eds.), *Developing and sustaining a research-supportive curriculum: A compendium of successful practices* (pp. 473–475). Washington, DC: Council on Undergraduate Research.

Gonzalez-Espada, W. J. & LaDue, D. S. (2006). Evaluation of the impact of the NWC REU program compared with other undergraduate research experiences. *Journal of Geoscience Education, 54*, 541–549.

Goodman, J. (2006). Undergraduate research: Intelligent design for the evolution of a program. *Council on Undergraduate Research Quarterly, 27*, 80–83.

Gose, B. (October 1, 2012). 4 massive open online courses and how they work. *Chronicle of Higher Education.* Retrieved July 16, 2013, from http://www.lexisnexis.com.

Gould, L. (Ed.) (2016). From the CURQ issue editor. *Council on Undergraduate Research Quarterly, 37 (1)*, 3.

Grabowski, J. J., Heely, M. E., & Brindley, J. A. (2008). Scaffolding faculty-mentored authentic research experiences for first-year students. *Council on Undergraduate Research Quarterly, 29 (1)*, 41–47.

Graham, C. R. (2006). Blended learning systems: Definition, current trends, and future directions. In C. J. Bonk & C. R. Graham (Eds.), *The handbook of blended learning* (pp. 3–21). San Francisco, CA: Pfeiffer.

Grant, G. J. & Haynes, P. J. (2001). Research in the undergraduate environment: What lessons can we learn from successful entrepreneurs? *Council on Undergraduate Research Quarterly, 21,* 180–184.

Gray, S. & Schermer, T. (2011). The senior capstone: Transformative experiences in the liberal arts. *Council on Undergraduate Research Quarterly, 32 (1),* 35.

Greening, T. & Kay, J. (2002). Undergraduate research experience in computer science education. *ACM SIGCSE Bulletin, 34 (3),* 151–155.

Greever, J. & Gallian, J. (1995). Challenging the myth: Has undergraduate research in mathematics come of age? *Council on Undergraduate Research Quarterly, 15,* 197–198.

Gregerman, S. R. (2009). Filling the gap: The role of undergraduate research in student retention and academic success. In M. K. Boyd & J. L. Wesemann (Eds.), *Broadening participation in undergraduate research: Fostering excellence and enhancing the impact* (pp. 245–256). Washington, DC: Council on Undergraduate Research.

Gregorian, V. (2005). Six challenges to the American university. In R. H. Hersh & J. Merrow (Eds.), *Declining by degrees: Higher education at risk* (pp. 77–96). New York, NY: Palgrave Macmillan.

Griffiths, R. (2004). Knowledge production and the research-teaching nexus: The case of the built environment disciplines. *Studies in Higher Education, 29,* 709–726.

Grobman, L. (2007). Affirming the independent researcher model: Undergraduate research in the humanities. *Council on Undergraduate Research Quarterly, 28 (1),* 23–28.

Grobman, L. (2011). Expanding honors research through undergraduate research: Another look at equity and access. *Council on Undergraduate Research Quarterly, 32 (1),* 29–34.

Grobman, L. & Kinkead, J. (2010a). Introduction: Illuminating undergraduate research in English. In L. Grobman & J. Kinkead (Eds.), *Undergraduate research in English studies* (pp. ix–xxxii). Urbana, IL: National Council of Teachers of English.

Grobman, L. & Kinkead, J. (Eds.) (2010b). *Undergraduate research in English studies.* Urbana, IL: National Council of Teachers of English.

Groover, R. S. (2014). A contract can help make undergraduate research successful. In N. H. Hensel & B. D. Cjeda (Eds.), *Tapping the potential of all: Undergraduate research at community colleges* (pp. 17–22). Washington, DC: Council on Undergraduate Research.

Grossman, P. D. (2014). The greatest change in disability law in 20 years. In M. L. Vance, N. E. Lipsitz, & K. Parks (Eds.), *Beyond the Americans with Disabilities Act: Inclusive policy and practice for higher education* (pp. 3–19). Washington, DC: NASPA.

Groth, R. E., Bergner, J. A., Burgess, C. R., Austin, J. W., & Holdai, V. (2016). Re-imagining education of mathematics teachers through undergraduate research. *Council on Undergraduate Research Quarterly, 36 (3),* 41–46.

Guertin, L. & Cerveny, N. (2012). Undergraduate research programs at two-year colleges. In J. Kinkead & L. Blockus (Eds.), *Undergraduate research offices and programs: Models & practices* (pp. 165–178). Washington, DC: Council on Undergraduate Research.

Guo, J. (2008). Using group-based projects to improve retention of students in computer science major. *Journal of Computing Sciences in Colleges, 23 (6),* 187–193.

Gurung, R. A. R., Chick, N. L., & Haynie, A. (Eds.) (2009). *Exploring signature pedagogies: Approaches to teaching disciplinary habits of mind.* Sterling, VA: Stylus.

Haase, S. J. & Fisk, G. D. (2008). Research collaboration as an effective avenue to promotion and tenure. *Council on Undergraduate Research Quarterly, 29 (1),* 6–8.

Hacker, A. & Dreifus, C. (2010). *Higher education? How colleges are wasting our money and failing our kids—and what we can do about it.* New York, NY: St. Martin's Griffin.

Haik, K. L. & Bullen, H. A. (2011). A risky proposition? Undergraduate research with low-income, first-generation, underrepresented STEM students. *Council on Undergraduate Research Quarterly, 31 (3),* 41.

Hakim, T. M. (2000). *At the interface of scholarship and teaching: How to develop and administer institutional undergraduate research programs.* Washington, DC: Council on Undergraduate Research.

Hall, L. E. (2007). *Who's afraid of Marie Curie? The challenges facing women in science and technology.* Emeryville, CA: Seal.

Hall, L. M. & Belch, H. A. (2000). Setting the context: Reconsidering the principles of full participation and meaningful access for students with disabilities. In H. A. Belch (Ed.), *Serving students with disabilities* (pp. 5–17). New Directions for Student Services, n. 91. San Francisco, CA: Jossey-Bass.

Halpern, A. R. & Blackburn, T. R. (2005). The rhetoric of the grant proposal. *Council on Undergraduate Research Quarterly, 25,* 187–190.

Halstead, J. A. (1997). Council on Undergraduate Research: A resource (and a community) for science educators. *Journal of Chemical Education, 74,* 148–149.

Hamilton, R. & Ingram, V. (1996). Teacher to teacher and student to student research partnerships: Mississippi College and Jackson Academy. *Council on Undergraduate Research Quarterly, 17,* 20–21, 38–39.

Hammond, D. M. & Lalor, M. M. (2009). Promoting STEM careers among undergraduates through interdisciplinary engineering research. *Council on Undergraduate Research Quarterly, 30 (2),* 26–33.

Hannum, W. (2002). Transforming the scholarly process through information technology. In K. J. Zahorski (Ed.), *Scholarship in the postmodern era: New venues, new values, new visions* (pp. 19–27). New Directions for Teaching and Learning, n. 90. San Francisco, CA: Jossey-Bass.

Hart, D. A. (Ed.) (2012a). *How to start an undergraduate research journal.* Washington, DC: Council on Undergraduate Research.

Hart, D. A. (2012b). Undergraduate research journals: Why and how? In D. A. Hart (Ed.), *How to start an undergraduate research journal* (pp. 10–18). Washington, DC: Council on Undergraduate Research.

Hathaway, R. S., Nagda, B. A., & Gregerman, S. R. (2002). The relationship of undergraduate research participation to graduate and professional education pursuit: An empirical study. *Journal of College Student Development, 43,* 614–631.

Hativa, N. (1995). What is taught in an undergraduate lecture? Differences between a matched pair of pure and applied disciplines. In N. Hativa & M. Marincovich (Eds.), *Disciplinary differences in teaching and learning: Implications for practice* (pp. 19–27). New Directions for Teaching and Learning, no, 64. San Francisco, CA: Jossey-Bass.

Hauhart, R. C. & Grahe, J. E. (2015). *Designing and teaching undergraduate capstone courses.* San Francisco, CA: Jossey-Bass.

Havholm, K. G. (2012). Connecting undergraduate research to state legislators: A model strategy. *Council on Undergraduate Research Quarterly, 33 (2),* 27.

Hawkins, L. B., Leone, C., & Jarvis-Mejia, S. (2011). The protégé-mentor relationship as a recruiting tool. *Council on Undergraduate Research Quarterly, 32 (2),* 47.

Hay, E., Snowball, D., Varallo, S., Hilton-Morrow, W., & Klien, S. (2014). Research-methods modules: Preparing students for the capstone in communication studies. *Council on Undergraduate Research Quarterly, 34 (4),* 6–10.

Hayes, E. (2000). Voice. In E. Hayes & D. D. Flannery (Eds.), *Women as learners: The significance of gender in adult learning* (pp. 79–109). San Francisco, CA: Jossey-Bass.

Healey, M. (2005). Linking research and teaching: Exploring disciplinary spaces and the role of inquiry-based learning. In R. Barnett (Ed.), *Reshaping the university: New relationships between research, scholarship, and teaching* (pp. 67–78). New York, NY: Society for Research into Higher Education & Open University Press.

Healey, M. & Jenkins, A. (2009). *Developing undergraduate research and inquiry*. Heslington, York, UK: Higher Education Academy. Retrieved August 5, 2009, from http://www.heacademy.ac.uk/assets/York/documents/resources/publications/DevelopingUnder graduate_Final.pdf.

Heath, T. (1992, October). *Predicting the educational aspirations and graduate plans of Black and White college and university students: When do dreams become realities?* Paper presented at the annual meeting of the Association for the Study of Higher Education, Minneapolis, MN. (ERIC Document Reproduction Service no. ED352915)

Hedley, J. & Schneider, B. (2009). The undergraduate student as scholar in the context of the research college. In L. L. Behling (Ed.), *Reading, writing, research: Undergraduate students as scholars in literary studies* (pp. 65–77). Washington, DC: Council on Undergraduate Research.

Heinemann, S. (Ed.) (2008). From the issue editor. *Council on Undergraduate Research Quarterly, 29 (2)*, 4.

Hensel, N. (2006a). From the executive officer. *Council on Undergraduate Research Quarterly, 27*, 50.

Hensel, N. (2006b). From the executive officer. *Council on Undergraduate Research Quarterly, 26*, 100–101.

Hensel, N. (2009). From the executive officer. *Council on Undergraduate Research Quarterly, 29 (3)*, 6–7.

Hensel, N. (2010). From CUR executive officer. *Council on Undergraduate Research Quarterly, 31 (1)*, 4.

Hensel, N. (2011a). From the CUR executive officer. *Council on Undergraduate Research Quarterly, 32 (1)*, 4–5.

Hensel, N. (2011b). From CUR executive officer. *Council on Undergraduate Research Quarterly, 31 (3)*, 3.

Hensel, N. (2011c). From the CUR executive officer. *Council on Undergraduate Research Quarterly, 32 (2)*, 4–5.

Hensel, N. (Ed.) (2012). *Characteristics of excellence in undergraduate research (COEUR)*. Washington, DC: Council on Undergraduate Research.

Hensel, N. H. & Cjeda, B. D. (Eds.) (2014). *Tapping the potential of all: Undergraduate research at community colleges*. Washington, DC: Council on Undergraduate Research.

Hensley, R. B. (2003). Technology as environment: From collections to connections. In M. M. Watts (Ed.), *Technology: Taking the distance out of learning* (pp. 23–30). New Directions for Teaching and Learning, n. 94. San Francisco, CA: Jossey-Bass.

Hersh, R. H. & Merrow, J. (2005). *Declining by degrees: Higher education at risk*. New York, NY: Palgrave Macmillan.

Hewlett, J. (2009). The search for synergy: Undergraduate research at the community college. In B. D. Cejda & N. Hensel (Eds.), *Undergraduate research at community colleges* (pp. 9–18). Washington, DC: Council on Undergraduate Research.

Hicok, B. (2009). Inviting our students to join the scholarly conversation. In L. L. Behling (Ed.), *Reading, writing, research: Undergraduate students as scholars in literary studies* (pp. 42–52). Washington, DC: Council on Undergraduate Research.

Higgins, T. B., Brown, K. L., Gillmore, J. G., Johnson, J. B., Peaslee, G. F., & Stanford, D. J. (2011). Successful student transitions from the community college to the four-year college facilitated by undergraduate research. *Council on Undergraduate Research Quarterly, 31 (3)*, 16–22.

Hill, C., Corbett, C., & St. Rose, A. (2010). *Why so few? Women in science, technology, engineering, and mathematics.* Washington, DC: AAUW.

Hill, J. L., Banks, M. O., & Floyd, A. (2009). The disparate evolution of undergraduate research: From individual to institutional efforts. In M. K. Boyd & J. L. Wesemann (Eds.), *Broadening participation in undergraduate research: Fostering excellence and enhancing the impact* (pp. 153–165). Washington, DC: Council on Undergraduate Research.

Hirsch, S. F., Lazarus, N., Wisler, A., Minde, J., & Cerasini, G. (2013). Pursuing research through focus groups: A capstone experience meets disciplinary, general education goals. *Council on Undergraduate Research Quarterly, 33 (4)*, 23–27.

Hluchy, M. M. (2002). Interdisciplinary grant proposals—writing and reviewing experiences with NSF's ILI, CCLI-A&I and CCLI-ND programs. *Council on Undergraduate Research Quarterly, 22*, 117–121.

Hoagland, E. (1999). Talking to policy-makers on the connection between research and undergraduate education. *Council on Undergraduate Research Quarterly, 19*, 151.

Hodapp, T. (1996). Industrial sabbaticals: Building corporate partnerships. *Council on Undergraduate Research Quarterly, 16*, 226–228.

Hoffman, P. W., Fletcher, H. L., & Dwyer, P. M. (2009). Using undergraduate research to connect with external constituencies. *Council on Undergraduate Research Quarterly, 29 (5)*, 16–19.

Hoke, K. & Gentile, L. (2008). Early involvement in undergraduate research at the University of Richmond. *Council on Undergraduate Research Quarterly, 29 (1)*, 18–23.

Holland, L. A., Tomechko, S., Leigh, A. M., Oommen, A., Bradford, A., & Burns, A. E. (2004). Real-time distance research with IP network videoconferencing: Extending undergraduate research opportunities. *Journal of Chemical Education, 81*, 1224–1228.

Hollinsed, C. (2007). Changes to the Petroleum Research Fund. *Council on Undergraduate Research Quarterly, 28 (2)*, 42–43.

Holman, R. (2006). A recipe for academic-industrial partnerships. *Council on Undergraduate Research Quarterly, 27 (1)*, 6–10.

Holmes, V., Nieuwkoop, L., & Miedema, C. (2011). Teaching algebra concepts through technology. *Council on Undergraduate Research Quarterly, 31 (3)*, 41.

Hoppe, S. E. (2010). Cameron University Undergraduate Research Project. *Council on Undergraduate Research Quarterly, 31 (2)*, 40.

Hossler, D. (2015). Origins of strategic enrollment management. In D. Hossler, B. Bontrager & Associates, *Handbook of strategic enrollment management* (pp. 3–17). San Francisco, CA: Jossey-Bass.

Howard Hughes Medical Institute (HHMI) (2016). *History.* Retrieved December 18, 2016, from http://www.hhmi.org/about/history.

Howard Hughes Medical Institute (HHMI) (2015). *Science education and research training.* Retrieved July 25, 2015, from http://www.hhmi.org/programs/science-education-research-training.

Howery, C. B. (2001). Promoting undergraduate research in sociology. *Council on Undergraduate Research Quarterly, 21*, 163–167.

Howitt, S. & Wilson, A. (2016). Scaffolded reflection as a tool for surfacing complex learning in undergraduate research projects. *Council on Undergraduate Research Quarterly, 36 (4)*, 33–38.

Hu, S., Kuh, G. D., & Gayles, J. G. (2007). Engaging undergraduate students in research activities: Are research universities doing a better job? *Innovative Higher Education, 32,* 167–177.

Hu, S., Kuh, G. D., & Li, S. (2008). The effects of engagement in inquiry-oriented activities on student learning and personal development. *Innovative Higher Education, 33,* 71–81.

Hu, S., Scheuch, K., Schwartz, R., Gayles, J. G., & Li, S. (2008). *Reinventing undergraduate education: Engaging college students in research and creative activities.* ASHE Higher Education Report, v. 33, n. 4. San Francisco, CA: Jossey-Bass.

Huber, M. T. (2004). *Balancing acts: The scholarship of teaching and learning in academic careers.* Sterling, VA: Stylus.

Huber, M. T. & Morreale, S. P. (Eds.) (2002). *Disciplinary styles in the scholarship of teaching and learning: Exploring common ground.* Washington, DC: American Association for Higher Education.

Humes, K. R., Jones, N. A., & Ramirez, R. R. (2011). *Overview of race and Hispanic origin: 2010.* Washington, DC: U.S. Census Bureau.

Hunnes, C. H. & Dooley, D. M. (2004). Research partnership between teaching-centered and research-intensive schools. *Journal of Chemical Education, 81,* 989–990.

Hunter, A. (2008). Transformative learning in international education. In V. Savicki (Ed.), *Developing intercultural competence and transformation: Theory, research, and application in international education* (pp. 92–107). Sterling, VA: Stylus.

Hunter, A., Laursen, S. L., & Seymour, E. (2007). Becoming a scientist: The role of undergraduate research in students' cognitive, personal, and professional development. *Science Education, 91 (1),* 36–74.

Hunter, A., Weston, T. J., Laursen, S. L., & Thiry, H. (2009). URSSA: Evaluating student gains from undergraduate research in the sciences. *Council on Undergraduate Research Quarterly, 29 (3),* 15–19.

Hurtado, S., Milem, J., Clayton-Pedersen, A., & Allen, W. (1999). *Enacting diverse learning environments: Improving the climate for racial/ethnic diversity in higher education.* ASHE-ERIC Higher Education Report, v. 26, n. 8. Washington, DC: The George Washington University, Graduate School of Education and Human Development.

Husic, D. W. (2006). Navigating through interdisciplinary pitfalls and pathways to success. *Council on Undergraduate Research Quarterly, 26,* 169–176.

Husic, D. (2009a). From the president. *Council on Undergraduate Research Quarterly, 30 (1),* 4–6.

Husic, D. (2009b). Advocacy and the political process: It's not for me. Is it? *Council on Undergraduate Research Quarterly, 29 (4),* 6–7.

Husic, D. (2009c). From CUR president. *Council on Undergraduate Research Quarterly, 30 (2),* 4–5.

Husic, D. (2010). From CUR president. *Council on Undergraduate Research Quarterly, 30 (3),* 5–6.

Hutchings, P. & Clarke, S. E. (2004). The scholarship of teaching and learning: Contributing to reform in graduate education. In A. E. Austin & D. H. Wulff (Eds.), *Paths to the professoriate: Strategies for enriching the preparation of future faculty* (pp. 161–176). San Francisco, CA: Jossey-Bass.

Ingram, J. C. (2009). Establishing relationships and partnerships to engage Native-American students in research. In M. K. Boyd & J. L. Wesemann (Eds.), *Broadening participation in undergraduate research: Fostering excellence and enhancing the impact* (pp. 269–280). Washington, DC: Council on Undergraduate Research.

Inquiries Journal (2016). *About Inquiries Journal.* Retrieved December 18, 2016, from http:// www.inquiriesjournal.com/about-inquiries-journal.

Ishiyama, J. (2001). Undergraduate research and the success of first-generation, low-income college students. *Council on Undergraduate Research Quarterly, 22,* 36–41.

Ishiyama, J. (2002a). Does early participation in undergraduate research benefit social science and humanities students? *College Student Journal, 36,* 380–386.

Ishiyama, J. (2002b, August/September). *Participation in undergraduate research and the development of political science students.* Paper presented at the annual meeting of the American Political Science Association, Boston, MA. (ERIC Document Reproduction Service No. ED473026)

Ishiyama, J. (2007). Expectations and perceptions of undergraduate research mentoring: Comparing first generation, low income White/Caucasian and African American students. *College Student Journal, 41 (3),* 540–549.

Jackson, J. & Guerrant, B. M. (2012). Exposing hidden barriers for faculty of color. In N. H. Hensel & E. L. Paul (Eds.), *Faculty support and undergraduate research: Innovations in faculty role definition, workload, and reward* (pp. 57–67). Washington, DC: Council on Undergraduate Research.

Jacob, N. (2008). Initiating partnerships in scientific discovery at a two-year college via the introductory curriculum. *Council on Undergraduate Research Quarterly, 29 (1),* 24–29.

Jacobs, G. (2000). Using the project approach in early childhood teacher preparation. In *Issues in Early Childhood Education: Curriculum, Teacher Education, & Dissemination of Education* (pp. 343–347). Proceedings of the Lilian Katz Symposium, Champaign, IL. (ERIC Document Reproduction Service no. ED470906)

Jacoby, B. (2015). *Service-learning essentials: Questions, answers, and lessons learned.* San Francisco, CA: Jossey-Bass.

Jakubowski, H. & Jianping, X. (2007). An innovative and reciprocal undergraduate summer science exchange program between the US and China. *Council on Undergraduate Research Quarterly, 28 (1),* 12–17.

Jarvis, L. H., Shaughnessy, J., Chase, L., & Barney, C. (2011). Integrating undergraduate research into faculty responsibilities: The impact on tenure and promotion decisions. *Council on Undergraduate Research Quarterly, 31 (4),* 7–9.

Jenkins, A. (2012). Preface: The role of research in university teaching, the potential of undergraduate research for student learning, and the importance of students publishing their research. In D. A. Hart (Ed.), *How to start an undergraduate research journal* (pp. 1–9). Washington, DC: Council on Undergraduate Research.

Jenkins, A., Breen, R., Lindsay, R. & Brew, A. (2003). *Reshaping teaching in higher education: Linking teaching with research.* Sterling, VA: Kogan Page.

Jenkins, A. & Healey, M. (2015). International perspectives on strategies to support faculty who teach students via research and inquiry. *Council on Undergraduate Research Quarterly, 35 (3),* 31–37.

Jessup-Anger, J. E. (2015). Theoretical foundations of learning communities. In M. Benjamin (Ed.), *Learning communities from start to finish* (pp. 17–27). New Directions for Student Services, n. 149. San Francisco, CA: Jossey-Bass.

Johnsen, S. K. & Goree, K. (2005). *Independent study for gifted learners.* Waco, TX: Prufrock.

Johnson, A. B. (2007). Using GIS technology to develop research skills—learning to think spatially and use GIS in higher education. In K. K. Karukstis & T. E. Elgren (Eds.), *Developing and sustaining a research-supportive curriculum: A compendium of successful practices* (pp. 103–107). Washington, DC: Council on Undergraduate Research.

Johnson, B. & Christensen, L. (2000). *Educational research: Quantitative and qualitative approaches.* Boston, MA: Allyn & Bacon.

Johnson, C. D., Hanson, L., & Kunka, J. L. (2011). De-centered discovery: Advancing an undergraduate research culture within the English major. In N.Y. Klos, J. O. Shanahan, & G.Young (Eds.), *Creative inquiry in the arts & humanities: Models of undergraduate research* (pp. 33–42).Washington, DC: Council on Undergraduate Research.

Johnson, D. C. & Gould, C. (2009). Special challenges of assessing undergraduate research in the arts and humanities. *Council on Undergraduate Research Quarterly, 29 (3)*, 33–38.

Johnson, D. W., Johnson, R. T., & Smith, K. A. (1991). *Cooperative learning: Increasing college faculty instructional productivity.* ASHE-ERIC Higher Education Report No. 4. Washington, DC:The George Washington University, School of Education and Human Development.

Johnson, E. S. & Clohessy, A. B. (2014). *Identification and evaluation of learning disabilities:The school team's guide to student success.*Thousand Oaks, CA: Corwin.

Johnson, R. C. (2011). Using summer research to attract pre-college underrepresented students to STEM fields. *Council on Undergraduate Research Quarterly, 31 (3)*, 7–15.

Johnson, W. B. (2007). *On being a mentor: A guide for higher education faculty.* New York, NY: Psychology Press.

Jones, J. I. T. & Bolyard, M. (2009). Integrating research into a large teaching laboratory. *Council on Undergraduate Research Quarterly, 30 (1)*, 39–43.

Jones, R. M. & Davis, S. N. (2014).Assessing faculty perspectives on undergraduate research: Implications from studies of two faculties. *Council on Undergraduate Research Quarterly, 34 (3)*, 37–42.

Jonides, J. (1995). *Evaluation and dissemination of an undergraduate program to improve retention of at-risk students.* University of Michigan, Ann Arbor, MI. (ERIC Document Reproduction Service No. ED 414841)

Jonte-Pace, D. & Gilbert, L. (2010). The Faculty-Student Research Assistant Program (FSRAP). *Council on Undergraduate Research Quarterly, 31 (1)*, 31.

Josselson, R. (1987). *Finding herself: Pathways to identity development in women.* San Francisco, CA: Jossey-Bass.

Josselson, R. (1996). *Revising herself: The story of women's identity from college to midlife.* New York, NY: Oxford University Press.

Journal of Student Research (2016). *Author guidelines.* Retrieved December 18, 2016, from http://www.jofsr.com/index.php/path/pages/view/authors.

JYI (Journal of Young Investigators) (2016). *Submission FAQ.* Retrieved December 18, 2016, from http://www.jyi.org/submit/submission-faq/.

Joyce, J. P. (2004). Establishing a social science undergraduate research program. In L. Kauffman & J. Stocks (Eds.), *Reinvigorating the undergraduate experience: Successful models supported by NSF's AIRE/RAIRE program* (pp. 3–4).Washington, DC: Council on Undergraduate Research.

Kamenetz, A. (2007). *Generation debt: How our future was sold out for student loans, credit cards, bad jobs, no benefits, and tax cuts for rich geezers – and how to fight back.* New York, NY: Riverhead.

Kardash, C. M. (2000). Evaluation of an undergraduate research experience: Perceptions of undergraduate interns and their faculty mentors. *Journal of Educational Psychology, 92*, 191–201.

Kardash, C. M., Wallace, M., & Blockus, L. (2008). Undergraduate research experiences: Male and female interns' perceptions of gains, disappointments, and self-efficacy. In R. Taraban & R. L. Blanton (Eds.), *Creating effective undergraduate research programs in science: The transformation from student to scientist* (pp. 191–205). New York, NY: Teachers College Press.

Karkowski, A. M. & Fournier, J. S. (2012). Undergraduate research as a catalyst for institutional change. *Council on Undergraduate Research Quarterly, 33 (1)*, 13–16.

Karkowski, A. M., Hutchinson, K., & Howell, K. (2012). Advancing institutional assessment via undergraduate research journals. In D. A. Hart (Ed.), *How to start an undergraduate research journal* (pp. 34–40). Washington, DC: Council on Undergraduate Research.

Karukstis, K. (2005a). Showcasing successful practices that enhance a research-supportive undergraduate curriculum. *Journal of Chemical Education, 82*, 1440–1441.

Karukstis, K. (2005b). Communicating the importance of undergraduate research to legislators. *Journal of Chemical Education, 82*, 1279–1280.

Karukstis, K. K. (2007a). Developing an understanding of the integration of research and society. In K. K. Karukstis & T. E. Elgren (Eds.), *Developing and sustaining a research-supportive curriculum: A compendium of successful practices* (pp. 401–402). Washington, DC: Council on Undergraduate Research.

Karukstis, K. (2007b). The impact of undergraduate research on America's global competitiveness. *Journal of Chemical Education, 84*, 912–914.

Karukstis, K. (2007c). Alliances to promote undergraduate research. *Journal of Chemical Education, 84*, 384–385.

Karukstis, K. K. (2010). A horizontal mentoring initiative for senior women scientists at liberal arts colleges. *Council on Undergraduate Research Quarterly, 31 (2)*, 33–39.

Karukstis, K. K. & Elgren, T. E. (Eds.) (2007). *Developing and sustaining a research-supportive curriculum: A compendium of successful practices*. Washington, DC: Council on Undergraduate Research.

Karukstis, K. K. & Hensel, N. (Eds.) (2010). *Transformative research at predominantly undergraduate institutions*. Washington, DC: Council on Undergraduate Research.

Keasley, A. & Johnson, A. (2009). Linking into the academic network: Supporting student success and program growth. In M. K. Boyd & J. L. Wesemann (Eds.), *Broadening participation in undergraduate research: Fostering excellence and enhancing the impact* (pp. 345–349). Washington, DC: Council on Undergraduate Research.

Kegan, R. (1982). *The evolving self: Problem and process in human development*. Cambridge, MA: Harvard University Press.

Kegan, R. (1994). *In over our heads: The mental demands of modern life*. Cambridge, MA: Harvard University Press.

Kellogg Commission on the Future of State and Land-Grant Universities (2001). *Returning to our roots: Executive summaries of the reports of the Kellogg Commission on the Future of State and Land-Grant Universities*. Washington, DC: National Association of State Universities and Land-Grant Colleges.

Kephart, K., Villa, E., Gates, A. Q., & Roach, S. (2008). The Affinity Research Group Model: Creating and maintaining dynamic, productive, and inclusive research groups. *Council on Undergraduate Research Quarterly, 28 (4)*, 13–24.

Kezar, A. J. (1999). The diverse campus: Broadening our ideal to include all voices. In J. D. Toma & A. J. Kezar (Eds.), *Reconceptualizing the collegiate ideal* (pp. 25–34). New Directions for Higher Education, no. 105. San Francisco, CA: Jossey-Bass.

Kezar, A. (2000). *Summer bridge programs: Supporting all students*. ERIC Digest. Washington, DC: ERIC Clearinghouse on Higher Education, George Washington University Graduate School of Education and Human Development. (ERIC Document Reproduction Service No. ED442421)

Khelifa, M., Sonleitner, N., Wooldridge, D., & Mayers, G. (2004). Integrating research into an undergraduate family sciences program. *Journal of Family and Consumer Sciences, 96 (2)*, 70–71.

Kierniesky, N. C. (2005). Undergraduate research in small psychology departments: Two decades later. *Teaching of Psychology, 32*, 84–90.

Kight, S., Gaynor, J. J., & Adams, S. D. (2006). Undergraduate research communities: A powerful approach to research training. *Journal of College Science Teaching, 35 (7)*, 34–39.

King, P. M. & Kitchener, K. S. (1994). *Developing reflective judgment: Understanding and promoting intellectual growth and critical thinking in adolescents and adults.* San Francisco, CA: Jossey-Bass.

Kinkead, J. (2003). Learning through inquiry: An overview of undergraduate research. In J. Kinkead (Ed.), *Valuing and supporting undergraduate research* (pp. 5–17). New Directions for Teaching and Learning, n. 93. San Francisco, CA: Jossey-Bass.

Kinkead, J. (2010). *Advancing undergraduate research: Marketing, communications, and fundraising.* Washington, DC: Council on Undergraduate Research.

Kinkead, J. & Blockus, L. (Eds.) (2012). *Undergraduate research offices & programs: Models & practices.* Washington, DC: Council on Undergraduate Research.

Kinkel, D. H. & Henke, S. E. (2006). Impact of undergraduate research on academic performance, educational planning, and career development. *Journal of Natural Resources & Life Science Education, 35*, 194–201.

Kitchens, M. B., Dolan, C. J., Hinshaw, J. H., & Johnson, D. E. (2010). Building a model for interdisciplinary research at a small college. *Council on Undergraduate Research Quarterly, 31 (1)*, 17–20.

Klein, J. T. (2010). *Creating interdisciplinary campus cultures: A model for strength and sustainability.* San Francisco, CA: Jossey-Bass.

Klinkner, P. A. (2001). The Arthur Levitt Public Affairs Center at Hamilton College: A social sciences laboratory. *Council on Undergraduate Research Quarterly, 21*, 168–169.

Klobas, J. E., Mackintosh, B., & Murphy, J. (2015). The anatomy of MOOCs. In P. Kim (Ed.), *Massive open online courses: The MOOC revolution* (pp. 1–22). New York, NY: Routledge.

Klos, N. Y. (2011). Beyond the thesis model: Making undergraduate research work for YOU. In N. Y. Klos, J. O. Shanahan, & G. Young (Eds.), *Creative inquiry in the arts & humanities: Models of undergraduate research* (pp. 15–21). Washington, DC: Council on Undergraduate Research.

Klos, N.Y., Shanahan, J. O., & Young, G. (Eds.) (2011). *Creative inquiry in the arts & humanities: Models of undergraduate research.* Washington, DC: Council on Undergraduate Research.

Knezek, C., Morreale, P., Keddis, R. & James, R. (2015). Ethics in practice: Research and technology. *Council on Undergraduate Research Quarterly, 36 (1)*, 4–11.

Knight, L. B. (1999). Undergraduate research & departmental funding. *Council on Undergraduate Research Quarterly, 19*, 106–108.

Knox, D. L., DePasquale, P. J., & Pulimood, S. M. (2006). A model for summer undergraduate research experiences in emerging technologies. *ACM SIGCSE Bulletin, 38 (1)*, 214–218.

Kolb, D. A. (1984). *Experiential learning: Experience as the source of learning and development.* Englewood Cliffs, NJ: Prentice-Hall.

Kopko, K. C., Edwards, A., Krause, E., & McGonigle, V. J. (2016). Assessing outcomes of National Science Foundation grants in the social sciences. *Council on Undergraduate Research Quarterly, 36 (3)*, 4–10.

Korbel, D. M., Lucia, J. H., Wenzel, C. M., & Anderson, B. G. (2011). Collaboration strategies to facilitate successful transition of students with disabilities in a changing higher education environment. In W. S. Harbour & J. W. Madaus (Eds.), *Disability services and campus dynamics* (pp. 17–25). New Directions for Higher Education, n. 154. San Francisco, CA: Jossey-Bass.

Kram, K. E. (1985). *Mentoring at work: Developmental relationships in organizational life.* Glenview, IL: Scott, Foresman.

Kreber, C. (2009). Supporting student learning in the context of diversity, complexity and uncertainty. In C. Kreber (Ed.), *The university and its disciplines: Teaching and learning within and beyond disciplinary boundaries* (pp. 3–18). New York, NY: Routledge.

Krone, J. (1997). Evaluating undergraduate research in mathematics and computer science. *Council on Undergraduate Research Quarterly, 18,* 77, 90.

Kronman, A. T. (2007). *Education's end: Why our colleges and universities have given up on the meaning of life.* New Haven, CT: Yale University Press.

Ku, K. (2009). Is technology transfer a winning proposition? In R. C. Miller & B. J. Le Boeuf (Eds.), *Developing university-industry relations: Pathways to innovation from the West Coast* (pp. 17–30). San Francisco, CA: Jossey-Bass.

Kuh, G. D. (2008). *High-impact educational practices: What they are, who has access to them, and why they matter.* Washington, DC: Association of American Colleges and Universities.

Kuh, G. D. (2009). The National Survey of Student Engagement: Conceptual and empirical foundations. In R. M. Gonyea & G. D. Kuh (Eds.), *Using NSSE in institutional research* (pp. 5–20). New Directions for Institutional Research, n. 141. San Francisco, CA: Jossey-Bass.

Kuh, G. D. (2010). Foreword. In J. E. Brownell & L. E. Swaner, *Five high-impact practices: Research on learning outcomes, completion, and quality* (pp. v–xi). Washington, DC: Association of American Colleges and Universities.

Kuh, G. D. (2013). Part 1: Taking HIPs to the next level. In G. D. Kuh & K. O'Donnell, *Ensuring quality & taking high-impact practices to scale* (pp. 1–14). Washington, DC: Association of American Colleges and Universities.

Kuh, G. D., Douglas, K. B., Lund, J. P., & Ramin-Gyurnek, J. (1994). *Student learning outside the classroom: Transcending artificial boundaries.* ASHE-ERIC Higher Education Report no. 8. Washington, DC: The George Washington University, Graduate School of Education and Human Development.

Kuh, G. D., Kinzie, J., Schuh, J. H., Whitt, E. J., & Associates (2005). *Student success in college: Creating conditions that matter.* San Francisco, CA: Jossey-Bass.

Kuh, G. D. & O'Donnell, K. (2013). *Ensuring quality & taking high-impact practices to scale.* Washington, DC: Association of American Colleges and Universities.

Kuh, G. D., Schuh, J. H., Whitt, E. J., & Associates (1991). *Involving colleges: Successful approaches to fostering student learning and development outside the classroom.* San Francisco, CA: Jossey-Bass.

Kvale, T., Connin, L., Teeple, J., Louden-Hanes, M., Henderson-Dean, B., & Edelbrock, M. (2012). Posters at the capitol: Undergraduate research in northwest Ohio. *Council on Undergraduate Research Quarterly, 33 (2),* 27.

Labster (n.d.). *About Labster.* Retrieved September 18, 2016, from https://www.labster.com/about/.

Lancy, D. F. (2003). What one faculty member does to promote undergraduate research. In J. Kinkead (Ed.), *Valuing and supporting undergraduate research* (pp. 87–92). New Directions for Teaching and Learning, n. 93. San Francisco, CA: Jossey-Bass.

Landrum, R. E. & Nelson, L. R. (2002). The undergraduate research assistantship: An analysis of the benefits. *Teaching of Psychology, 29,* 15–19.

Lane, N. F. (1994). Keynote address given at the fifth national conference of the Council on Undergraduate Research. *Council on Undergraduate Research Quarterly, 15,* 73–76.

Langenberg, D. N. & Spicer, D. Z. (2001). The modern campus. In G. R. Maughan (Ed.), *Technology leadership: Communication and information systems in higher education* (pp. 3–15). New Directions for Higher Education, n. 115. San Francisco, CA: Jossey-Bass.

Langford, J. (2011). Models of undergraduate research in the humanities: The Severan database project. In N.Y. Klos, J. O. Shanahan, & G. Young (Eds.), *Creative inquiry in the arts & humanities: Models of undergraduate research* (pp. 49–58). Washington, DC: Council on Undergraduate Research.

Langley-Turnbaugh, S., Whitney, J., Lovewell, L., & Moeller, B. (2014). Benefits of research fellowships for undergraduates with disabilities. *Council on Undergraduate Research Quarterly, 35 (2)*, 39–45.

Lanza, J. (1998). Whys and hows of undergraduate research. *Bioscience, 38*, 110–112.

LaPlant, J. T. (2010). Undergraduate research in times of poor fiscal health. *Council on Undergraduate Research Quarterly, 30 (4)*, 8.

LaPlant, J. T. (2011a). Undergraduate research and the tenure and promotion process. *Council on Undergraduate Research Quarterly, 31 (4)*, 5–6.

LaPlant, J.T. (2011b). Undergraduate research as a campus recruitment and marketing tool. *Council on Undergraduate Research Quarterly, 32 (2)*, 6–7.

LaPlant, J.T. (Ed.) (2013a). From the issue editor. *Council on Undergraduate Research Quarterly, 33 (4)*, 5.

LaPlant, J.T. (Ed.) (2013b). From the CURQ issue editor. *Council on Undergraduate Research Quarterly, 34 (2)*, 5.

LaPlant, J.T. (2013c). Building undergraduate research experiences into general education. *Council on Undergraduate Research Quarterly, 33 (4)*, 5–6.

LaPlant, J.T. (Ed.) (2014). From the CURQ issue editor. *Council on Undergraduate Research Quarterly, 34 (4)*, 4.

LaPlant, J.T. (Ed.) (2015). From the CURQ issue editor. *Council on Undergraduate Research Quarterly, 35 (3)*, 4.

Lattuca, L. R. (2001). *Creating interdisciplinarity: Interdisciplinary research and teaching among college and university faculty*. Nashville, TN: Vanderbilt University Press.

Lattuca, L. R. & Creamer, E. G. (2005). Learning as professional practice. In E. G. Creamer & L. R. Lattuca (Eds.), *Advancing faculty learning through interdisciplinary collaboration* (pp. 3–11). New Directions for Teaching and Learning, n. 102. San Francisco, CA: Jossey-Bass.

Lattuca, L. R. & Stark, J. S. (1995). Modifying the major: Discretionary thoughts from ten disciplines. *The Review of Higher Education, 18*, 315–344.

Laursen, S., Hunter, A., Seymour, E., Thiry, H., & Melton, G. (2010). *Undergraduate research in the sciences: Engaging students in real science*. San Francisco, CA: Jossey-Bass.

Leadership Alliance (2016a). *Developing outstanding leaders*. Retrieved December 18, 2016, from http://theleadershipalliance.org/about.

Leadership Alliance (2016b). *SR-EIP: The Summer Research Early Identification Program*. Providence, RI: author. Retrieved December 18, 2016, from http://www.theleadershipalliance.org/sites/default/files/sr-eip-brochure-2016.pdf.

Lee-Keller, H. (2009). "Scholarship automatically reminds me of grant money": Rethinking, revaluing, and re-envisioning undergraduate students and scholarship. In L. L. Behling (Ed.), *Reading, writing, research: Undergraduate students as scholars in literary studies* (pp. 11–27). Washington, DC: Council on Undergraduate Research.

Leek, D. (2014). Developing U.S. students' skills in communication research through ethnographies of speech in different London settings. *Council on Undergraduate Research Quarterly, 35 (2)*, 14–19.

Leggon, C. B. (2001). The scientist as academic. In S. R. Graubard (Ed.), *The American academic profession* (pp. 221–244). New Brunswick, NJ: Transaction.

LeMahieu, M. (2009). Creative inquiry: Facts, values, and undergraduate research in the humanities. In L. L. Behling (Ed.), *Reading, writing, research: Undergraduate students as scholars in literary studies* (pp. 29–41). Washington, DC: Council on Undergraduate Research.

Levesque, M. J. & Wise, M. (2001). The Elon Experience: Supporting undergraduate research across all disciplines. *Council on Undergraduate Research Quarterly, 21,* 113–116.

Levine, A. (2005). Worlds apart: Disconnects between students and their colleges. In R. H. Hersh & J. Merrow (Eds.), *Declining by degrees: Higher education at risk* (pp. 155–167). New York, NY: Palgrave Macmillan.

Levy, P. (2011). Embedding inquiry and research into mainstream higher education: A UK perspective. *Council on Undergraduate Research Quarterly, 32 (1),* 36–42.

Lichter, R. L. (1995). A supportive environment for research in undergraduate institutions: A resonance hybrid. *Council on Undergraduate Research Quarterly, 15,* 125–129.

Locks, A. M. & Gregerman, S. R. (2008). Undergraduate research as an institutional retention strategy: The University of Michigan model. In R. Taraban & R. L. Blanton (Eds.), *Creating effective undergraduate research programs in science: The transformation from student to scientist* (pp. 11–32). New York, NY: Teachers College Press.

Longtine, C. & Jones, M. (2011). The crossroads of U.S. demographics and higher education: A tale of disparate futures. *Council on Undergraduate Research Quarterly, 31 (3),* 29–37.

Lopatto, D. (2002a, June). *Follow up to the summer 2001 ROLE survey: Spring 2002.* Paper presented at the Council on Undergraduate Research National Conference, New London, CT.

Lopatto, D. (2002b, June). *Dropping the other shoe: Correspondence between qualitative and quantitative analysis of student reported benefits of undergraduate research experiences.* Paper presented at the Council on Undergraduate Research National Conference, New London, CT.

Lopatto, D. (2003). The essential features of undergraduate research. *Council on Undergraduate Research Quarterly, 23,* 139–142.

Lopatto, D. (2006). Undergraduate research as a catalyst for liberal learning. *Peer Review, 8 (1),* 22–25.

Lopatto, D. (2008). Exploring the benefits of undergraduate research experiences: The SURE survey. In R. Taraban & R. L. Blanton (Eds.), *Creating effective undergraduate research programs in science: The transformation from student to scientist* (pp. 112–132). New York, NY: Teachers College Press.

Lopatto, D. (2010). *Science in solution: The impact of undergraduate research on student learning.* Washington, DC: Council on Undergraduate Research & Research Corporation for Science Advancement.

Lorig, T. S. (1996). Courting companies for research support: A guide for would-be suitors. *Council on Undergraduate Research Quarterly, 16,* 211–214.

Losh, E. (2014). *The war on learning: Gaining ground in the digital university.* Cambridge, MA: MIT Press.

Louis, R. (2008). Collaboration at the Crossroads: A community-based arts research initiative. *Council on Undergraduate Research Quarterly, 29 (2),* 22–25.

Love, P. G. & Love, A. G. (1995). *Enhancing student learning: Intellectual, social, and emotional integration.* ASHE-ERIC Higher Education Report no. 4. Washington, DC: The George Washington University, Graduate School of Education and Human Development.

Luyben, P. D. (2005). Field studies in applied behavioral analysis and direct instruction. *Council on Undergraduate Research Quarterly, 26,* 66–68.

Lynch, C. A. (2008). A matter of mission: Information technology and the future of higher education. In R. N. Katz (Ed.), *The tower and the cloud: Higher education in the age of cloud computing* (pp. 43–50). Washington, DC: Educause.

Mabrouk, P. A. (2003). Research learning contracts: A useful tool for facilitating successful undergraduate research experiences. *Council on Undergraduate Research Quarterly, 24,* 26–30.

Mabrouk, P. A. & Peters, K. (2000). Student perspectives on undergraduate research experiences in chemistry and biology. *Council on Undergraduate Research Quarterly, 21,* 25–33.

MacDonald, G. (2009). Integrating interpreting, hearing, and deaf students in summer research. In M. K. Boyd & J. L. Wesemann (Eds.), *Broadening participation in undergraduate research: Fostering excellence and enhancing the impact* (pp. 199–210). Washington, DC: Council on Undergraduate Research.

Macfarlane, B. (2009). *Researching with integrity: The ethics of academic enquiry.* New York, NY: Routledge.

Mack, T. (2011). Assenting echo: The genesis and evolution of an undergraduate research journal. In N. Y. Klos, J. O. Shanahan, & G. Young (Eds.), *Creative inquiry in the arts & humanities: Models of undergraduate research* (pp. 67–74). Washington, DC: Council on Undergraduate Research.

Mahlab, M. (2010). Who benefits? Peer mentors at Grinnell College. *Council on Undergraduate Research Quarterly, 31 (2),* 7–10.

Malachowski, M. R. (1999). Promoting undergraduate research in non-science areas at predominantly undergraduate institutions. *Council on Undergraduate Research Quarterly, 19,* 126–130.

Malachowski, M. R. (2001). CUR comment: Should CUR expand to embrace all disciplines? *Council on Undergraduate Research Quarterly, 21,* 156–158.

Malachowski, M. R. (2003). A research-across-the-curriculum movement. In J. Kinkead (Ed.), *Valuing and supporting undergraduate research* (pp. 55–68). New Directions for Teaching and Learning, n. 93. San Francisco, CA: Jossey-Bass.

Malachowski, M. R. (2012). Living in parallel universes: The great faculty divide between product-oriented and process-oriented scholarship. In N. H. Hensel & E. L. Paul (Eds.), *Faculty support and undergraduate research: Innovations in faculty role definition, workload, and reward* (pp. 7–18). Washington, DC: Council on Undergraduate Research.

Malachowski, M. R. & Dwyer, T. J. (2011). Requiring research for all students in a major: Opportunities and challenges. *Council on Undergraduate Research Quarterly, 32 (1),* 23–28.

Malachowski, M. R., Hensel, N., Ambos, E., Karukstis, K., & Osborn, J. (2014). The evolution of CUR Institutes: From serving individuals to serving campuses, systems, and consortia. *Council on Undergraduate Research Quarterly, 35 (1),* 34–35.

Malachowski, M. R., Osborn, J. M., Karukstis, K. K., & Ambos, E. L. (Eds.) (2015). *Enhancing and expanding undergraduate research: A systems approach.* New Directions for Higher Education, n. 169. San Francisco, CA: Jossey-Bass.

Malachowski, M. R. & Webster, M. (2008). Transforming our institutions into research-rich environments. *Council on Undergraduate Research Quarterly, 29 (2),* 43–47.

Malcom, S. M. (1995). Perspectives on the future of undergraduate research and education. *Council on Undergraduate Research Quarterly, 16,* 16–18.

Manak, J. A. & Young, G. (2014). Incorporating undergraduate research into teacher education: Preparing thoughtful teachers through inquiry-based learning. *Council on Undergraduate Research Quarterly, 35 (2),* 35–38.

Manske, J. M. (2001). Students with disabilities: Unique challenges and opportunities for science and math programs. *Council on Undergraduate Research Quarterly, 22,* 27–31.

Marcia, J. E. (1966). Development and validation of ego-identity status. *Journal of Personality and Social Psychology, 3*, 551–558.

Markie, P. J. (1994). *A professor's duties: Ethical issues in college teaching.* Lanham, MD: Rowman & Littlefield.

Martinetti, M. P., Leynes, P. A., Medvecky, C. M., Benson, A. L., & Paul, E. L. (2009). Undergraduate research teams: Creating a vertical infrastructure to increase participation. In M. K. Boyd & J. L. Wesemann (Eds.), *Broadening participation in undergraduate research: Fostering excellence and enhancing the impact* (pp. 227–229). Washington, DC: Council on Undergraduate Research.

Martins, G. B. & Roth, B. J. (2011). Scientific research for high-school [sic] students. *Council on Undergraduate Research Quarterly, 31 (3)*, 41.

Marusak, R. A. (2002). Selling to skeptics: A guide to the PUI researcher for submitting successful MRI proposals. *Council on Undergraduate Research Quarterly, 23*, 82–84.

Massey, W. E. (1996). Predicting the future for research in higher education: An address to the biennial celebration of the Council on Undergraduate Research in Durham, North Carolina, June 26, 1996. *Council on Undergraduate Research Quarterly, 17*, 94–98.

Mateja, J. (2006). Undergraduate research: Needed more today than ever before. *Council on Undergraduate Research Quarterly, 27*, 27–32.

Mateja, J. (2011). It's time to take the next step. *Council on Undergraduate Research Quarterly, 32 (1)*, 9–12.

Matich-Maroney, J. & Moore, P. J. (2016). Flipping the classroom in an undergraduate social work research course. *Council on Undergraduate Research Quarterly, 37 (2)*, 24–29.

Mattis, M. C. (2007). Upstream and downstream in the engineering pipeline: What's blocking US women from pursuing engineering careers? In R. J. Burke & M. C. Mattis (Eds.), *Women and minorities in science, technology, engineering and mathematics: Upping the numbers* (pp. 334–362). Northampton, MA: Elgar.

May, S. R., Cook, D. L., & Panu, A. M. (2012). A quantitative model for predicting which features of undergraduate research aid acceptance into graduate education. *Council on Undergraduate Research Quarterly, 32 (3)*, 18–22.

Mayhew, M. J., Rockenbach, A. N., Bowman, N. A., Seifert, T. A., & Wolniak, G. C., with Pascarella E. T. & Terenzini, P. T. (2016). *How college affects students, volume 3: 21st century evidence that higher education works.* San Francisco, CA: Jossey-Bass.

McConnaughay, K. & Rueckert, L. (Eds.) (2004). *Council on Undergraduate Research Quarterly, 25 (1)*.

McConnaughay, K. & Rueckert, L. (Eds.) (2006). *Council on Undergraduate Research Quarterly, 26 (3)*.

McDaniel, M. (2011). Beyond mainstreaming. *Council on Undergraduate Research Quarterly, 31 (3)*, 38–40.

McDorman, T. (2004). Promoting undergraduate research in the humanities: Three collaborative approaches. *Council on Undergraduate Research Quarterly, 25*, 39–42.

McGee, D. J. (2003). Undergraduate research at Drew University: The Drew Summer Science Institute. *Council on Undergraduate Research Quarterly, 23*, 118–120.

McKay, S. E. & Lashlee, R. W. (2007). Providing an appropriate research environment for a physical science department. *Council on Undergraduate Research Quarterly, 27*, 131–134.

McKeachie, W. J. & Svinicki, M. (2006). *McKeachie's teaching tips: Strategies, research, and theory for college and university teachers* (12th ed.). Boston, MA: Houghton Mifflin.

McKillip, J. (2009). Transformative undergraduate research: Students as the authors of and authorities on their own education. *Council on Undergraduate Research Quarterly, 30 (2)*, 10–15.

McNely, B. J. (2010). Cultivating rhetorical dispositions through curricular change in technical and professional communication. In L. Grobman & J. Kinkead (Eds.), *Undergraduate research in English studies* (pp. 229–244). Urbana, IL: National Council of Teachers of English.

Medina, A, Jr. (2012). Connecting undergraduate research at PUIs to legislators: Designating a state and federal liaison. *Council on Undergraduate Research Quarterly, 33 (2)*, 8–12.

Meier, D. & Wood, G. (Eds.) (2004). *Many children left behind: How the No Child Left Behind Act is damaging our children and our schools.* Boston, MA: Beacon.

Mekolichick, J. & Gibbs, M. K. (2012). Understanding college generational status in the undergraduate research mentored relationship. *Council on Undergraduate Research Quarterly, 33 (2)*, 40–46.

Merkel, C. A. & Baker, S. M. (2002). *How to mentor undergraduate researchers: Elements of mentoring, expectations, practical information.* Washington, DC: Council on Undergraduate Research.

Merrimack College (n.d.). *Lawrence Math & Science Partnership.* Retrieved December 21, 2016, from http://www.merrimack.edu/academics/experiential_learning/service_learning/stevens/lawrence_math_and_science_partnership.php.

Mickley, G. A. (2007). College-wide curricular reform to provide faculty-student collaborative scholarly experiences at Baldwin-Wallace College. In K. K. Karukstis & T. E. Elgren (Eds.), *Developing and sustaining a research-supportive curriculum: A compendium of successful practices* (pp. 398–400). Washington, DC: Council on Undergraduate Research.

Milem, J. F., Chang, M. J., & Antonio, A. L. (2005). *Making diversity work on campus: A research-based perspective.* Washington, DC: Association of American Colleges and Universities.

Miller, B. A. (2007). *Assessing organizational performance in higher education.* San Francisco, CA: Jossey-Bass.

Miller, R. C. (2009). University-industry research agreements. In R. C. Miller & B. J. Le Boeuf (Eds.), *Developing university-industry relations: Pathways to innovation from the West Coast* (pp. 7–16). San Francisco, CA: Jossey-Bass.

Miller, R. C. & Le Boeuf, B. J. (2009). Context and constraints. In R. C. Miller & B. J. Le Boeuf (Eds.), *Developing university-industry relations: Pathways to innovation from the West Coast* (pp. 1–6). San Francisco, CA: Jossey-Bass.

Miller, R. C., Le Boeuf, B. J., & Associates (2009). *Developing university-industry relations: Pathways to innovation from the West Coast.* San Francisco, CA: Jossey-Bass.

Mills, N. S. (2010). Non-traditional sources of research funding at predominantly undergraduate institutions. In K. K. Karukstis & N. Hensel (Eds.), *Transformative research at predominantly undergraduate institutions* (pp. 105–116). Washington, DC: Council on Undergraduate Research.

Misceo, G. F. & O'Hare, J. M. (2002). Integrating scholarship in undergraduate education. *Council on Undergraduate Research Quarterly, 22*, 154–159.

Molecular Education and Research Consortium in Undergraduate Computational Chemistry (MERCURY) (2015). *Research philosophy.* Retrieved July 26, 2015, from http://mercury.chem.hamilton.edu/modules/content/index.php?id=35.

Morris, N. & Labhard, L. (2005). Benefits of undergraduate research in family and consumer sciences. *Journal of Family and Consumer Sciences, 97 (1)*, 75–76.

Morris, S. J., McConnaughay, K. D., & Wolffe, R. J. (2009). Empowering undergraduates to lead teams of researchers with different levels of experience and perspectives. In M. K. Boyd & J. L. Wesemann (Eds.), *Broadening participation in undergraduate research: Fostering excellence and enhancing the impact* (pp. 179–190). Washington, DC: Council on Undergraduate Research.

Morrow, M. A. & Tobin, K. (2012). Communicating student research at SUNY New Paltz to state and local elected officials. *Council on Undergraduate Research Quarterly, 33 (2),* 13–18.

Muir, G. & van der Linden, G. (2008, June). *Using research collaborations with undergraduates to examine scholarship of teaching and learning (SoTL) issues.* Poster session presented at the Council on Undergraduate Research National Conference, St. Joseph, MN.

Muller, L. (2006). Research collaboration with learning-disabled students: Strategies for successful student-faculty partnerships. *Journal of College Science Teaching, 36 (3),* 26–29.

Multhaup, K. S., Davoli, C. C., Wilson, S. F., Geghman, K. D., Giles, K. G., Martin, J. M. P., & Salter, P. S. (2010). Three models for undergraduate-faculty research: Reflections by a professor and her former students. *Council on Undergraduate Research Quarterly, 31 (1),* 21–26.

Mulvey, P. J. & Nicholson, S. (2002). Physics and astronomy senior report: Classes of 1999 and 2000. *AIP Report,* June, 2002, pp. 1–10. (ERIC Document Reproduction Service no. ED467007)

Mumper, M., Gladieux, L. E., King, J. E., & Corrigan, M. E. (2011). The federal government and higher education. In P. G. Altbach, P. J. Gumport, & R. O. Berdahl (Eds.), *American higher education in the twenty-first century: Social, political, and economic challenges* (3rd ed.) (pp. 113–138). Baltimore, MD: Johns Hopkins University Press.

Munroe, D. (2016). Interdisciplinary community-connected capstone courses: A model for engaging undergraduates with public policy. *Council on Undergraduate Research Quarterly, 36 (3),* 11–20.

Murphy, J., Kalbaska, N., Horton-Tognazzini, L., & Cantoni, L. (2015). Online learning and MOOCs: A framework proposal. In I. Tussyadiah & A. Inversini (Eds.), *Information and Communication Technologies in Tourism 2015: Proceedings of the International Conference in Lugano, Switzerland, February 3–6, 2015* (pp. 847–858). Cham, Switzerland: Springer International.

Murray, J. L. (2014). Course-based research on students' own institution introduces historical inquiry. *Council on Undergraduate Research Quarterly, 34 (3),* 30–36.

Murray, J. L., Fortney, S. D., Gioni, A. E., Goldnick, Z. G., LeValley, K. L., & Sechler, S. R. (2014). Personalizing history using course-based research on a student's own university. *CURQ on the Web, 34 (3),* 4–15.

Murray, J. L., Naimoli, P. H., Kagan, R. S., Kirnan, S. M., & Snider, B. R. (2004). Reflections on the use of undergraduate research to support student affairs assessment. *Journal of College Student Development, 45,* 243–252.

Myers, K. A., Lindburg, J. J., & Nied, D. M. (2013). *Allies for inclusion: Disability and equity in higher education.* ASHE Higher Education Report, v. 39, n. 5. San Francisco, CA: Jossey-Bass.

Nagda, B. A., Gregerman, S. R., Jonides, J., von Hippel, W., & Lerner, J. S. (1998). Undergraduate student-faculty research partnerships affect student retention. *The Review of Higher Education, 22,* 55–72.

Nakamura, J., Shernoff, D. J., & Hooker, C. H. (2009). *Good mentoring: Fostering excellent practice in higher education.* San Francisco, CA: Jossey-Bass.

Nash, R. J. (2001). *Religious pluralism in the academy: Opening the dialogue.* New York, NY: Lang.

National Academy of Sciences, National Academy of Engineering, & Institute of Medicine (2007a). *Rising above the gathering storm: Energizing and employing America for a brighter economic future.* Washington, DC: National Academies Press.

National Academy of Sciences, National Academy of Engineering, & Institute of Medicine (2007b). *Beyond bias and barriers: Fulfilling the potential of women in academic science and engineering.* Washington, DC: National Academies Press.

National Academy of Sciences, National Academy of Engineering, & Institute of Medicine (2010). *Rising above the gathering storm, revisited: Rapidly approaching category 5.* Washington, DC: National Academies Press.

National Center for Education Statistics (2013). *Table 318.30: Bachelor's, master's, and doctoral degrees conferred by postsecondary institutions, by sex of student and discipline division: 2011–12.* Retrieved July 29, 2015, from https://nces.ed.gov/programs/digest/d13/tables/dt13_318.30.asp.

NCHC (National Collegiate Honors Council) (2013). *Definition of honors education.* Retrieved December 15, 2016, from http://nchchonors.org/wp-content/uploads/2014/02/Definition-of-Honors-Education.pdf.

NCHC (National Collegiate Honors Council) (2015). *About NCHC.* Retrieved December 15, 2016, from http://nchchonors.org/public-press/about-nchc/.

National Commission for the Protection of Human Subjects of Biomedical and Behavioral Research (1978). *The Belmont report: Ethical principles and guidelines for the protection of human subjects of research.* Washington, DC: U.S. Department of Health, Education, and Welfare.

National Commission on Excellence in Education (1983). *A nation at risk: The imperative for educational reform.* Washington, DC: United States Department of Education.

National Education Goals Panel (1993). *The national education goals report: Building a nation of learners.* Washington, DC: United States Department of Education. Retrieved July 9, 2004, from http://www.ed.gov/pubs/goals/report/goalsrpt.txt.

NIH (National Institute of Health) (n.d.). *Who we are.* Retrieved December 16, 2016, from https://www.nih.gov/about-nih/who-we-are.

National Leadership Council for Liberal Education & America's Promise (2007). *College learning for the new global century.* Washington, DC: Association of American Colleges and Universities.

National Research Council (2006). *To recruit and advance: Women students and faculty in science and engineering.* Washington, DC: National Academies Press.

NSF (National Science Foundation) (n.d.a). *NSF at a glance.* Retrieved December 16, 2016, from http://www.nsf.gov/about/glance.jsp.

NSF (National Science Foundation) (n.d.b). *Guide to programs/Browse funding opportunities.* Retrieved December 16, 2016, from http://www.nsf.gov/funding/browse_all_funding.jsp.

NSF (National Science Foundation) (2004). *A guide for proposal writing.* NSF report no. 04–016. Arlington, VA: NSF.

NSF (National Science Foundation) (2013). *Research experiences for undergraduates (REU).* NSF report no. 13–542. Arlington, VA: NSF.

NSF (National Science Foundation) (2014). *Facilitating research at primarily undergraduate institutions.* NSF report no. 14–579. Arlington, VA: NSF.

NSF (National Science Foundation) (2015a). *Women, minorities, and persons with disabilities in science and engineering: 2015.* NSF report no. 15–311. Arlington, VA: NSF.

NSF (National Science Foundation) (2015b). *Louis Stokes Alliances for Minority Participation (LSAMP) program solicitation.* NSF report no. 15–594. Arlington, VA: NSF.

NSF (National Science Foundation) (2016). *Proposal and award policies and procedures guide: Part I—grant proposal guide.* NSF report no. 16–1. Arlington, VA: NSF.

Nazaire, D. W. & Usher, B. M. (2015). Leveraging federal work-study to support undergraduate research. *Council on Undergraduate Research Quarterly, 36 (2),* 9–17.

Neary, M. (2014). Student as producer: Research-engaged teaching frames university-wide curriculum development. *Council on Undergraduate Research Quarterly, 35 (2)*, 28–34.

Nelson, G. D. (2002). Science for all Americans. In J. L. Narum & K. Conover (Eds.), *Building robust learning environments in undergraduate science, technology, engineering, and mathematics* (pp. 29–32). New Directions for Higher Education, n. 119. San Francisco, CA: Jossey-Bass.

Nerad, M., Aanerud, R., & Cerny, J. (2004). "So you want to become a professor!" Lessons from the PhDs—ten years later study. In A. E. Austin & D. H. Wulff (Eds.), *Paths to the professoriate: Strategies for enriching the preparation of future faculty* (pp. 137–158). San Francisco, CA: Jossey-Bass.

Newman, F., Couturier, L., & Scurry, J. (2004). *The future of higher education: Rhetoric, reality, and the risks of the market.* San Francisco, CA: Jossey-Bass.

Newman, I., Daniels, M., & Faulkner, X. (2003). Open ended group projects a 'tool' for more effective teaching. *Proceedings of the Fifth Australasian Conference on Computing Education, 20*, 95–103.

Nichols, D. F. & Lyon, J. S. (2013). Improving student and parental perceptions of faculty research via an event showcasing faculty research. *Council on Undergraduate Research Quarterly, 33 (3)*, 35–41.

Nnadozie, E., Ishiyama, J., & Chon, J. (2001). Undergraduate research internships and graduate school success. *Journal of College Student Development, 42*, 145–155.

No child left behind act of 2001 (2002). Retrieved July 9, 2004, from http://www.ed.gov/print/policy/elsec/leg/esea02/index.html.

Noddings, N. (2007). *When school reform goes wrong.* New York, NY: Teachers College Press.

Noice, H. (1999). The independent research organization as a funding resource. *Council on Undergraduate Research Quarterly, 19*, 109–111.

Noice, H. (2003). Summer fellowships: One size does not fit all. *Council on Undergraduate Research Quarterly, 23*, 111–112.

Noji, K.Y. (2011). Marketing and recruiting through undergraduate research teams. *Council on Undergraduate Research Quarterly, 32 (2)*, 16–21.

Nyhus, P. J., Cole, F. R., Firmage, D. H., & Lehmann, P. S. (2002). Enhancing education through research in the environmental science laboratory: Integrating GIS and project-based learning at Colby College. *Council on Undergraduate Research Quarterly, 23*, 34–40.

Nyhus, P. J., Cole, F. R., Firmage, D. H., & Yeterian, E. H. (2002). Enhancing the integration of research and education using an interdisciplinary undergraduate research symposium. *Council on Undergraduate Research Quarterly, 23*, 16–23.

Oates, K. (2001, Summer-Fall). Promoting progressive pedagogies: A case for community based undergraduate research. *AAC&U Peer Review*, 19–20.

Oberlin Group (2016). *A brief history of the Oberlin Group.* Retrieved October 4, 2016, from http://www.oberlingroup.org/brief-history-oberlin-group.

O'Clock, P. M. & Rooney, C. J. (1996). Exposing undergraduates to research through a mentoring program. *Journal of Accounting Education, 14*, 331–346.

O'Hare, M. (2007). Faculty commitment to an inquiry-based curriculum: The Discovery Program. In K. K. Karukstis & T. E. Elgren (Eds.), *Developing and sustaining a research-supportive curriculum: A compendium of successful practices* (pp. 507–521). Washington, DC: Council on Undergraduate Research.

Olson-McBride, L., Hassemer, H., & Hoepner, J. (2016). Broadening participation: Engaging academically at-risk freshmen in undergraduate research. *Council on Undergraduate Research Quarterly, 37 (1)*, 4–10.

O'Meara, K. A. (2005). Effects of encouraging multiple forms of scholarship nationwide and across institutional types. In K. A. O'Meara & R. E. Rice (Eds.), *Faculty priorities reconsidered: Rewarding multiple forms of scholarship* (pp. 255–289). San Francisco, CA: Jossey-Bass.

O'Meara, K. A. & Rice, R. E. (Eds.) (2005). *Faculty priorities reconsidered: Rewarding multiple forms of scholarship.* San Francisco, CA: Jossey-Bass.

O'Neill, N. (2009). Undergraduate research within a framework of inclusive excellence. In M. K. Boyd & J. L. Wesemann (Eds.), *Broadening participation in undergraduate research: Fostering excellence and enhancing the impact* (pp. 31–40). Washington, DC: Council on Undergraduate Research.

Orr, A. J. (2011). The benefits and challenges of interdisciplinary undergraduate research abroad. *Council on Undergraduate Research Quarterly, 31 (4),* 42–46.

Osborn, J. M. (2008). From the president. *Council on Undergraduate Research Quarterly, 29 (1),* 5–6.

Osborn, J. M. (2009). From the president. *Council on Undergraduate Research Quarterly, 29 (3),* 4–5.

Osgood, D., Morris, L., & Rice, K. (2009). How can an interdisciplinary research program be managed effectively? *Council on Undergraduate Research Quarterly, 30 (2),* 16–20.

Oslund, C. M. (2015). *Disability services and disability studies in higher education: History, contexts, and social impacts.* New York, NY: Palgrave.

Overath, R. D., Zhang, D., & Hatherill, J. R. (2016). Implementing course-based research increases student aspirations for STEM degrees. *Council on Undergraduate Research Quarterly, 37 (2),* 4–10.

Owens, K. S. & Murkowski, A. J. (2009). A model of interdisciplinary undergraduate research experiences at a community college. In B. D. Cejda & N. Hensel (Eds.), *Undergraduate research at community colleges* (pp. 19–31). Washington, DC: Council on Undergraduate Research.

Packard, B. W. (2016). *Successful STEM mentoring initiatives for underrepresented students: A research-based field guide for faculty and administrators.* Sterling, VA: Stylus.

Pagano, T. (2009). Conducting research with early undergraduates and students with special needs. In M. K. Boyd & J. L. Wesemann (Eds.), *Broadening participation in undergraduate research: Fostering excellence and enhancing the impact* (pp. 211–214). Washington, DC: Council on Undergraduate Research.

Palloff, R. M. & Pratt, K. (2005). *Collaborating online: Learning together in community.* San Francisco, CA: Jossey-Bass.

Palloff, R. M. & Pratt, K. (2007). *Building online learning communities: Effective strategies for the virtual classroom* (2nd ed.). San Francisco, CA: Jossey-Bass.

Parish, C. (2004). Undergraduate research symposia: A review of the MERCURY conference for undergraduate computational chemistry. *Council on Undergraduate Research Quarterly, 24,* 140–141.

Parker, J. (2012). International comparisons of the integration of research into undergraduate degrees in the social sciences. *Council on Undergraduate Research Quarterly, 32 (3),* 28–33.

Parks, S. D. (2011). *Big questions, worthy dreams: Mentoring emerging adults in their search for meaning, purpose, and faith* (2nd ed.) San Francisco, CA: Jossey-Bass.

Parnell, R., Berutich, L., Henn, A., & Koressel, N. (2014). The campus as a four-year undergraduate learning laboratory on sustainability: Linking facilities, operations, curriculum, and community engagement. *Council on Undergraduate Research Quarterly, 35 (1),* 11–19.

Pascarella, E. T. & Terenzini, P. T. (1991). *How college affects students: Findings and insights from twenty years of research.* San Francisco, CA: Jossey-Bass.

Pascarella, E. T. & Terenzini, P. T. (2005). *How college affects students, volume 2: A third decade of research.* San Francisco, CA: Jossey-Bass.

Patton, L. D., Renn, K. A., Guido, F. M., & Quaye, S. J. (2016). *Student development in college: Theory, research, and practice* (3rd ed.). San Francisco, CA: Jossey-Bass.

Paul, B. (2010a). From CUR President. *Council on Undergraduate Research Quarterly, 31 (2),* 2.

Paul, B. (2010b). From CUR President. *Council on Undergraduate Research Quarterly, 31 (1),* 2.

Paul, B. (2011). From the CUR President. *Council on Undergraduate Research Quarterly, 31 (4),* 2.

Paul, E. L. (2003). Undergraduate research for the public good: Engaging undergraduates in community-based research. *Council on Undergraduate Research Quarterly, 23,* 180–185.

Paul, E. L. (2006). Community-based research as scientific and civic pedagogy. *Peer Review, 8 (1),* 12–15.

Pawlow, L. & Retzlaff, W. (2012). Undergraduate researchers become change agents for sustainability. *Council on Undergraduate Research Quarterly, 33 (1),* 28–32.

Pearson, K. N., Brown, K. L., Dershem, H. L., Winnett-Murray, K., Barney, C. C., & Lee, M. N. F. (2009). Enriching a culture of research: Expanding opportunities to a broader community. In M. K. Boyd & J. L. Wesemann (Eds.), *Broadening participation in undergraduate research: Fostering excellence and enhancing the impact* (pp. 167–178). Washington, DC: Council on Undergraduate Research.

Peeler, A. (2013). Biblical studies research in Introduction to the New Testament. *Council on Undergraduate Research Quarterly, 33 (4),* 34.

Pence, L. E., Workman, H. J., & Riecke, P. (2003). Effective laboratory experiences for students with disabilities: The role of the student laboratory assistant. *Journal of Chemical Education, 80,* 295–298.

Penn, G. (1999). *Enrollment management for the 21st century: Institutional goals, accountability, and fiscal responsibility.* ASHE-ERIC Higher Education Report, v. 26, n. 7. Washington, DC: The George Washington University, Graduate School of Education and Human Development.

Perez, J. A. (2003). Undergraduate research at two-year colleges. In J. Kinkead (Ed.), *Valuing and supporting undergraduate research* (pp. 69–77). New Directions for Teaching and Learning, n. 93. San Francisco, CA: Jossey-Bass.

Perry, W. G. (1999). *Forms of ethical and intellectual development in the college years: A scheme.* San Francisco, CA: Jossey-Bass. (Original work published 1968)

Pierce, B. A. (2005). Connecting undergraduate science research with the community. *Council on Undergraduate Research Quarterly, 25,* 180–186.

Pierce, S. R. (2001). Mission possible: Mission-based decisions can offer immediate and dramatic benefits. *Council on Undergraduate Research Quarterly, 21,* 117–121.

Plater, W. M. (2011). The context for international service learning: An invisible revolution is underway. In R. G. Bringle, J. A. Hatcher, & S. G. Jones (Eds.), *International service learning: Conceptual frameworks and research* (pp. 29–56). Sterling, VA: Stylus.

Plunkett, S. W., Saetermoe, C. L., & Quilici, J. L. (2014). Increasing the chances that under-represented students will enter doctoral programs in mental health. *Council on Undergraduate Research Quarterly, 35 (1),* 36–42.

Polack-Wahl, J. A. & Squire, P. N. (2003). Overcoming obstacles to undergraduate research at a small institution. *Journal of Computing Sciences in Colleges, 18 (5),* 128–135.

Porter, S. (2015). *To MOOC or not to MOOC: How can online learning help to build the future of higher education?* Waltham, MA: Chandos.

Posnick, M. (2014). A capstone experience: From research to performance. *Council on Undergraduate Research Quarterly, 34 (4)*, 11–17.

Posselt, J. & Black, K. (2007). Students to scholars: An undergraduate research curriculum facilitating graduate school enrollment. In K. K. Karukstis & T. E. Elgren (Eds.), *Developing and sustaining a research-supportive curriculum: A compendium of successful practices* (pp. 556–559). Washington, DC: Council on Undergraduate Research.

PKAL (Project Kaleidoscope) (2000). *A collection of statements 2000–2001.* Washington, DC: author.

PKAL (Project Kaleidoscope) (2016). *New online homes for PKAL & the PKAL LSC.* Retrieved December 23, 2016, from http://www.pkal.org/archives.cfm.

Pryor, J. H., Hurtado, S., DeAngelo, L., Palucki Blake, L., & Tran, S. (2009). *The American freshman: National norms fall 2009.* Los Angeles, CA: Higher Education Research Institute, UCLA.

Pryor, J. H., Hurtado, S., DeAngelo, L., Sharkness, J., Romero, L. C., Korn, W. K., & Tran, S. (2008). *The American freshman: National norms for fall 2008.* Los Angeles, CA: Higher Education Research Institute, UCLA.

Puglia, M. L. (2001). Laboratory experiences and the vision-impaired student: A personal journey. *Council on Undergraduate Research Quarterly, 22*, 32–34.

Pukkila, P. J., Arnold, M. S., Li, A. A., & Bickford, D. M. (2013). The graduate research consultant program: Embedding undergraduate research across the curriculum. *Council on Undergraduate Research Quarterly, 33 (4)*, 28–33.

Pukkila, P., DeCosmo, J., Swick, D. C., & Arnold, M. S. (2007). How to engage in collaborative curriculum design to foster undergraduate inquiry and research in all disciplines. In K. K. Karukstis & T. E. Elgren (Eds.), *Developing and sustaining a research-supportive curriculum: A compendium of successful practices* (pp. 341–357). Washington, DC: Council on Undergraduate Research.

Pukkila, P. J., Parikh, N. R., & Woodard, H. (2009). Catalyzing sustainable partnerships: Expanding a pilot program for rising first-year students. In M. K. Boyd & J. L. Wesemann (Eds.), *Broadening participation in undergraduate research: Fostering excellence and enhancing the impact* (pp. 137–139). Washington, DC: Council on Undergraduate Research.

Pukkila, P. J., Taylor, D. E., & Gray-Little, B. (2001). Why establish an office of undergraduate research? *Council on Undergraduate Research Quarterly, 21*, 177–179.

Pusch, M. D. & Merrill, M. (2008). Reflection, reciprocity, responsibility, and committed relativism: Intercultural development through international service-learning. In V. Savicki (Ed.), *Developing intercultural competence and transformation: Theory, research, and application in international education* (pp. 297–321). Sterling, VA: Stylus.

Pusser, B. (2010). Of a mind to labor: Reconceptualizing student work and higher education. In L. W. Perna (Ed.), *Understanding the working college student: New research and its implications for policy and practice* (pp. 134–154). Sterling, VA: Stylus.

Pyles, R. A. & Levy, F. (2009). Opening the door to early student involvement in scholarly activity: Coordinating efforts and providing financial support. In M. K. Boyd & J. L. Wesemann (Eds.), *Broadening participation in undergraduate research: Fostering excellence and enhancing the impact* (pp. 134–136). Washington, DC: Council on Undergraduate Research.

Quaye, S. J. & Harper, S. R. (Eds.) (2015). *Student engagement in higher education: Theoretical perspectives and practical approaches for diverse populations* (2nd ed.). New York, NY: Routledge.

Quinones, C. & Marsteller, P. A. (2005). The Summer Undergraduate Research Experience (SURE) at Emory University. *Council on Undergraduate Research Quarterly, 25*, 126–131.

Ramaley, J. A. (2002). New truths and old verities. In J. L. Narum & K. Conover (Eds.), *Building robust learning environments in undergraduate science, technology, engineering, and mathematics* (pp. 15–19). New Directions for Higher Education, n. 119. San Francisco, CA: Jossey-Bass.

Ramirez, M., McNicholas, J., Gilbert, B., Saez, J., & Siniawski, M. (2015). Creative funding strategies for undergraduate research at a primarily undergraduate liberal arts institution. *Council on Undergraduate Research Quarterly, 36 (2),* 5–8.

Randall, G. K. & Collins, N. (2011). The value of undergraduate research for recruitment. *Council on Undergraduate Research Quarterly, 32 (2),* 46–47.

Ravitch, D. (2009). Time to kill 'No Child Left Behind.' *Education Week, 28 (33),* 36, 30.

Reggio, P. (Ed.) (2000). *Council on Undergraduate Research Quarterly, 21 (2).*

Reggio, P. H. (2002). 2001 CUR proposal writing institute a resounding success! *Council on Undergraduate Research Quarterly, 22,* 141–142.

Reinarz, A. G. & White, E. R. (Eds.) (2001). *Beyond teaching to mentoring.* New Directions for Teaching and Learning, n. 85. San Francisco, CA: Jossey-Bass.

Reinen, L., Grosfils, E., Gaines, R., & Hazlett, R. (2006). Integrating research into a small geology department's curriculum. *Council on Undergraduate Research Quarterly, 26,* 109–114.

Reingold, I. D. (2000). Proposal writing: CUR's newest institute. *Council on Undergraduate Research Quarterly, 21,* 85.

Reiter, K. D. (2014). The early English landscape: An interdisciplinary field course. *Council on Undergraduate Resesearch Quarterly, 35 (2),* 46–47.

RCSA (Research Corporation for Science Advancement) (2015). *Cottrell Scholars: Guidelines.* Retrieved December 18, 2016, from http://rescorp.org/cottrell-scholars/cottrell-scholar-award/guidelines.

Rice, R. E. (2002). Beyond *Scholarship Reconsidered:* Toward an enlarged vision of the scholarly work of faculty members. In K. J. Zahorski (Ed.), *Scholarship in the postmodern era: New venues, new values, new visions* (pp. 7–17). New Directions for Teaching and Learning, n. 90. San Francisco, CA: Jossey-Bass.

Rice, T. & Redlawsk, D. P. (2009). Why civic service. In D. P. Redlawsk & T. Rice (Eds.), *Civic service: Service-learning with state and local government partners* (pp. 1–22). San Francisco, CA: Jossey-Bass.

Riordan, T. (2005). Introduction. In T. Riordan & J. Roth (Eds.), *Disciplines as frameworks for student learning: Teaching the practice of the disciplines* (pp. xi–xix). Sterling, VA: Stylus.

Riordan, T. & Roth, J. (Eds.) (2005). *Disciplines as frameworks for student learning: Teaching the practice of the disciplines.* Sterling, VA: Stylus.

Robins, K. & Webster, F. (2002). The virtual university? In K. Robins & F. Webster (Eds.), *The virtual university? Knowledge, markets, and management* (pp. 3–19). New York, NY: Oxford University Press.

Robison, K. M. (2014). Teaching and researching incarcerated women: Undergraduates explore education as a human right. *Council on Undergraduate Research Quarterly, 34 (3),* 13–18.

Rocheleau, J. & Speck, B. W. (2007). *Rights and wrongs in the college classroom: Ethical issues in postsecondary teaching.* Boston, MA: Anker.

Rocheleau, S., Muschio, G., Malazita, J., Petrovich, M., & Mohan, J. (2013). STAR scholars and digital cultural heritage. *Council on Undergraduate Research Quarterly, 34 (2),* 27–32.

Rogers, J. M. (2010). An undergraduate research methods course in rhetoric and composition: A model. In L. Grobman & J. Kinkead (Eds.), *Undergraduate research in English studies* (pp. 74–92). Urbana, IL: National Council of Teachers of English.

Rogers, V. D. (2003). Surviving the "culture shock" of undergraduate research in the humanities. *Council on Undergraduate Research Quarterly, 23*, 132–135.

Rohs, C. R. (2011). Undergraduate research and the tenure and promotion process. *Council on Undergraduate Research Quarterly, 31 (4)*, 13–18.

Roksa, J. & Arum, R. (2012). Life after college: The challenging transitions of the *Academically Adrift* cohort. *Change, 44 (4)*, 8–14.

Ronco, S. & Engstrom, R. (2003). Interdisciplinary REU sites at the University of South Dakota. *Council on Undergraduate Research Quarterly, 24*, 18–21.

Ronnenberg, S. C. & Sadowski, J. (2011). Recognizing undergraduate research in criteria for faculty promotion and tenure. *Council on Undergraduate Research Quarterly, 31 (4)*, 10–12.

Rosser, S. V. (2012). *Breaking into the lab: Engineering progress for women in science.* New York, NY: New York University Press.

Rotenberg, R. (2005). *The art & craft of college teaching: A guide for new professors & graduate students.* Chicago, IL: Active Learning.

Rowlett, R. S., Blockus, L., & Larson, S. (2012). Characteristics of excellence in undergraduate research (COEUR). In N. Hensel (Ed.), *Characteristics of excellence in undergraduate research (COEUR)* (pp. 2–19). Washington, DC: Council on Undergraduate Research.

Rueckert, L. (Ed.) (2008). From the issue editor. *Council on Undergraduate Research Quarterly, 29 (1)*, 4.

Rueckert, L. (2009). Assessing outcomes. *Council on Undergraduate Research Quarterly, 29 (3)*, 8–9.

Russell, S. H. (2008). Undergraduate research opportunities: Facilitating and encouraging the transition from student to scientist. In R. Taraban & R. L. Blanton (Eds.), *Creating effective undergraduate research programs in science: The transformation from student to scientist* (pp. 53–80). New York, NY: Teachers College Press.

Russell, P. J., Rivenburg, J. W., Creedon, C. F., Anderson, G., & Yager, N. A. (2004). Peer mentors in faculty/student research projects and in the classroom. In L. Kauffman & J. Stocks (Eds.), *Reinvigorating the undergraduate experience: Successful models supported by NSF's AIRE/RAIRE program* (pp. 11–12). Washington, DC: Council on Undergraduate Research.

Ryan, S., Scott, B., Freeman, H., & Patel, D. (2000). *The virtual university: The Internet and resource-based learning.* Sterling, VA: Kogan Page.

Sabatini, D. A. (1997). Teaching and research synergism: The undergraduate research experience. *Journal of Professional Issues in Engineering Education and Practice, 123*, 98–102.

Saitta, E., Morrison, B., Waldrop, J. B., & Bowdon, M. A. (2016). Introduction: Joining the flipped classroom conversation. In J. B. Waldrop & M. A. Bowdon (Eds.), *Best practices for flipping the college classroom* (pp. 1–16). New York, NY: Routledge.

Sandover, S., Partridge, L., Dunne, E., & Burkill, S. (2012). Undergraduate researchers change learning and teaching: A case study in Australia and the United Kingdom. *Council on Undergraduate Research Quarterly, 33 (1)*, 33–39.

Savicki, V. (2008). Preface. In V. Savicki (Ed.), *Developing intercultural competence and transformation: Theory, research, and application in international education* (pp. xiii–xx). Sterling, VA: Stylus.

Sax, L. J. (2008). *The gender gap in college: Maximizing the developmental potential of women and men.* San Francisco, CA: Jossey-Bass.

Schammel, C. M. G., Schisler, N., Thompson, L. K., Pollard, A. J., Schammel, D. P., McKinley, B., & Trocha, S. D. (2008). Training undergraduates in clinical research: The Furman Oncology Research Team (FORT). *Council on Undergraduate Research Quarterly, 28 (4)*, 31–38.

Schantz, M. S. (2008). Undergraduate research in the humanities: Challenges and prospects. *Council on Undergraduate Research Quarterly, 29 (2),* 26–29.

Schilt, P. & Gilbert, L. A. (2008). Undergraduate research in the humanities: Transforming expectations at a research university. *Council on Undergraduate Research Quarterly, 28 (4),* 51–55.

Schneider, C. G. (2005). Making excellence inclusive: Liberal education & America's promise. *Liberal Education, 91 (2),* 6–17.

Schneider, C. G. (2015). The LEAP challenge: Transforming for students, essential for liberal education. *Liberal Education 101 (1/2),* 6–15.

Schneider, K. R., Sullivan, L., & Collado, E. (2016). A centralized undergraduate research database: Collaboration between institutional research and university-wide research programs. *Council on Undergraduate Research Quarterly, 36 (4),* 19–25.

ScholarBridge (2015). *ScholarBridge: Connecting current and future scholars.* Retrieved June 30, 2016, from http://www.scholarbridge.com/.

Schroeder, M. J. (2008). The scholar team initiative: A framework to enhance undergraduate research, product-development, and project-management skills. *Council on Undergraduate Research Quarterly, 28 (4),* 25–29.

Schuck, J. & Kroeger, S. (1993). Essential elements in effective service delivery. In S. Kroeger & J. Schuck (Eds.), *Responding to disability issues in student affairs* (pp. 59–68). New Directions for Student Services, n. 64. San Francisco, CA: Jossey-Bass.

Schultheis, A. S., Farrell, T. M., & Paul, E. L. (2011). Promoting undergraduate research through revising tenure and promotion policy. *Council on Undergraduate Research Quarterly, 31 (4),* 25–31.

Schummer, T., Lukosch, S., & Haake, J. M. (2005). Teaching distributed software development with the project method. *Proceedings of the 2005 Conference on Computer Support for Collaborative Learning: Learning 2005: The Next 10 Years!,* 577–586.

Schuster, J. H. & Finkelstein, M. J. (2006). *The American faculty: The restructuring of academic work and careers.* Baltimore, MD: Johns Hopkins University Press.

Scordilis, S. P. & Litwin, T. S. (2005). Integrating technology, science and undergraduate education at Smith College: The creation of student-faculty research centers. *Council on Undergraduate Research Quarterly, 25,* 138–140.

Scott, D. (1995). Global-scale concerns and local undergraduate research. *Council on Undergraduate Research Quarterly, 16,* 63–65.

Scott, D. (1996). Academic-industry relations done the right way. *Council on Undergraduate Research Quarterly, 16,* 197–199.

Scott, D. M. (1994). Looking ahead to the year 2000. *Council on Undergraduate Research Quarterly, 15,* 70–72.

Seal, B. C., Wynne, D., & MacDonald, G. (2002). Deaf students, teachers, and interpreters in the chemistry lab. *Journal of Chemical Education, 79,* 239–243.

Sears, R. R. & Yoder, L. S. M. (2014). Fostering students' commitment to service through international field research. *Council on Undergraduate Research Quarterly, 35 (2),* 20–27.

Segura-Totten, M. (2012). Bringing everyone to the table: A strategy for creating an undergraduate research center supporting all academic fields. In J. Kinkead & L. Blockus (Eds.), *Undergraduate research offices and programs: Models & practices* (pp. 214–219). Washington, DC: Council on Undergraduate Research.

Selby, R. (2008). Designing transformation in international education. In V. Savicki (Ed.), *Developing intercultural competence and transformation: Theory, research, and application in international education* (pp. 1–10). Sterling, VA: Stylus.

Seymour, E., Hunter, A., Laursen, S. L., & DeAntoni, T. (2004). Establishing the benefits of research experiences for undergraduates in the sciences: First findings from a three-year study. *Science Education, 88,* 493–534.

Shachter, A. M. (2007). Responsible conduct in research instruction in undergraduate research programs. In K. K. Karukstis & T. E. Elgren (Eds.), *Developing and sustaining a research-supportive curriculum: A compendium of successful practices* (pp. 209–239). Washington, DC: Council on Undergraduate Research.

Shanahan, J. O. (2011). Scaffolding research skills in the humanities curriculum. In N. Y. Klos, J. O. Shanahan, & G. Young (Eds.), *Creative inquiry in the arts & humanities: Models of undergraduate research* (pp. 7–14). Washington, DC: Council on Undergraduate Research.

Shanahan, J. O., Liu, X., Manak, J., Miller, S. M., Tan, J., & Yu, C. W. (2015). Research-informed practice, practice-informed research: The integral role of undergraduate research in professional disciplines. *Council on Undergraduate Research Quarterly, 35 (4),* 6–16.

Shapiro, C. A. & Sax, L. J. (2011). Major selection and persistence for women in STEM. In J. G. Gayles (Ed.), *Attracting and retaining women in STEM* (pp. 5–18). New Directions for Institutional Research, n. 152. San Francisco, CA: Jossey-Bass.

Shapiro, N. S. & Levine, J. H. (1999). *Creating learning communities: A practical guide to winning support, organizing for change, and implementing programs.* San Francisco, CA: Jossey-Bass.

Shaw, V. N. (2004). *Career-making in postmodern academia: Process, structure, and consequence.* Lanham, MD: Hamilton.

Shellito, C., Shea, K., Weissmann, G., Mueller-Solger, A., & Davis, W. (2001). Successful mentoring of undergraduate researchers: Tips for creating positive student research experiences. *Journal of College Science Teaching, 30,* 460–464.

Shields, G. C. (2002). The benefits of forming a consortium for an NSF-MRI proposal. *Council on Undergraduate Research Quarterly, 23,* 80–81.

Shields, G. C. (2010). Creating a comprehensive summer undergraduate research program despite fiscal challenges. *Council on Undergraduate Research Quarterly, 30 (4),* 18–21.

Shields, G. C., Hewitt, G. J., & North, L. (2010). Using pre-college research to promote student success and increase the number of science majors. *Council on Undergraduate Research Quarterly, 31 (1),* 43–47.

Shokair, S. M. (2002). The University of California-Irvine Undergraduate Research Symposium—a research university perspective. *Council on Undergraduate Research Quarterly, 22,* 160–164.

Shors, T. & McFadden, S. H. (2009). Facilitating learning through interdisciplinary undergraduate research involving retrospective epidemiological studies and memories of older adults. *Council on Undergraduate Research Quarterly, 30 (2),* 34–38.

Shrier, C. (2007). The anatomy of a science scholar. In K. K. Karukstis & T. E. Elgren (Eds.), *Developing and sustaining a research-supportive curriculum: A compendium of successful practices* (pp. 550–552). Washington, DC: Council on Undergraduate Research.

Shrum, R. K. (2011). Oral history as a model for undergraduate research. In N. Y. Klos, J. O. Shanahan, & G. Young (Eds.), *Creative inquiry in the arts & humanities: Models of undergraduate research* (pp. 59–66). Washington, DC: Council on Undergraduate Research.

Shulman, L. S. (2005). Signature pedagogies in the professions. *Daedalus, 134 (3),* 52–59.

Shulman, L. S. (2007). Foreword. In R. Bacchetti & T. Ehrlich (Eds.), *Reconnecting education & foundations: Turning good intentions into educational capital* (pp. xi–xv). San Francisco, CA: Jossey-Bass.

Silberman, M. (1996). *Active learning: 101 strategies to teach any subject.* Boston, MA: Allyn & Bacon.

Simmons, J. A., Anderson, L. J., Bowne, D. R., Dosch, J. J., Gartner, T. B., Hoopes, M. F., Kuers, K., Lindquist, E. S., McCay, T. S., Pohlad, B. R., Thomas, C. L., & Shea, K. L. (2016). Collaborative research networks provide unique opportunities for faculty and student researchers. *Council on Undergraduate Research Quarterly, 36 (4)*, 12–18.

Simon, J. A. (2000). Legal issues in serving students with disabilities in postsecondary education. In H. A. Belch (Ed.), *Serving students with disabilities* (pp. 69–81). New Directions for Student Services, n. 91. San Francisco, CA: Jossey-Bass.

Sims, J. D., Le, J., Emery, B., & Smith, J. (2012). Beyond the quantitative headcount: Considering the un-captured qualitative impact of engaging undergraduates in research. *Council on Undergraduate Research Quarterly, 32 (3)*, 23–27.

Singer, J. & Weiler, D. (2009). A longitudinal student outcomes evaluation of the Buffalo State College summer undergraduate research program. *Council on Undergraduate Research Quarterly, 29 (3)*, 20–25.

Singer, J. & Zimmerman, B. (2012). Evaluating a summer undergraduate research program: Measuring student outcomes and program impact. *Council on Undergraduate Research Quarterly, 32 (3)*, 40–47.

Singer, J. K. (2007). Integrating undergraduate research into the curriculum—SUNY, College at Buffalo. In K. K. Karukstis & T. E. Elgren (Eds.), *Developing and sustaining a research-supportive curriculum: A compendium of successful practices* (pp. 391–394). Washington, DC: Council on Undergraduate Research.

Slavin, R. E. (2015). *Educational psychology: Theory and practice* (11th ed.). Boston. MA: Pearson.

Slezak, J. (2007). Research at two-year colleges. *Journal of Chemical Education, 84*, 1108.

Slobodzian, J. T. & Pancsofar, N. (2014). Integrating undergraduate research into teacher training: Supporting the transition from learner to educator. *Council on Undergraduate Research Quarterly, 34 (3)*, 43–47.

Slobodzian, J., Pancsofar, N., Hall, M., & Peel, A. (2016). A closer look at the pragmatic model of mentored undergraduate research in a school of education. *Council on Undergraduate Research Quarterly, 37 (1)*, 41–45.

Slocum, R. D. & Scholl, J. D. (2013). NSF support of research at primarily undergraduate institutions. *Council on Undergraduate Research Quarterly, 34 (1)*, 31–40.

Smart, J. C. & Ethington, C. A. (1995). Disciplinary and institutional differences in undergraduate education goals. In N. Hativa & M. Marincovich (Eds.), *Disciplinary differences in teaching and learning: Implications for practice* (pp. 49–57). New Directions for Teaching and Learning, n. 64. San Francisco, CA: Jossey-Bass.

Smith, B. L. & Williams, L. B. (2007). Academic and student affairs: Fostering student success. In B. L. Smith & L. B. Williams (Eds.), *Learning communities and student affairs: Partnering for powerful learning* (pp. 1–33). Olympia, WA: The Evergreen State College, Washington Center for Improving the Quality of Undergraduate Education.

Smyser, M. (2003). Maximum mobility and function. *American School & University, 75 (11)*, 24, 26–28.

Snyder, T. D., de Brey, C., & Dillow, S. A. (2016). *Digest of education statistics 2014* (NCES 2016–006). Washington, DC: National Center for Education Statistics, U.S. Department of Education.

Spears, J. (2009). Saluki Research Rookies Program: Building partnerships across campus. *Council on Undergraduate Research Quarterly, 30 (1)*, 25–28.

Speck, B. W. (2001). Why service-learning? In M. Canada & B. W. Speck (Eds.), *Developing and implementing service-learning programs* (pp. 3–13). New Directions for Higher Education, n. 114. San Francisco, CA: Jossey-Bass.

Spencer, S. E. & Tuma, K. (Eds.) (2007). *The guide to successful short-term programs abroad* (2nd ed.). Washington, DC: NAFSA.

Spieles, D. J. & Cunfer, G. (2002). Collaborative integration of geographic information systems (GIS) in co-curricular undergraduate research. *Council on Undergraduate Research Quarterly, 23,* 41–44.

Spronken-Smith, R. (2010). Undergraduate research and inquiry-based learning: Is there a difference? Insights from research in New Zealand. *Council on Undergraduate Research Quarterly, 30 (4),* 28–35.

SUNY New Paltz (State University of New York at New Paltz) (n.d.). *The Benjamin Center for Public Policy Initiatives.* Retrieved December 21, 2016, from http://www.newpaltz.edu/benjamincenter/.

Stearns, P. N. (2009). *Educating global citizens in colleges and universities: Challenges and opportunities.* New York, NY: Routledge.

Steele, S. R. (2008). Web-based surveys facilitate undergraduate research and knowledge. *Journal of Economic Education, 39 (1),* 41–49.

Steneck, N. H. (2007). *ORI introduction to the responsible conduct of research.* Washington, DC: Office of Research Integrity, U.S. Department of Health and Human Services.

Stocks, J. (2006). From the guest editor. *Council on Undergraduate Research Quarterly, 27,* 52–53.

Stocks, J. (Ed.) (2010). From the issue editor. *Council on Undergraduate Research Quarterly, 30 (3),* 10.

Stocks, J. (Ed.) (2011a). From the issue editor. *Council on Undergraduate Research Quarterly, 32 (1),* 6.

Stocks, J. (2011b). Undergraduate research for all? *Council on Undergraduate Research Quarterly, 32 (1),* 6–7.

Stocks, J. (Ed.) (2013). From the issue editor. *Council on Undergraduate Research Quarterly, 34 (1),* 5.

Stocks, J. (Ed.) (2014). From the CURQ issue editor. *Council on Undergraduate Research Quarterly, 35 (1),* 4.

Stocks, J. & Gregerman, S. (2009). Interdisciplinary research projects supported by the NCUR/Lancy program. *Council on Undergraduate Research Quarterly, 30 (2),* 21–25.

Stocks, J., Ramey, J. B., & Lazarus, B. (2004). Involving faculty at research universities in undergraduate research. In L. Kauffman & J. Stocks (Eds.), *Reinvigorating the undergraduate experience: Successful models supported by NSF's AIRE/RAIRE program* (pp. 7–8). Washington, DC: Council on Undergraduate Research.

Stoecker, R. (2003). Community-based research: From practice to theory and back again. *Michigan Journal of Community Service Learning, 9,* 35–46.

Stone, C., Van Horn, C., & Zukin, C. (2012). *Chasing the American dream: Recent college graduates and the great recession.* New Brunswick, NJ: John J. Heldrich Center for Workforce Development, Edward J. Bloustein School of Planning and Public Policy, Rutgers, The State University of New Jersey. (ERIC Document Reproduction Service no. ED535270)

Strand, K. J. (2000). Community-based research as pedagogy. *Michigan Journal of Community Service Learning, 7,* 85–96.

Strand, K. & Jansen, E. (2013). Novel transdisciplinary undergraduate research provides a developmental pathway. *Council on Undergraduate Research Quarterly, 34 (1),* 7–11.

Strand, K., Marullo, S., Cutforth, N., Stoecker, R., & Donohue, P. (2003). *Community-based research and higher education: Principles and practices.* San Francisco, CA: Jossey-Bass.

Strange, C. (2000). Creating environments of ability. In H. A. Belch (Ed.), *Serving students with disabilities* (pp. 19–30). New Directions for Student Services, n. 91. San Francisco, CA: Jossey-Bass.

Strassburger, J. (1995). Embracing undergraduate research. *Council on Undergraduate Research Quarterly, 16,* 120–122.

Strayhorn, T. L. (2012). *College students' sense of belonging: A key to educational success for all students.* New York, NY: Routledge.

Student Opportunity Center (2016). *What we do.* Retrieved June 30, 2016, from https://www.studentopportunitycenter.com/#/about.

Sukumaran, B., Jahan, K., Dorland, D., Everett, J., Kadlowec, J., Gephardt, Z., & Chin, S. (2006). Engineering clinics: An integration of research into the undergraduate engineering curriculum. *Council on Undergraduate Research Quarterly, 26,* 115–121.

Swift, J. (2012). The critical role of faculty in advancing undergraduate research. In N. H. Hensel & E. L. Paul (Eds.), *Faculty support and undergraduate research: Innovations in faculty role definition, workload, and reward* (pp. 19–25). Washington, DC: Council on Undergraduate Research.

Sykes, C. J. (1988). *ProfScam: Professors and the demise of higher education.* Washington, DC: Regnery Gateway.

Szymanski, D. W., Hadlock, C., & Zlotkowski, E. (2012). Using public-sector research projects to engage undergraduates. *Council on Undergraduate Research Quarterly, 33 (2),* 19–26.

Tagg, J. (2003). *The Learning Paradigm College.* Bolton, MA: Anker.

Tangney, S. (2009). Live fast, die young, and leave a good-looking corpse: What's really behind the push for undergraduate scholarship—and what should be. In L. L. Behling (Ed.), *Reading, writing, research: Undergraduate students as scholars in literary studies* (pp. 53–64). Washington, DC: Council on Undergraduate Research.

Taniguchi, M. I. (2003). Internet metaphors matter. In M. M. Watts (Ed.), *Technology: Taking the distance out of learning* (pp. 13–21). New Directions for Teaching and Learning, n. 94. San Francisco, CA: Jossey-Bass.

Tannenbaum, M. (2006). Research and the curriculum. *Council on Undergraduate Research Quarterly, 26,* 102–103.

Tanner, K. & Allen, D. (2007). Cultural competence in the college biology classroom. *CBE—Life Sciences Education, 6,* 251–258.

Tapping America's Potential (2008). *Gaining momentum, losing ground.* Washington, DC: Business Roundtable. Retrieved July 15, 2008, from the Tapping America's Potential website: http://www.tap2015.org/news/tap_2008_progress.pdf.

Taraban, R. (2008). What is undergraduate research and why should we support it? In R. Taraban & R. L. Blanton (Eds.), *Creating effective undergraduate research programs in science: The transformation from student to scientist* (pp. 3–10). New York, NY: Teachers College Press.

Taylor, M. C. (2010). *Crisis on campus: A bold plan for reforming our colleges and universities.* New York, NY: Knopf.

Temple, L., Sibley, T. Q., & Orr, A. J. (2010). *How to mentor undergraduate researchers.* Washington, DC: Council on Undergraduate Research.

Thabet, W. Y. (1994). Undergraduate research significance and funding: A perspective from Union College. *Council on Undergraduate Research Quarterly, 15,* 87–90.

The attack of the MOOCs (July 20, 2013). *The Economist.* Retrieved July 24, 2013, from http://www.economist.com/news/business/21582001-army-new-online-courses-scaring-wits-out-traditional-universities-can-they.

Thompson, J. D., Hawkes, R. W., & Avery, R. W. (1969). Truth strategies and university organization. *Educational Administration Quarterly*, *5 (2)*, 4–25.

Thornton, J. E., Beinstein-Miller, J., Gandha, T., & deWinstanley, P. (2004). Priming the pumps: Developing and assessing research-like experiences in courses. In L. Kauffman & J. Stocks (Eds.), *Reinvigorating the undergraduate experience: Successful models supported by NSF's AIRE/RAIRE program* (pp. 15–16). Washington, DC: Council on Undergraduate Research.

Thorsheim, H., LaCost, H., & Narum, J. L. (2010). Peer mentoring of undergraduate research in community colleges: A "transplantable" model for workshops. *Council on Undergraduate Research Quarterly*, *31 (2)*, 26–32.

Tiffin, J. & Rajasingham, L. (2003). *The global virtual university*. New York, NY: RoutledgeFalmer.

Tinto, V. (1993). *Leaving college: Rethinking the causes and cures of student attrition* (2nd ed.). Chicago, IL: University of Chicago Press.

Towle, D. W., Hand, P. H., Kent, B., McKernan, M., & Lawson, T. G. (2003). An intensive short-course in molecular biology for undergraduates. *Council on Undergraduate Research Quarterly*, *24*, 79–84.

Tritelli, D. (2014). Looking back at one hundred years of the Association of American Colleges and Universities: An interview with Presidents John W. Chandler, Paula P. Brownlee, and Carol Geary Schneider. *Liberal Education*, *100 (4)*, 6–19.

Tritton, T. R. (2002). *The environment for scientific research by undergraduates: Some thoughts on reading the Academic Excellence study*. Tucson, AZ: Research Corporation. (ERIC Document Reproduction Service no. ED469491)

Troischt, P. W., Koopmann, R. A., O'Donoghue, A., Odekon, M. C., & Haynes, M. P. (2016). The undergraduate ALFALFA team: A collaborative model for undergraduate research in major long-term astronomy projects. *Council on Undergraduate Research Quarterly*, *36 (4)*, 4–11.

Trolian, T. L. & Fouts, K. S. (2011). No Child Left Behind: Implications for college student learning. *About Campus*, *16 (3)*, 2–7.

Trosset, C., Lopatto, D., & Elgin, S. (2008). Implementation and assessment of course-embedded undergraduate research experiences: Some explorations. In R. Taraban & R. L. Blanton (Eds.), *Creating effective undergraduate research programs in science: The transformation from student to scientist* (pp. 33–49). New York, NY: Teachers College Press.

Turner, J. E. (2005). The institutionalization of undergraduate research at the Virginia Military Institute (VMI). *Council on Undergraduate Research Quarterly*, *25*, 108–112.

Turrens, J. F. (2003). Undergraduate research at the University of South Alabama. *Council on Undergraduate Research Quarterly*, *23*, 116–117.

Uffelman, L. K. (1995). Victorian periodicals: Research opportunities for faculty-undergraduate research. *Council on Undergraduate Research Quarterly*, *15*, 207–208.

Undergraduate Research Community (URC) (2016). *Undergraduate Research Journal for the Human Sciences*. Retrieved December 18, 2016, from http://kon.org/CFP/cfp_urjhs.html.

Urry, J. (2002). Globalizing the academy. In K. Robins & F. Webster (Eds.), *The virtual university? Knowledge, markets, and management* (pp. 20–29). New York, NY: Oxford University Press.

U.S. Department of Education (2006). *A test of leadership: Charting the future of U.S. higher education*. Washington, DC: author.

U.S. Department of Education (2011). *Frequently asked questions*. Retrieved December 16, 2016, from http://www2.ed.gov/programs/triomcnair/faq.html.

U.S. Department of Energy (2016). *SULI program overview*. Retrieved December 16, 2016, from http://science.energy.gov/wdts/suli/.

U.S. News & World Report (2007). *America's best colleges 2007: College search.* Retrieved June 21, 2007, from http://www.usnews.com/usnews/edu/college/tools/search.php.

Van Dusen, G. C. (1997). *The virtual campus: Technology and reform in higher education.* ASHE-ERIC Higher Education Report v. 25, n. 5. Washington, DC: The George Washington University, Graduate School of Education and Human Development.

Van Dusen, G. C. (2000). *Digital dilemma: Issues of access, cost, and quality in media-enhanced and distance education.* ASHE-ERIC Higher Education Report v. 27, n. 5. San Francisco, CA: Jossey-Bass.

Van Galen, D. A. (1995). Undergraduate research in an international setting: An environmental science project in Norway. *Council on Undergraduate Research Quarterly, 16,* 85–88.

Vaughan, M. (2011). Differing college-level tenure models and the culture of undergraduate research. *Council on Undergraduate Research Quarterly, 31 (4),* 19–24.

Vaught, S. (2009). Telling tales in two cities: How historical undergraduate research can inform urban policy and dismiss urban legends. *Council on Undergraduate Research Quarterly, 29 (4),* 28–32.

VentureWell (2016). *E-team program.* Retrieved December 18, 2016, from http://venturewell.org/student-grants/.

Vieyra, M., Carlson, A., Leaver, E., & Timmerman, B. (2013). Undergraduate research: I am not sure what it is, but I don't have time to do it anyway. *Council on Undergraduate Research Quarterly, 33 (3),* 27–34.

Vieyra, M., Gilmore, J., & Timmerman, B. (2011). Requiring research may improve retention in STEM fields for underrepresented women. *Council on Undergraduate Research Quarterly, 32 (1),* 13–19.

Visick, J. E. (2006). Compensation for summer research with undergraduates: Issues and options. *Council on Undergraduate Research Quarterly, 26,* 182–184.

Waddill, P. & Einstein, G. (1996). Collaboration between researchers at primarily undergraduate institutions and major research institutions. *Council on Undergraduate Research Quarterly, 16,* 218–221.

Wade, C. B., Gragson, D., Wubah, D., & Nalley, A. (2000, June). *Academic/industrial success stories involving primarily undergraduate institutions.* Presentation conducted at the Council on Undergraduate Research National Conference, Wooster, OH.

Wadsworth, D. (2005). Ready or not? Where the public stands on higher education reform. In R. H. Hersh & J. Merrow (Eds.), *Declining by degrees: Higher education at risk* (pp. 23–38). New York, NY: Palgrave Macmillan.

Waite, S. & Davis, B. (2006a). Developing undergraduate research skills in a faculty of education: Motivation through collaboration. *Higher Education Research & Development, 25,* 403–419.

Waite, S. & Davis, B. (2006b). Collaboration as a catalyst for critical thinking in undergraduate research. *Journal of Further and Higher Education, 30,* 405–419.

Walczak, M. & Richey, M. (2016). Directed undergraduate research courses: A viable academic-year option. *Council on Undergraduate Research Quarterly, 37 (1),* 46–47.

Walker, G. E., Golde, C. M., Jones, L., Bueschel, A. C., & Hutchings, P. (2008). *The formation of scholars: Rethinking doctoral education for the twenty-first century.* San Francisco, CA: Jossey-Bass.

Walkington, H., Edwards-Jones, A., & Grestly, K. (2013). Strategies for widening students' engagement with undergraduate research journals. *Council on Undergraduate Research Quarterly, 34 (1),* 24–30.

Wall, V. A. & Evans, N. J. (Eds.) (2000). *Toward acceptance: Sexual orientation issues on campus.* Lanham, MD: University Press of America.

Walpole, M. (1997, March). *College and class status: The effect of social class background on college impact and outcomes.* Paper presented at the annual meeting of the American Educational Research Association, Chicago, IL. (ERIC Document Reproduction Service no. ED408885)

Walpole, M. (1998, April). *Social mobility and highly-selective colleges: The effect of social class background on college involvement and outcomes.* Paper presented at the annual meeting of the American Educational Research Association, San Diego, CA. (ERIC Document Reproduction Service no. ED428306)

Walsh, M. J. (2007a). SUMR: Colgate University's program to support faculty mentoring student summer research. In K. K. Karukstis & T. E. Elgren (Eds.), *Developing and sustaining a research-supportive curriculum: A compendium of successful practices* (pp. 410–411). Washington, DC: Council on Undergraduate Research.

Walsh, M. J. (2007b). Colgate University's Upstate Institute Field School: Community-based research and learning. In K. K. Karukstis & T. E. Elgren (Eds.), *Developing and sustaining a research-supportive curriculum: A compendium of successful practices* (pp. 483–484). Washington, DC: Council on Undergraduate Research.

Walter, C. W. (2013). Home energy assessments in a general education first-year seminar. *Council on Undergraduate Research Quarterly, 33 (4),* 34.

Ward, K. (2003). *Faculty service roles and the scholarship of engagement.* ASHE-ERIC Higher Education Report v. 29, n. 5. San Francisco, CA: Jossey-Bass.

Ward, R. M. & Dixon, L. (2008). The first-year research experience: Miami University's Scholastic Enhancement Program—Undergraduate Research Option. *Council on Undergraduate Research Quarterly, 29 (1),* 36–40.

Washburn, J. (2005). *University, Inc.: The corporate corruption of higher education.* New York, NY: Basic.

Watford, B. A. (2007). Undergraduate student support programs. In R. J. Burke & M. C. Mattis (Eds.), *Women and minorities in science, technology, engineering, and mathematics: Upping the numbers* (pp. 276–313). Northampton, MA: Elgar.

Watkins, L. M. (2009). Strengthening inter-institutional ties: Extending research partnerships to a two-year campus. In M. K. Boyd & J. L. Wesemann (Eds.), *Broadening participation in undergraduate research: Fostering excellence and enhancing the impact* (pp. 77–87). Washington, DC: Council on Undergraduate Research.

Way, T. P. (2006). A virtual laboratory model for encouraging undergraduate research. *ACM SIGCSE Bulletin, 38 (1),* 203–207.

Webb, F. J. & Cortez, A. R. (2009). Developing scholars: Targeting excellence using the axiom of achievement. In M. K. Boyd & J. L. Wesemann (Eds.), *Broadening participation in undergraduate research: Fostering excellence and enhancing the impact* (pp. 257–268). Washington, DC: Council on Undergraduate Research.

Webber, K. L., Fechheimer, M., & Kleiber, P. B. (2012). Defining and measuring participation in undergraduate research at the University of Georgia. *Council on Undergraduate Research Quarterly, 32 (3),* 15–17.

Webster, L. D. & Mirielli, E. J. (2007). Student reflections on an academic service learning experience in a computer science classroom. *Proceedings of the 8th ACM SIGITE Conference on Information Technology Education,* 207–212.

Webster, S. K. & Karpinsky, N. (2015). Using COEUR to assess the undergraduate research environment: A three-stage model for institutional assessment. *Council on Undergraduate Research Quarterly, 36 (1),* 32–39.

Weigel, V. B. (2002). *Deep learning for a digital age: Technology's untapped potential to enrich higher education.* San Francisco, CA: Jossey-Bass.

Weimer, M. (2002). *Learner-centered teaching: Five key changes to practice.* San Francisco, CA: Jossey-Bass.

Weiss, G. M. (2013). Smartphone sensor mining research: Successes and lessons. *Council on Undergraduate Research Quarterly, 34 (2)*, 17–21.

Wenzel, T. (Ed.) (2001a). From the editor. *Council on Undergraduate Research Quarterly, 22 (2)*, 52.

Wenzel, T. J. (2001b). What is an appropriate teaching load for a research-active faculty member at a predominantly undergraduate institution? *Council on Undergraduate Research Quarterly, 21*, 104–107.

Werner, T. C. & Sorum, C. E. (2003). Enriching undergraduate research and scholarly activity opportunities in all disciplines at Union College. *Council on Undergraduate Research Quarterly, 23*, 186–190.

Wettack, S. (2007). Administrative contributions to a research-supportive curriculum. In K. K. Karukstis & T. E. Elgren (Eds.), *Developing & sustaining a research-supportive curriculum: A compendium of successful practices* (pp. 565–577). Washington, DC: Council on Undergraduate Research.

Whatley, K. M. & Miller, J. W. (2001). The UNCA Undergraduate Research Program: An evolution. *Council on Undergraduate Research Quarterly, 22*, 86–90.

White, H. B., III (2007). Stimulating attitudes of inquiry with problem-based learning. In K. K. Karukstis & T. E. Elgren (Eds.), *Developing and sustaining a research-supportive curriculum: A compendium of successful practices* (pp. 9–19). Washington, DC: Council on Undergraduate Research.

White, K., Ward, R., Agarwal, M., Bennett, T., & Varahramyan, K. (2013). Innovation to enterprise: Undergraduate researchers as entrepreneurs. *Council on Undergraduate Research Quarterly, 34 (1)*, 12–17.

Whitt, M. E. & Henningsen, M. (2010). Partners in scholarship: The making of an anthology. In L. Grobman & J. Kinkead (Eds.), *Undergraduate research in English studies* (pp. 13–29). Urbana, IL: National Council of Teachers of English.

Williams, D. A., Berger, J. B., & McClendon, S. A. (2005). *Toward a model of inclusive excellence and change in postsecondary institutions.* Washington, DC: Association of American Colleges and Universities.

Williams, J. R. & Johnson, K. E. (2007). Implementing a capstone honors research experience in psychology. In K. K. Karukstis & T. E. Elgren (Eds.), *Developing and sustaining a research-supportive curriculum: A compendium of successful practices* (pp. 259–261). Washington, DC: Council on Undergraduate Research.

Willison, J. & O'Regan, K. (2007). Commonly known, commonly not known, totally unknown: A framework for students becoming researchers. *Higher Education Research & Development, 26*, 393–409.

Wilshire, B. (1990). *The moral collapse of the university: Professionalism, purity, and alienation.* Albany, NY: State University of New York Press.

Wilson, A. (2012). Using the National Survey of Student Engagement to measure undergraduate research participation. *Council on Undergraduate Research Quarterly, 32 (3)*, 9–14.

Wilson, A. & Howitt, S. (2012). Is more always better? An Australian experiment with a research-intensive undergraduate degree. *Council on Undergraduate Research Quarterly, 33 (2)*, 28–33.

Wilson, K. J. & Crowe, M. (2010). Undergraduate research: A powerful pedagogy to engage sophomores. In M. S. Hunter, B. F. Tobolowsky, J. N. Gardner, S. E. Evenbeck, J. A. Pattengale, M. A. Schaller, L. A. Schreiner, & Associates, *Helping sophomores succeed:*

Understanding and improving the second-year experience (pp. 177–188). San Francisco, CA: Jossey-Bass.

Wilson, K., Crowe, M., Singh, J., Stamatoplos, A., Rubens, E., Gosney, J., Dimaculangan, D., Levy, F., Zrull, M., & Pyles, R. (2009). Using electronic portfolios to measure student gains from mentored research. *Council on Undergraduate Research Quarterly, 29 (3)*, 26–32.

Wilson, R., Cramer, A., & Smith, J. L. (2004). Research is another word for education. In L. Kauffman & J. Stocks (Eds.), *Reinvigorating the undergraduate experience: Successful models supported by NSF's AIRE/RAIRE program* (pp. 1–2). Washington, DC: Council on Undergraduate Research.

Wilson, V. P. (2009). Transforming the academy: Fulfilling the promise of leadership. In M. K. Boyd & J. L. Wesemann (Eds.), *Broadening participation in undergraduate research: Fostering excellence and enhancing the impact* (pp. 319–329). Washington, DC: Council on Undergraduate Research.

Wingspread Group on Higher Education (1993). *An American imperative: Higher expectations for higher education.* Racine, WI: Johnson Foundation.

Winningham, R. G., Templeton, J. H., Dutton, B. E., & Scheck, S. H. (2009). A grassroots, faculty-driven initiative to institutionalize undergraduate research: The ins and outs of cultivating administrative support. *Council on Undergraduate Research Quarterly, 30 (1)*, 29–34.

Wittner, D. G. (2007). Making history: Developing a research tradition with Utica College's history majors. *Council on Undergraduate Research Quarterly, 28 (1)*, 29–32.

Wolverton, A., Nagaoka, L., & Wolverton, M. (2015). *Breaking in: Women's accounts of how choices shape STEM careers.* Sterling, VA: Stylus.

Wong, N. Y. J. (2004, May-June). *An exploratory research study of Massachusetts Institute of Technology's Undergraduate Research Opportunities Program (UROP): The impact of student-supervisor relationships.* Paper presented at the Annual Forum of the Association for Institutional Research, Boston, MA. (ERIC Document Reproduction Service no. ED491017)

Wood, J. L. & Palmer, R. T. (2015). *Black men in higher education: A guide to ensuring student success.* New York, NY: Routledge.

Woolfolk, A. (2017). *Educational psychology: Active learning edition* (13th ed.). Boston, MA: Pearson.

Wozniak, C. (2011). Freshman fellows: Recruiting and retaining great students through research opportunities. *Council on Undergraduate Research Quarterly, 32 (2)*, 8–15.

Wubah, D. A., Schaefer, D., Brakke, D. F., Downey, D., Gasparich, G. E., & McDonald, G. (2000). Retention of minority students through research. *Council on Undergraduate Research Quarterly, 20*, 120–126.

Xie, Y. & Shauman, K. A. (2003). *Women in science: Career processes and outcomes.* Cambridge, MA: Harvard University Press.

Yaffe, K., Bender, C., & Sechrest, L. (2012). What is a mentor? *Council on Undergraduate Research Quarterly, 33 (2)*, 34–38.

Yavelow, J. (2006). Rider University Science Advisory Board: A mechanism for successful partnering between the university, industry and the community. *Council on Undergraduate Research Quarterly, 27 (1)*, 18–21.

Yost, D. S. & Soslau, E. (2009). School-based service-learning as action research. In T. Kelshaw, F. Lazarus, & J. Minier (Eds.), *Partnerships for service-learning: Impacts on communities and students* (pp. 206–234). San Francisco, CA: Jossey-Bass.

Young, G. (2008). Interdisciplinary research seminars in the arts and humanities at Montana State University. *Council on Undergraduate Research Quarterly, 29 (2)*, 30–33.

Young, G. (2011). Undergraduate research in the arts and humanities. In N. Y. Klos, J. O. Shanahan, & G. Young (Eds.), *Creative inquiry in the arts & humanities: Models of undergraduate research* (pp. 87–91). Washington, DC: Council on Undergraduate Research.

Young, G. & Nelson, M. (2010). NCUR: A look back as CUR and NCUR join forces. *Council on Undergraduate Research Quarterly, 31 (1)*, 27–30.

Young, J. R. (December 4, 2012). Providers of free MOOC's now charge employers for access to student data. *Chronicle of Higher Education*. Retrieved July 16, 2013, from http://search.proquest.com/docview/1237570917?accountid=9784.

Zeidel, R. F. & Kramschuster, K. (2013). What happened on your birthday: A model for building undergraduate research into the general education U.S. history survey. *Council on Undergraduate Research Quarterly, 33 (4)*, 34.

Zemsky, R., Wegner, G. R., & Massy, W. F. (2006). *Remaking the American university: Market-smart and mission-centered*. New Brunswick, NJ: Rutgers University Press.

Zubizarreta, J. (2004). *The learning portfolio: Reflective practice for improving student learning*. San Francisco, CA: Anker.

Zusman, A. (2005). Challenges facing higher education in the twenty-first century. In P. G. Altbach, R. O. Berdahl, & P. J. Gumport (Eds.), *American higher education in the twenty-first century: Social, political, and economic challenges*, 2nd ed. (pp. 115–160). Baltimore, MD: Johns Hopkins University Press.

Zydney, A. L., Bennett, J. S., Shahid, A., & Bauer, K. W. (2002a). Impact of undergraduate research experience in engineering. *Journal of Engineering Education, 91*, 151–157.

Zydney, A. L., Bennett, J. S., Shahid, A., & Bauer, K. W. (2002b). Faculty perspectives regarding the undergraduate research experience in science and engineering. *Journal of Engineering Education, 91*, 291–297.

INDEX